Idiomatic Expressions
and
Grammatical Constructions

CSLI Lecture Note Number 230

IDIOMATIC EXPRESSIONS AND GRAMMATICAL CONSTRUCTIONS

PAUL KAY, LAURA A. MICHAELIS,
IVAN A. SAG & DAN FLICKINGER

CSLI
PUBLICATIONS
Center for the Study of
Language and Information
Stanford, California

Printed in the United States
29 28 27 26 25 1 2 3 4 5

Names: Kay, Paul, 1934- author. | Michaelis, Laura A., author. | Sag, Ivan A., 1949-2013, author. | Flickinger, Daniel P., author.

Title: Idiomatic expressions and grammatical constructions / Paul Kay, Laura A. Michaelis, Ivan A. Sag, Daniel P. Flickinger.

Description: Stanford, Calif. : CSLI Publications, 2025. | Series: CSLI Lecture Notes Number ; 230 | Includes bibliographical references and index. | Summary: "The investigations reported in the these chapters constituting this work were undertaken separately and their results were not meant to be potential chapters of a single book. Nevertheless, the result has been that these investigations form a whole in jointly reflecting the interaction and mutual reinforcement of three guiding principles of recent work in Sign-Based Construction Grammar (SBCG) and to a not insignificant degree in constructional Head-Driven Phrase Structure Grammar (HPSG)" – Provided by publisher.

Identifiers: LCCN 2024045413 (print) | LCCN 2024045414 (ebook) | ISBN 9780937073414 (paperback) | ISBN 9780937073278 (ebook)

Subjects: LCSH: Construction grammar. | Idioms. | English language – Syntax.

Classification: LCC P163.5 .K39 2025 (print) | LCC P163.5 (ebook) — DDC 425.01/836–dc23/eng/20241026

LC record available at `https://lccn.loc.gov/2024045413`

LC ebook record available at `https://lccn.loc.gov/2024045414`

CIP

∞ The acid-free paper used in this book meets the minimum requirements of the American National Standard for Information Sciences—Permanence of Paper for Printed Library Materials, ANSI Z39.48-1984.

CSLI Publications is located on the campus of Stanford University.

Visit our web site at
`http://cslipublications.stanford.edu/`
for comments on this and other titles, as well as for changes and corrections by the author and publisher.

to Ivan Sag (1949–2013)

a treasured colleague and friend

Contents

Preface

The investigations reported in the three chapters constituting the bulk of the present work were undertaken separately and their results were not imagined to be potential chapters of a single book. Nevertheless, the result has been that these three investigations form a whole in jointly reflecting the interaction and mutual reinforcement of three guiding principles of recent work in Sign-Based Construction Grammar (SBCG) and to a not insignificant degree in constructional Head-Driven Phrase Structure Grammar (HPSG). These principles are reflected in the three quotations of the epigraph.

(1) Many idioms are syntactically protean; they have meaningful parts whose denotations may be combined syntactically according to the standard compositional properties associated with the assumed syntactic form.

(2) A grammar of a natural language contains, among other things, (i) a lexicon consisting in entries that canonically specify representation in a physical medium (normally sound or visual appearance), a corresponding meaning, and, critically, a specification at some level of abstraction of the representational and meaning properties of its required accompaniments (its semantic and syntactic dependents), and
(ii) a body of rules (here Constructions[1]) that operate on a lexical object to augment, replace, or (occasionally) reduce the set of properties that characterize it.

(3) Idiomaticity is a gradient, rather than dichotomous, phenomenon.

The framework employed here is SBCG. Since SBCG is a constructionist framework it can represent a large idiomatic phrasal type with

[1]'Construction' (capitol C) is a member of a type formally defined in SBCG; 'construction' (lowercase c) is the traditional linguistic term of art.

its own Construction. For example, a negative question such as *Don't you want more cake?* does not simply mean: 'True or false: you don't want more cake?' The meaning of an expression of this kind can not be calculated in full from the meanings of negation and interrogation applied to the denotations of its content words. In particular, the italicized expression expresses a suggestion that the gloss in single quotes does not. It is for situations of this kind that SBCG provides a feature CONSTRUCTIONAL-CONTENT as part of the SEM(antics) value of a sign (Sag 2012: 146, note). Syntactically (as well as semantically), a grammar of English must distinguish the Negative Question Construction, illustrated in (4a), which permits the contracted negative auxiliary, from the similarly inverted protasis clause of the counterfactual conditional construction (4b), which does not permit it, as illustrated in (4c). Moreover, (4a) has only the 'suggestion' reading, while the uncontracted (4d) has two, scopally distinct, interrogative readings: 'Is it not the case that he helped you earlier' and 'Is it the case that he did not help you earlier?'

(4) a. Hadn't he helped you earlier?
b. Had he not helped you earlier, you would not have finished on time.
c. *Hadn't he helped you earlier, you would not have finished on time.
d. Had he not helped you earlier?

However, many phrasal, especially sentential, constructions of English have been described in the construction grammar literature as, like negative questions, requiring an individual phrasal or sentential Construction, or as inheriting selectively from a network of phrasal or sentential Constructions. But most of these constructions of English, and similar ones of German, have been shown to yield to more succinct and economical analyses in terms of lexical rules that output lexemes or words which straightforwardly interact with the *ordinary* syntactic structures of the language to produce the phrases and clauses that exemplify the construction (Müller 2006, 2002, Müller & Wechsler 2014a, 2014b).[2] The same authors have presented data involving recursion that cannot in principle be represented by inheritance systems alone.

With regard to a constructional analysis of sentences like those in (5), Kay and Fillmore (1999) report having first considered a lexical

[2] In SBCG, lexical rules are expressed as Derivational Constructions; the Müller and Wechsler papers cited were not presented in SBCG and do not represent lexical rules in this particular way. Their relevance to the present work is not thereby diminished.

analysis and then, unwisely as it now appears, rejected it for an analysis that posits an abstract syntactic entity which can be realized as either a full clause, like (5a), or a verb phrase, like (5b). The abstract syntactic entity is never fully explained nor do the authors argue for postulation of this new kind of grammatical object. Sag (2012, 174-6) provides an SBCG analysis of the WXDY construction, which closely parallels the abstract syntactic object analysis. That analysis, like the analysis in Chapter 1, makes use of the central proposal of Chapter 1, the presence in the lexicon of special words dedicated to the idioms in which, and only in which, they can occur.[3] There are thus two primary mechanisms underlying our analysis of idioms and relatively idiom-like constructions. One is the postulation of special, idiom-dedicated words and the other is lexical rules, which are implemented in SBCG as a type of derivational Construction. The analyses of Müller and Wechsler cited above employ lexical rules, as do the analyses of the present chapters 2 and 3.

(5) a. What is your name doing in my book? (Kay & Fillmore 1999: 3, (148b))
  b. I wonder what the salesman will say this house is doing without a kitchen. (Kay and Fillmore 1999: 3, (148a))

It may appear obvious, but is perhaps nevertheless worth observing, that reliance on special idiom words is characteristic of the idiomatic end of the idiomaticity scale. Lexical rules tend to play an increasing role as one departs from maximal idiomaticity in the direction of canonicity. The following three chapters are arranged in the order of decreasing idiomaticity.

Chapter 1, 'A lexical theory of phrasal idioms', anchors the idiomatic end of the scale. It deals with the self-evidently most idiomatic material of the three chapters in introducing special idiom words as part of a theory of syntactically flexible idioms. The analysis of the chapter is based on the insight of Nunberg, Sag, & Wasow (1994, earlier Wasow et al. (1984)) that idioms enjoying significant syntactic freedom of expression – countenancing passive, various clefts, conjunction, extractions, etc.– are best analyzed as containing special idiom words, familiar words with special idiom meanings. Limitations on the syntactic freedom of such idioms, when they occur, are generally explicable in terms of the meanings of the idiom words and the semantic constraints of the syntactic structures in question. In the parade example of this kind of idiom, *spill the beans*, the idiom word *spill* is taken to mean

[3] Sag's account cites an earlier, manuscript version of Chapter 1.

something like 'divulge' and the idiom word *beans* is taken to mean something like 'secret(s)'. The chief theoretical success of the SBCG implementation is to formally restrict each idiom word to occurrence in its appropriate contexts: for example, blocking an expression such as (6a), while licensing the otherwise identical version in which the idiom word *spilling* replaces *divulging*.

(6) a. *Unfortunately, he couldn't resist divulging the **beans** to everyone.
    b. Unfortunately, he couldn't resist divulging the **secret(s)** to everyone.

In Chapter 2, 'Copy raising as a lexical rule' the Copy Raising Construction specifies no idiomatic lexical entries in licensing sentences like (7), but it does have two idiom-like characteristics. (1) The Construction consists in a lexical rule that changes each of the four perception verbs *seem, appear, look* and *sound* into a weak epistemic verb of 'seeming'. Admitting that one wouldn't ordinarily classify copy raising (CR) as an idiom *per se*, the restriction of CR to just these four verbs is an idiom-like property. (2) The CR lexical rule endows the common output verb of 'seeming' with the potential of licensing a bound possessive pronoun; bound possessive pronouns only otherwise appear in indisputable idioms, such as *lose one's cool, go/be out of one's mind, blow one's nose...* (In copy raising, the coreference between the matrix subject and the possessor pronoun in the complement subject, when it occurs, requires no special machinery when the complement clause is properly analyzed.) We consider copy raising less idiomatic than the idioms considered in Chapter 1 because copy raising does not require any special, idiomatic lexical entries. In Chapter 3, what we term *split-subject* sentences, such as in (8), have neither of the idiomatic properties of CR, although the abstract, non-maximal (or 'leaf') Construction that figures in sentences like (8) and four other clausal types that feature the idiosyncratic combination of raising and postverbal agreement is a lexical rule.

(7) Trump$_i$ looked like he$_i$ was going to win in January.

(8) Yet, there seem to emerge some persons in this world who are more highly intuitive than average.

We observe in (8) the split of canonical subject properties between two distinct constituents, raising and subject-verb agreement. The lexical rule that licenses this distribution of subject properties is idiosyncratic in disaggregating the characteristic properties of the erstwhile subject constituent. Chapter 3, 'Partial Inversion', considers five closely related syntactic patterns, illustrated by the examples in (9). One might wish to refer to these closely related constructions as 'formal idioms,' "syntactic patterns dedicated to semantic and pragmatic purposes not knowable from their form alone" (Fillmore et al. 1988: 505). Attested examples of these constructions are shown in (9):

(9) a. Oblique Inversion (OI): Inside it buzzed a flying insect, furry-bodied and gray.
  b. Presentational-*there* (P-*there*): There will arise someday, a great civilization around San Francisco Bay.
  c. Deictic Inversion (DI): Here come the robot lawyers.
  d. Existential-*there* (E-*there*): There are likely to be problems with the finale.
  e. Reversed Specificational *be* (RS-*be*): My biggest worry are the injury risks.

Although there are evident differences among the examples in (9) that require distinct clause-level Constructions, all five of these (attested) examples display the important similarities of (i) agreeing with the postverbal constituent, (ii) permitting raising as visible in the (invented) examples of (10), and (iii) focusing the agreeing constituent.

(10) a. OI: But then appeared to emerge a new fear.
  b. P-*there*: And from this consciousness ... there seemed to arise a feeling that they had been betrayed.
  c. DI: Here seemed to come the proof.
  d. E-*there*: There seemed to be some discrepancies.
  e. RS-*be*: The biggest problem appear to be the increased costs.

These similarities are noteworthy for their common divergence from the canonical case, in which a single constituent displays all the properties which together comprise the notion of subject. They are captured by a lexical Construction that describes a derivational relationship between a canonical intransitive verb (the Construction's daughter sign) and a verb (the mother sign) that distributes subject properties among two distinct members of the 'output' verb's valence list. This construction constitutes a formal idiom in part because the mother sign has semantic properties not owed to the daughter sign. In (9a), for example, the verb *buzz* is seen to combine with a locative expression (*inside [the jar]*) that it does not otherwise select.

A brief introduction to SBCG is provided in section 2 of Chapter 2. Some readers may prefer to look at that section before beginning Chapter 1.

1

A Lexical Theory of Phrasal Idioms

Paul Kay, Ivan A. Sag and Dan Flickinger

1.1 Introduction

Among the most important desiderata for a theory of idioms, also known as multiword expressions (MWEs), are the following four. First, idioms divide into classes whose distinct properties, described below, need to be theoretically accommodated. Second, the theory should get the semantics right. It should, for example, represent the fact that (1a) and (1b) have roughly the same meaning, which can be glossed as (1c):[1]

(1) a. let the cat out of the bag
   b. spill the beans
   c. reveal a/the secret(s)

Third, the theory should get the syntax right. For example, it should predict that (2a) is utterly unacceptable while (2b) is not, despite the fact that (3a) and (3b) mean roughly the

[0]We would like to thank Frank Richter, Manfred Sailer, and Thomas Wasow for discussion of some of the issues raised here, Stephen Wechsler for comments on an earlier draft, and especially Stefan Müller for detailed comments and extensive discussion. None are to be blamed for the good advice we have failed to accept.

[1]All unstarred examples in this paper were attested on the web at the time of drafting, unless otherwise noted.

same thing.[2]

We know that idiomatic *ghost* is meaningful independently of the fact that it passivizes because, unlike idiomatic *bucket*, it can be semantically modified, as illustrated in (4).

(2) a.*The bucket was kicked ...
 b. The ghost was given up ...

(3) a. kick the bucket
 b. give up the ghost

(4) a. Gonna be out of video producing for a lil bit, my camera gave up the recording ghost yesterday...
 b. I took a single year of classes before my parents gave up the budgetary ghost...
 c. Who now remembers the general relief when the increasingly odd Blair gave up the political ghost?

Finally, the theory of idioms should be part and parcel of a general theory of grammar; the theory of idioms should add as little machinery to one's overall grammatical approach as possible, ideally nothing. We will expand on all these desiderata using the framework of Sign-Based Construction Grammar (SBCG), as developed in Boas and Sag (2012) (see in particular Sag (2012)). Our theory of idioms will be lexicalist; in particular, we will divide the lexicon into words that appear only in idioms, such as *cat, bag, spill* and *beans* in (1) and the words that are pronounced exactly like these that appear in nonidiom contexts such as in (5) (cf. Nunberg et al. (1994) [henceforth NSW] and also Wasow et al.

[2] It is difficult to find two idioms with similar extensions only one of which passivizes. For readers who find (2b) unacceptable, a quick Google search will reveal that examples of the passive form of this idiom are not hard to find. Most examples appear to be metaphorical, about abandonment of projects or activities rather than actual deaths, but there are some examples about actual loss of life as well, e.g.
(i) Then, in January of '72, the ghost was given up. It's still difficult to write about Patchen's death.
(ii) Gazing into that jar ... the poison as pure as Alpine snow ... he had witnessed ... the awful instant when the ghost was given up, the wings settling down into the first magnificence of death.

(1984)). O'Grady (1998), in a dependency-based approach, introduced the concept of a chain of lexical dependencies – christened a "catena" by Osborne (2012) – as the underlying structure of idioms. The basic intuition is similar to that of the current approach, although many details of the implementation are different.

(5) The vet held onto the dog and let the cat out of the bag. (invented example)

We will in fact propose a three-way split in the lexicon. In addition to non-idiomatic words and the words occurring only as arguments of idiom predicators, there are the idiom predicators themselves, such as *let* and *spill* in (1). Phrases headed by these words are not restricted to occurrence in idiom contexts (*Kim spilled the beans* can be embedded in a nonidiom context, as in *Someone said Kim spilled the beans*). The words like idiomatic *spill* pattern with nonidioms in this regard. But these words play the special role in phrasal idioms of requiring some or all of their argument phrases to be headed by idiom words. An idiom predicator thus bridges between the idiom context it governs and the nonidiom context in which the phrases that it projects occur.

A key problem in formulating a theory of idioms which, like ours, accords meaning to many idiom words and concomitantly allows a certain amount of syntactic freedom to the occurrences of these words, is to limit that freedom of occurrence appropriately. For example, if we analyze *beans* of *spill the beans* as meaningful (meaning something like 'secret(s)') and idiomatic *spill* as meaning something like 'reveal', and use these assumptions to explain why idiomatic *beans* can be modified and *spill* can be passivized, as in (6), we must also prevent *beans* meaning 'secret(s)' from occurring in environments like (7), where *beans* is not lexically licensed by idiomatic *spill*:

(6) The Pam Anderson beans were spilled long ago, but who's joining the Baywatch babe in the Dancing With

the Stars spotlight this year?

(7) *John Dean refused to keep the Watergate beans.

Several dimensions of difference among idioms have been observed in the literature (for reviews, see Fillmore et al. (1988) and Sag et al. (2002) and the references cited therein). The dimension we will focus on primarily is the general correlation between the syntactic plasticity of an idiom and its semantic compositionality (noted originally by NSW; see also Abeillé (1995) for a TAG treatment of rich data on partial syntactic flexibility of idioms in French). In footnote 2 above, we mentioned that *kick* of *kick the bucket* does not passivize, whereas *give* of *give up the ghost* shows some signs of passivizing. We noted in the text that these expressions convey roughly the same meaning but, crucially, in the *kick the bucket* case the meaning is presumably a simple predicate 'die', while in the *give up the ghost* case it appears to be a more complex, decomposable predicate like 'lose (one's) life/soul'. NSW's hypothesis, which we pursue further here, is that meaningfulness of the words of an idiom correlates with their syntactic potential; specifically, meaningful idiom words can be modified and can appear in syntactic contexts that meaningless ones cannot. Noting observations by Ackerman & Webelhuth and by Shenk regarding limited syntactic flexibility in semantically non-decomposable idioms in German and Dutch, NSW observe that the structures in these languages calling for special devices to "scramble" constituents – such as those proposed by Reape and Kathol (later published as Reape 1994 and Kathol 2000) – and which do not entail interpretive consequences (as does, for example, English topicalization) are precisely the syntactic contexts that permit meaningless idiom words to be "displaced."

Following Sag et al. (2002), we distinguish three types of (English) idioms:

Fixed Expressions: Expressions which appear to contain more than one word but which display idiosyncratic syntactic combination (and *a fortiori* no semantic compositionality). Examples include *by and large, right away, first off, all of a sudden.* These can, without loss of generality, be listed as single words in the lexicon, despite their spelling suggesting a multiword history.

Semi-Fixed Expressions: Idioms which obey normal syntactic constraints but which are nonetheless quite frozen as well as being semantically non-compositional. Examples are *black and white, kith and kin, bright-eyed and bushy-tailed, it takes one to know one.* One is tempted to accord members of this class the syntactic structures that they appear to exemplify, but since they strongly resist both morphological and syntactic manipulation, parsimony argues for encoding them as single words. However, since they can be interrupted by epistemic or intensifying adverbs, they cannot be considered single words:[3]

(8) a. It sure/surely/certainly takes one to know one.
b. So we huddle together as kith and as kin.
c. surprisingly bright eyed and bushy tailed

The class of semi-fixed expressions also includes idioms that are syntactically frozen and semantically noncompositional but morphologically alternating. Relevant examples are **kick/kicks/kicked/kicking** *the bucket* and **buy/buys/bought/buying** *a pig in a poke.* The inflectional potential of *kick*, for example, shows that *kicked the bucket* is not a fixed expression, but rather a verb phrase constructed according to the familiar English pattern. After introducing the next and final type, we return to the analysis of this and other semi-fixed expressions.

Syntactically Flexible Expressions: Idioms with the following properties:

---

[3]The appearance of 'epithets' within these idioms, as in *kith and* **bloody** *kin*, cannot be taken as evidence of phrasal structure if it is found that they obey the same phonological constraints as those interrupting uncontroversial words, e.g. *out-***bloody***-rageous*, *fan-***freakin***-tastic.*

(9) a. they exhibit modulations of syntax or morphology (or both),
b. their meaning cannot be composed from the 'literal' (nonidiomatic) interpretations of their parts, but
c. they are analyzable in terms of parts whose special (idiomatic) meanings can be modified or quantified under certain circumstances.

Parade examples are *pull strings* and *spill the beans*, which have been analyzed as containing special idiom words *pull* 'manipulate', *strings* 'access', and *spill* 'reveal', *beans* 'secret(s)'. Idioms of this type are widely taken to have the same syntactic structure as the homophonous nonidiomatic expressions, which in turn explains why they can be inflected, modified and dislocated syntactically. This is the type of idiom that we will be mostly concerned with in this paper.

We begin the introduction of the main features of SBCG in a preliminary discussion of flexible expressions. Then, as noted, we take up an example of a semi-fixed expression and finally return to some complex flexible expressions. Fixed expressions are not discussed further.

1.2 The Analysis of Syntactically Flexible Expressions

SBCG is equipped with a multiple-inheritance hierarchy of typed features structures of the familiar kind.[4] Readers acquainted with HPSG or with the kind of Berkeley Construction Grammar presented in, for example, Kay and Fillmore (1999), should find nothing very surprising in the tools and notations introduced in this paper.[5]

The most important type of feature structure in SBCG is the *sign*, with its various subtypes: *word*, *lexeme* and *phrase* (Sag (2012):71). Each sign has a FORM feature, whose value is a morphological representation of the expression, notated

[4]See Sag et al. (2003) for an elementary presentation.

[5]For those familiar with the latter but not the former, read the embedded bracketed attribute-value matrices (AVMs) as embedded boxes. Angled brackets (⟨...⟩) denote lists.

here in standard English orthography. The other features of the sign are PHONology, ARG-ST (argument-structure), SYNtax, SEMantics, and CONTEXT. The value of SYN is a feature structure that specifies a value for features like CATegory, VALence, and MRKG (marking). CAT values are feature structures, assigned to various word-class types, that specify values for appropriate features, including Lexical Identity (LID), whose value is a list of frames. [6]

The value of the ARG-ST feature is a list of the arguments – syntactic and/or semantic – of a predicating lexeme. Members of the ARG-ST list reappear in the list value of the VAL feature, unless extracted or given null realization.[7]

The VAL feature takes as value a list of signs, corresponding to the elements that an expression can combine with: the syntactico-semantic arguments of the predicator in order of decreasing obliqueness, or accessibility (⟨Subject, Direct Object, ...⟩). Expressions like NPs and clauses have the empty list as their VAL value, as they are intuitively 'saturated'; i.e. they already contain (canonically, at least) all of the predicator's arguments.

The values of SEM include specifications for the features INDex and FRAMES. We assume an indefinitely large list of referential indices 1,2,.... Non-referring expressions such as idiomatic *bucket* receive the specification [SEM [INDEX *none*]]. The FRAMES feature takes a list of elementary predications[8] as its value. In certain cases, the FRAMES list of an expression is empty.

Our analysis appeals to a frame-based conception of semantics (Fillmore (1982, 1985), Fillmore and Baker (2010)), in which we assume a bifurcation of the universe of frames

[6]Typically this will be a singleton list, but the list definition is adopted in anticipation of possible cases in which non-singleton frame lists for listemes or derived lexemes should arise. CAT specifications 'percolate' in headed constructs from the head lexeme to higher projections. See Sag (2012) for details.

[7]This paper is not concerned with extraction or null realization processes, nor with the PHON or CONTEXT features. Again, see Sag (2012).

[8]Roughly the RELS of Minimal Recursion Semantics in Copestake et al. (2005).

into canonical frames (*c-frames*) and idiom-frames (*i-frames*).

For example, *i-beans[secret]-fr* models the idiomatic sense of *beans* in *spill the beans*. It is an *i-frame* that can be loosely paraphrased as *secret* and is distinct from the nonidiomatic sense of *beans*, which we represent simply as *beans-fr*, a *c-frame*.[9]

(10) (i) Shah Rukh Khan spilled many beans about his upcoming film Happy New Year which has huge starcast of Deepika Padukone, Abhishek Bachchan, Sonu Sood and Boman Irani.

(ii) Instead of throwing a rock, he is throwing all her family secrets and dirty laundry out to the media. He enjoys it. You can see it in his smirk as he spills bean after bean of little juicy nasty tidbits about Palin.

(iii) MilSuper...can you spill a bean or two?

Lexemes are identified in our theory in terms of a feature LEXICAL-ID (LID), whose value identifies each lexeme (and the phrases it projects) by its principal frame.[10] In the case of nonidiomatic lexemes and meaningful idiomatic lexemes, the LID value is the main frame of the lexeme.[11]

---

[9] Although the idiom word *beans* appears to have plural form, the corresponding *i-beans-fr* 'secret or secrets' seems often not to denote a plurality of countable entities but an abstract (mass) entity. However, an anonymous referee suggests cases in which (a) it combines with *many*, (b) can occur in the "N after N"-construction, and (c) occurs with the singular article *a*.

[10] For readers familiar with HPSG, the LID feature subsumes the function of the PFORM feature and accomplishes the analogous function for lexical heads of all categories.

[11] For conciseness, we follow the abbreviation conventions of Sag (2012). Thus, (i), depending on the context, abbreviates either (ii) or (iii), and (iv) further abbreviates (v):

(i) NP[LID L]

(ii) $\begin{bmatrix} \textit{sign} & \\ \text{SYN} & \begin{bmatrix} \text{CAT} & \begin{bmatrix} \textit{noun} & \\ \text{LID} & L \end{bmatrix} \\ \text{VALENCE} & \langle\rangle \end{bmatrix} \end{bmatrix}$

(iii) $\begin{bmatrix} \textit{syntax-object} & \\ \text{CAT} & \begin{bmatrix} \textit{noun} & \\ \text{LID} & L \end{bmatrix} \\ \text{VALENCE} & \langle\rangle \end{bmatrix}$

(iv) NP$_i$

(v) NP [SEM [INDEX i]]

(11)

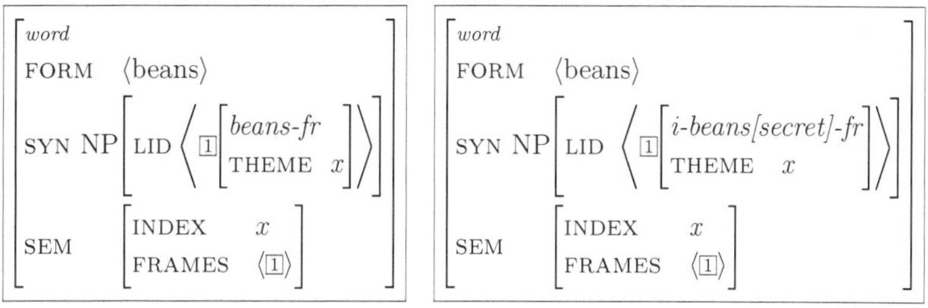

The phrases these words project are distinguished as non-idiomatic or idiomatic in terms of their LID value, because the LID value of the lexical head is identified with that of the phrase it heads by the Head Feature Principle (Pollard and Sag (1994)) or some similar constraint, as indicated in (12):

(12)

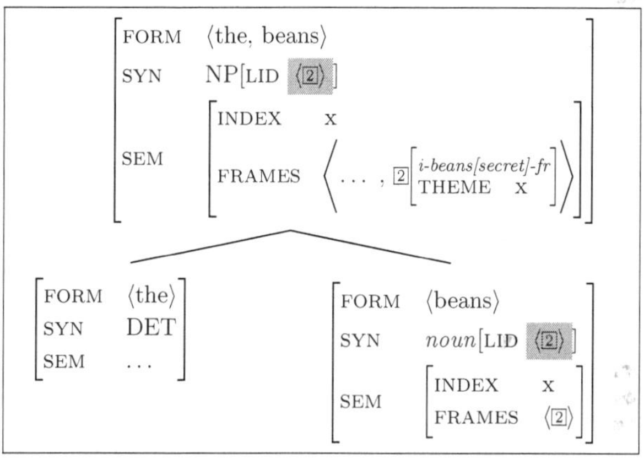

The basic mechanism for preventing idiom words from appearing in contexts where they are not lexically governed by the appropriate idiom predicator involves the feature ARG-ST. Ordinary, non-idiom predicators are lexically specified as requiring all members of their ARG-ST list to be nonidiomatic. By contrast, an idiomatic predicator like idiomatic *spill* requires a direct object that is idiomatic, i.e. one whose LID value (and hence that of its lexical head) contains a particular *i-frame*, as in (13b).[12]

[12]We follow the abbreviation conventions of Copestake et al. (2005) in (i)

(13) a.

$$\boxed{\begin{bmatrix} \textit{trans-v-lxm} & \\ \text{FORM} & \langle \text{spill} \rangle \\ \text{ARG-ST} & \left\langle \text{NP}_x[\text{LID } \langle \textit{c-frame} \rangle] \text{ , NP}_y[\text{LID } \langle \textit{c-frame} \rangle] \right\rangle \\ \text{SYN} & \begin{bmatrix} \text{LID} & \left\langle \boxed{1} \textit{spill(s,x,y)} \right\rangle \end{bmatrix} \\ \text{SEM} & \begin{bmatrix} \text{INDEX} & \text{s} \\ \text{FRAMES} & \langle \boxed{1} \rangle \end{bmatrix} \end{bmatrix}}$$

b.

$$\boxed{\begin{bmatrix} \textit{trans-v-lxm} & \\ \text{FORM} & \langle \text{spill} \rangle \\ \text{ARG-ST} & \left\langle \text{NP}_x[\text{LID } \langle \textit{c-frame} \rangle] \text{ , NP}_y[\text{LID } \langle \textit{i-beans[secret]} \rangle] \right\rangle \\ \text{SYN} & \begin{bmatrix} \text{LID} & \left\langle \boxed{1} \textit{spill[reveal](s,x,y)} \right\rangle \end{bmatrix} \\ \text{SEM} & \begin{bmatrix} \text{INDEX} & \text{s} \\ \text{FRAMES} & \langle \boxed{1} \rangle \end{bmatrix} \end{bmatrix}}$$

Because these predicators and their complements also pass their frames up to be part of the meaning of the phrases they license (in accordance with general principles of semantic composition), the idiomatic sense of the direct object *beans* will be part of the phrase's meaning only when the predicator *spill* has introduced the appropriate *i-frame*. A nonidiomatic object can only cooccur with predicators that fail to require an idiomatic object. Note that predicators like idiomatic *spill*

---

for the corresponding frame descriptions shown in (ii). Here and throughout, UNDGR abbreviates UNDERGOER. Notice that we use *s* variables for quantifying over situations, which function as Davidsonian event arguments, and we omit the feature LABEL except where necessary for label identification:

(i) *l: beans(x)* *l:spill(s,x,y)* *l:i-beans[secret](x)* *l:spill[reveal](s,x,y)*

(ii)

$$\begin{bmatrix} \textit{beans-fr} & \\ \text{LABEL} & \text{l} \\ \text{THEME} & \text{x} \end{bmatrix} \quad \begin{bmatrix} \textit{spill-fr} & \\ \text{LABEL} & \text{l} \\ \text{SIT} & \text{s} \\ \text{ACTOR} & \text{x} \\ \text{UNDGR} & \text{y} \end{bmatrix} \quad \begin{bmatrix} \textit{i-beans[secret]-fr} & \\ \text{LABEL} & \text{l} \\ \text{THEME} & x \end{bmatrix} \quad \begin{bmatrix} \textit{spill[reveal]-fr} & \\ \text{LABEL} & \text{l} \\ \text{SIT} & \text{s} \\ \text{ACTOR} & \text{x} \\ \text{UNDGR} & \text{y} \end{bmatrix}$$

Representations of feature structures (Sag 2012:74ff) are enclosed in boxes; representations of descriptions of feature structures (including constructions) are not enclosed in boxes.

are themselves identified via *c-frames*, allowing the phrases they project to occur in nonidiomatic contexts. The reader should bear in mind that the basic mechanism allowing idiom words to occur just when governed by the appropriate lexical governor is that non-idiom predicators are lexically specified to accept only arguments whose LID value is canonical, as in (13a). Recalling that the value of VAL is identical to that of ARG-ST, modulo extraction and null realization such as control, this will always lead to a nonidiomatic VP like (14):

(14)

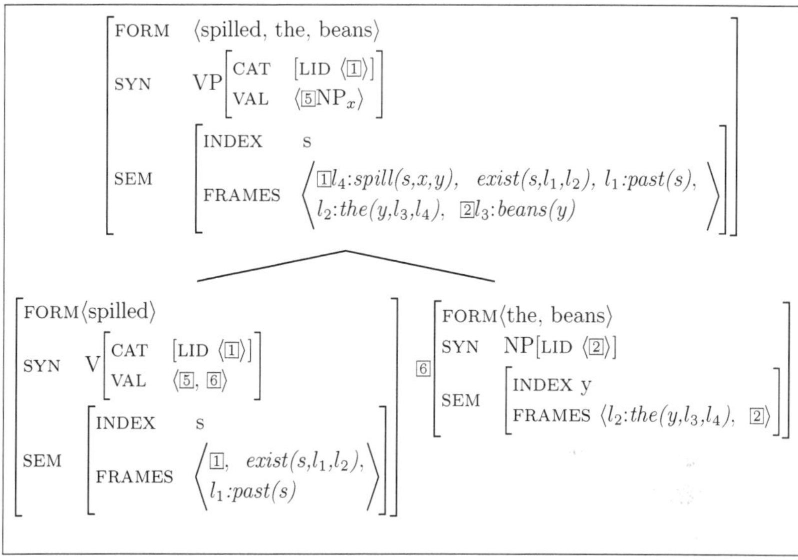

And the idiomatic (13b) will project structures like (15), where the semantics includes the direct object's *i-frame*:

(15)

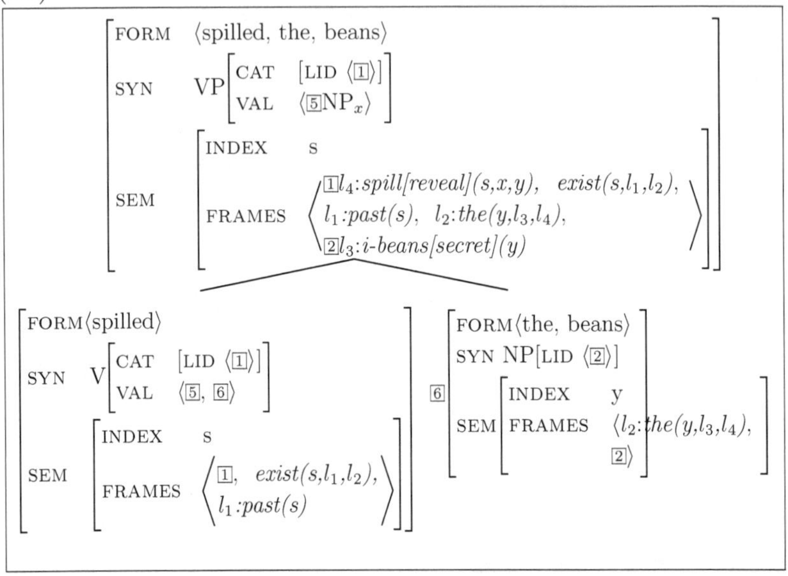

Our analysis thus treats *Kim spilled the beans* as ambiguous. (13a) will give rise to an S whose FRAMES list is as shown in (16a), and (13b) will likewise project an S whose FRAMES list is (16b):

(16) a. $l_0{:}\exists(s,l_1,l_2)$, $l_1{:}past(s)$, $l_2{:}the(y,l_3,l_4)$, $l_3{:}beans(y)$, $l_4{:}spill(s,Kim,y)$

b. $l_0{:}\exists(s,l_1,l_2)$, $l_1{:}past(s)$, $l_2{:}the(y,l_3,l_4)$, $l_3{:}i\text{-}beans[secret](y)$, $l_4{:}spill[reveal](s,Kim,y)$

The *l*s here are just labels (see Copestake et al. (2005)) that can be eliminated by replacing an argument *l* by the formula labelled by *l*, as shown in (17):

(17) a. (16a) = $\exists(s,past(s),\ the(y,\ beans(y),\ spill(s,Kim,y)))$

b. (16b) = $\exists(s,past(s),\ the(y,\ i\text{-}beans[secret](y),\ spill[reveal](s,Kim,y)))$

(17b) is the idiomatic reading, which can be read as 'there is some past situation in which there is a contextually provided secret that Kim reveals'.

1.3 The Analysis of Semi-Fixed Expressions

We return now to the question of how an idiom like *kick the bucket* should be analyzed. To begin with, the absence of a progressive usage, shown in (18a), can be explained by assuming punctuality in the meaning of the idiom, contrasted with (b) and (c) using the related idiom with *ghost*, which is not constrained to a punctual meaning.

(18) a.*He was kicking the bucket when she walked in.
b. Erasmus seized him by the throat, threw him down, and giving him a violent kick in the neck, a rattle in the throat announced that he was giving up the ghost.
c. Lowe and Cushing sank bleeding to the basket floor as the balloon was giving up the ghost, its descent accelerating as the weight of its fabric overpowered the ...

Example (19) shows that the gerund is possible for *kick the bucket*, so if the gerund and present participle are taken to employ the same morphological object, the progressive cannot be blocked morphologically.

(19) I think the correlation between her kicking the bucket and the surgery is a daft point.

The first interesting question that arises is whether to attribute the meaning 'die' to *kick* alone or to the full VP *kick(s/ed/ing) the bucket.* We propose to analyze *kick the bucket* by positing two lexemes, an idiom-predicator verb *kick* meaning 'die' (punctually) which requires as object a meaningless noun *bucket*[13] marked by *the.*

[13]A referee, noting the existence of *bucket list*, raises the question of including all the semantics of the idiom in idiomatic *kick*. Motivation for this move comes from the observation that there exist several variants of the idiom in which *bucket* is lacking.

(i)The old guy kicked off, eh?

(ii)... you were morally obligated to eat the flesh of Aunt Rose when she kicked it - regardless how she died (or what you thought of Aunt Rose).

(iii)I'm old but, before I kick, I'm going to visit Montana where, from what I'm

To account for the absence of Passive, one might simply posit a restriction on the VERBFORM (VF) value of *kick*. Such an analysis, apart from being stipulative, does not yet deal with the entire problem raised here, since Passive is not the only construction where this idiom is blocked. No idiomatic readings are available for any of the examples in (20), for example:

(20) a. Which (gunman's) bucket did he kick?
b. What he kicked was the bucket.
c. It was the bucket that he kicked.
d. In Kim's case, the bucket kicked easily.

We propose that Questions, *WH*-clefts, *It*-clefts and Middle all impose semantic or pragmatic constraints on the (displaced) direct object of the verb, which would make these constructions incompatible with any analysis of idiomatic *kicked* that required a semantically vacuous direct object. The relevant fact is not that expletive nouns cannot occur as passive subjects, which in fact they can.

(21) a. There was believed to be another worker at the site besides the neighbors who witnessed the incident.
b. It was rumored that Great Britain, in apparent violation of the terms of the Clayton-Bulwer treaty, had taken possession of certain islands in the Bay of Honduras.

It is rather that passive does not apply to verbal lexemes that select an expletive direct object.[14]

(22) a. *It is just being winged (essentially) by this man.

told, there's no friggin city lights and just lie on my back and look at the night sky.

[14]We are indebted to an anonymous referee for the observation that expletives selected by verbal listeme are blocked from becoming passive subjects. The Passive Construction is a derivational construction containing a mother lexeme and a single daughter lexeme. The constraint on passivizing expletive objects is implemented by assigning a value distinct from *none* to the INDEX of the second member of the ARG-ST list of the daughter verbal lexeme in the Passive Construction.

(Cf. attested: Even this man is essentially just winging it.)

b. *It was totally lost by John and Kristen when one answer was given! (Cf. attested: John and Kristen totally lost it when one answer was given!)

c. *It was blown by Becca when she wore a juicy couture jumpsuit to the final rose ceremony.(Cf. attested:: Becca blew it when she wore a juicy couture jumpsuit to the final rose ceremony.)

This strictly lexical analysis of *kick the bucket* accounts in addition for both the inflectional freedom of the head *kick* and the fact that the *bucket* NP can be interrupted by metalinguistic operators like *proverbial*, *metaphorical*, etc., as in (23):

(23) a. I feel like I've seen so much of the world already, but there's still a lot I want to do before I kick the proverbial bucket...

b. My Kindle kicked the metaphorical bucket on the 25th.[15]

Since idiomatic *kick* specifies about its NP complement only that it is an NP headed by the idiom word *bucket*, the insertion of epithets or semantically external modifiers in examples like those in (23) causes no problem, while passivization and semantic modification of the idiomatic word *bucket* are precluded by that noun's lexically specified meaninglessness.[16]

We now turn to our analysis of the idiomatic common noun *bucket* in SBCG terms. This involves a listeme (lexical entry) that is like the one for nonidiomatic *bucket*, except

[15]As a referee points out, *kick the bucket* can also be interrupted by domain-delimiting adjectives (Ernst 1981), e.g., *In a metaphorical sense, Ingraham has kicked the political bucket.* We take such cases to represent, not modification of *bucket*, but exemplification of the external modification trope whose parade example is P.G. Wodehouse's *pensive cigarette.*

[16]The metalinguistic modifier can nevertheless select the idiomatic word *bucket* by selecting for its LID value, which indicates a subtype of *i-bucket[null]-fr*.

that (1) the FRAMES list is empty, (2) the INDEX value is *none* and (3) the frame contained in the LID value is of type *i-bucket[null]-fr*:

(24)
$$\begin{bmatrix} \textit{cn-lxm} & \\ \text{FORM} & \langle\text{bucket}\rangle \\ \text{SYN} & \begin{bmatrix}\text{CAT} & [\text{LID}\ \ \langle \textit{i-bucket[null]-fr}\rangle] \\ \text{VAL} & \langle\rangle\end{bmatrix} \\ \text{SEM} & \begin{bmatrix}\text{IND} & \textit{none}\\ \text{FRAMES} & \langle\rangle\end{bmatrix}\end{bmatrix}$$

The label *cn-lxm* indicates that idiomatic *bucket* is a common noun lexeme, a subtype of *lexeme*. The first syntactic specification requires that the LID feature have the value ⟨*i-bucket-fr*⟩, the list containing just a feature structure of type *i-bucket-fr*.[17] As indicated above, the type hierarchy recognizes two kinds of frames: canonical frames (subtypes of *c-frame*) and idiomatic frames (subtypes of *i-frame*). In the case of meaningless idiomatic lexemes, those with an empty FRAMES list and *none* as their INDEX value, like idiomatic *bucket*, the LID value is a semantically inert *i-frame* that simply identifies the lexeme for purposes of selection by the relevant predicator. As before, since CAT features percolate in headed constructs from the head lexeme to higher projections, the identity of idiomatic *bucket* as the head of a noun phrase like *the bucket* or *the proverbial bucket* will be visible to idiomatic *kick*.

Before turning our attention to idiomatic *kick*, let us consider the construction that licenses the NP headed by idiomatic *bucket*. The Head-Functor Construction, formulated in (25), licenses constructs of type *hd-func-cxt*, a subtype of *headed-construct*; a *headed-construct* specifies one of its daughters as the head daughter and further specifies that

[17] We sometimes write *i-bucket-fr* instead of *i-bucket-null-fr* when it is clear from context that the null version is intended.

the head daughter's syntactic category (SYN|CAT) value is shared by the mother, encoding the principle of head feature percolation.[18]

(25) **Head-Functor Construction:** (↑*headed-cxt*):

$$\mathit{hd\text{-}func\text{-}cxt} \Rightarrow \begin{bmatrix} \text{MTR} & [\text{SYN}\ X![\text{MRKG}\ M\,]] \\ \text{DTRS} & \left\langle \begin{bmatrix}\text{SYN} \begin{bmatrix}\text{CAT}\ [\text{SELECT}\ Y\,] \\ \text{MRKG}\ \ M\end{bmatrix}\end{bmatrix}, Y{:}[\text{SYN}\ X] \right\rangle \\ \text{HDDTR} & \text{Y} \end{bmatrix}$$

In our discussion of *spill the beans*, we have already sketched a construct licensed by this construction; see (12) above.

We notice in the title line of (25) the notation ↑*headed-cxt*, which is to be read as '*headed-construct* is an immediate supertype of *head-functor-construct*'. Constructs play an important role in SBCG: they are like local trees licensed in a Context-Free Grammar (CFG); similarly, the combinatoric constructions that license these constructs are analogous to context-free rewrite rules. Since a construct is modeled as a feature structure, it too is specified in AVM notation: its MTR (MOTHER) feature's value is a sign and its DTRS (DAUGHTERS) feature's value is a non-empty list of signs.

Just as 'VP → VP ADV' places constraints on a type of head-modifier structures in a CFG, the Head-Functor Construction constrains a class of headed structures in a SBCG. Note that the constraints in both cases are local, making reference only to two levels of structure. The notation for SBCG constructions presents a double arrow with the type name of a construct on its left, here *head-functor-construct* (*hd-func-cxt*), and on its right an AVM expressing the defining properties of the class of constructs named on the left. A sign is thus either licensed by lexical entries, *listemes*, or else it

[18]Based on the analyses of Allegranza (2007), Van Eynde (2006, 2007), Sag (2012), and Kay and Sag (2012), we posit a SELECT feature, according to which specifiers, markers, and modifiers select their heads, in effect collapsing the categories of specifier, modifier, and marker.

is 'constructionally licensed' as the mother of a well-formed construct.[19]

The defining constraint on the class of *hd-func-cxt*s says something about the mother, the daughters and the head-daughter. The notation in the MTR's value says that the SYN value is the same as that associated elsewhere with the variable X, except that the local value has the marking value indicated by the variable M. (The latter, 'except', clause is the interpretation of the '!' following the X; cf. Sag 2012:125-6, fn. 71.) The DTRS value specifies a list of two daughters. Taking the second daughter first, its SYN value is tagged X, which, when taken together with the occurrence of 'X!' in the MTR's SYN value, says that the MTR's syntax value is that of its second daughter except for the specification [MRKG M]. The second daughter is tagged Y, which identifies it as the head daughter (i.e. the value of the HDDTR feature just below). Turning now to the first daughter (the functor), we note that its MRKG value is M, and its SYN|CAT|SELECT value is Y, the variable also assigned to the head daughter. The M specifies that in constructs of type *hd-func-cxt* the mother inherits its MARKING value from the non-head daughter (while it inherits the rest of its syntax from the head daughter, as we have seen). The Y indicates that the 'functor' daughter selects the head daughter. In the case of idiomatic *kick the bucket*, this specification will allow *the* to select a nominal phrase headed by idiomatic *bucket.* We assume that English has a meaningless *the*, which occurs in this and other idioms, such as *chew the fat* 'converse', *drop the ball* 'err', *bite the dust* 'die', *fly the coop* 'escape', *buy the farm*, 'die', and *shoot the breeze* 'chat'. The listeme for meaningless *the* specifies [FRAMES ⟨*i-the[null]-fr*⟩] and correspondingly [LID ⟨*i-the[null]-fr*⟩]. It also specifies the unique marking value ⟨*i-the[null]-fr*⟩ (see Section 5).

[19]There are also unilevel constructions in the lexicon, called *lexical class constructions.* We are not concerned with them in this paper; see Sag (2012):15 and elsewhere.

The predicators of this group of idioms take NP arguments with the LID of the NP's head noun and the MRKG value ⟨*i-the[null]-fr*⟩. For example, idiomatic *kick* is specified [ARG-ST ⟨NP, NP[LID *i-bucket[null]-fr*⟩, MRKG ⟨*i-the[null]-fr*⟩]. The Head-Functor Construction licenses the combination of non-quantifier *the* and idiomatic *bucket* (or a *bucket*-headed phrase with appropriate modification) into an NP obeying the constraints that idiomatic *kick* will require of its pseudo-object.

Before considering the special lexical entry for idiomatic *kick* we consider the construction that licenses phrases consisting of predicators with their non-subject complements, i.e. the construction that will enable *kick* to combine with *the... bucket.* The Predicational Head-Complement Construction licenses head-complement phrases—VPs, PPs, APs, and Common Noun Phrases (CNPs)—in which all non-subject complement requirements (non-subject *valents*) of a predicator are realized as sisters to the head. As in the Head-Functor-Construction, we note in the title line of (26) that this construction[20] also licenses a subclass of headed constructs:

(26) **Predicational Head-Complement Construction (↑*headed-cxt*):**

$$\textit{pred-hd-comp-cxt} \Rightarrow \begin{bmatrix} \text{MTR} & [\text{SYN } X \;!\; [\text{VAL } \langle Y \rangle]] \\ \text{DTRS} & \langle\, Z \,\rangle \oplus L{:}\textit{nelist} \\ \text{HDDTR} & Z{:}\begin{bmatrix} \textit{word} \\ \text{SYN } X{:}\begin{bmatrix} \text{CAT} & [\text{XARG } Y] \\ \text{VAL} & \langle Y \rangle \oplus L \end{bmatrix} \end{bmatrix} \end{bmatrix}$$

Our earlier discussion exhibited two constructs, (14) and (15), that are licensed by (26).

[20]Rui Chaves (p.c.) has called attention to a flaw in this version of the construction, though the matter is not relevant here, but see the corrected definition (84) and attendant discussion in chapter 2 for details.

As in the Head-Functor Construction (25), MTR, DTRS, and HDDTR features are all constrained by (26). Looking first at the DTRS value, we note that it is a composite list, composed of a singleton list containing a sign tagged Z, which we see below is identified with the head daughter, followed by a non-empty list, tagged L. Viewed as a local tree this class of constructs is characterized by a list of one or more daughters of which the head daughter is the first. Looking down now at the head daughter, tagged Z, we see that it is of type *word* and that its SYN value, tagged X, has specifications for CAT and VAL features. The CAT feature specifies that its external argument (XARG) is tagged Y—which we see again in the MTR's SYN|VAL list. In general, the XARG feature, as a CAT feature, is projected upwards from the lexical head in all headed constructs, making visible at all 'bar' levels the subject requirement of a lexical predicator. Normally, the XARG value is identified with the first element of the VAL list, which lists the unsaturated argument requirements of a predicator.[21] The VAL list of the head daughter consists of a singleton list containing the XARG (subject-to-be), tagged Y, which is identified with the unique member of the VAL list of the mother, followed by a non-empty list tagged L, whose members, we see in the DTRS value, are identified with the non-head daughters. The Predicational Head-Complement Construction will license a VP headed by idiomatic *kick* followed by an NP headed by idiomatic *bucket*.

We have seen how the Head-Functor Construction licenses an NP headed by idiomatic *bucket*, selected by *the*, and possibly containing semantically external modification: e.g. *proverbial* or *metaphorical*. We have also discussed the construction that assembles verb phrases and their non-subject complements. It remains to complete the picture by considering the listeme for idiomatic *kick*, given in (27):

[21] The VAL list corresponds fairly closely with the SUBCAT list of Pollard and Sag (1994). For further discussion of the XARG feature, especially regarding its relation to issues of locality and long distance dependency, see Sag (2010b).

(27)
$$\begin{bmatrix} \textit{strans-v-lxm} & \\ \text{FORM} & \langle \text{kick} \rangle \\ \text{SYN} & \begin{bmatrix} \text{VAL} \ \langle \ \text{NP}_i, \ \text{NP}\begin{bmatrix} \text{SYN}\begin{bmatrix} \text{CAT}|\text{LID} & \langle \textit{i-bucket-fr} \rangle \\ \text{MRKG} & \textit{the} \end{bmatrix} \end{bmatrix} \rangle \end{bmatrix} \\ \text{SEM} & \begin{bmatrix} \text{FRAMES} & \left\langle \begin{bmatrix} \textit{die-punctually-fr} \\ \text{DECEDENT} \ \ i \end{bmatrix} \right\rangle \end{bmatrix} \end{bmatrix}$$

As shown in (27), idiomatic *kick* is a transitive lexeme whose object is semantically empty and whose base morphological form is *kick*. This lexeme has two valence requirements. The first is for a potential subject NP with index i. The second is for an NP identified in terms of *i-bucket-fr*, an idiomatic frame that never contributes to the sentence's meaning. The semantics of the lexeme *kick* consists of the predicate 'die punctually' whose argument is identified with the index of its potential subject. The second valent requirement will ensure that this verb projects a VP containing a single NP, whose head lexeme is idiomatic *bucket* and whose functor ('specifier') is meaningless *the*. The resulting VP will express a predicate 'die punctually' that is 'looking for' a subject NP to provide the DECEDENT argument to complete the predication.

This concludes our analysis of *kick the bucket*. Notice that the present approach eliminates the need for special devices for the analysis of semi-fixed expressions. Instead, they are analyzed in the same way as syntactically flexible expressions, leaving their restricted properties to be explained in terms of the idiosyncrasies of their listemes in interaction with ordinary phrasal constructions.

1.4 Super-Flexible Idioms

The idioms we have examined so far exhibit varying degrees of flexibility. In this section we explore the analysis of idioms whose variability includes more than multiple morphological realizations or the positional variation of a single idiom word. We first examine *side the bread is buttered on* and *What's X doing Y?*, which interact with *wh*-constructions in interesting ways, yet exhibit certain differences which, we claim, can be simply treated in terms of diverse lexical constraints and their interaction with the constraints imposed by English combinatorial constructions and other listemes.

Consider first the sentences in (28):

(28) a. Yes, a little line drawn in the sand to let Bibi know which side his bread is buttered on.
b. I know which side my bread is buttered on.
c. Google should know which side its bread is buttered on.
d. And don't think for a minute that the "scientific community", especially the Al Gore global warming community, doesn't know what side their bread is buttered on.

We have not found any linguistic analyses of this idiom. Popular accounts usually say—or more often imply—that it has the following properties:

A. The matrix verb is *know*, possibly negated.
B. The specifier of *bread* is a genitive pronoun.
C. The pronominal specifier of *bread* is bound to the subject of *know*.
D. The NP headed by *side* must cooccur with an interrogative *wh*-word determiner.
E. The *bread-is-buttered-on* phrase is an embedded interrogative clause.
F. The immediate governor of the phrase headed by *buttered* is *be*, presumably the passive auxiliary.
G. The preposition *on* is stranded.

The next section may be viewed as a methodological exercise. The idiom is more abstract than suggested by the above picture. In fact none of the properties (A–G) is a necessary one. Often, when one notices a recurring grammatical pattern and begins to investigate its constructional status, one finds that the truly idiomatic part—the irreducible stuff that is unpredictable from anything else in the grammar—is more abstract than the pattern one originally recognized. Following this reduction of the scope of the syntactic investigation, we will look at the semantics of the idiom. Then a somewhat more formal analysis of the construction will be presented, in an effort to persuade the reader of the analytic versatility of Sign-Based Construction Grammar.

1.4.1 Limiting the Scope of the Bread-Buttering Idiomaticity

A. It is immediately apparent that many verbs other than *know* can serve as governors in this pattern.

(29) a. Come on, this guy figured out which side his bread is buttered on ...

b. Looking at the headlines, I notice that US Senators from both parties are paying careful attention to the side their bread's buttered on.[22]

It appears that (at least) any verb that can take an embedded interrogative complement can appear as the governing verb in this pattern.

B. The specifier of *bread* need not be a pronoun. It may be a genitive noun phrase, either proper or common, or it may be the definite article *the*. The constraint seems to be only

[22]Some readers may not consider examples like this one, in which the specifier of *side* is not a *WH*-phrase, legitimate examples of ordinary English, but the web contains too many examples of this type to consider them all word play:

(i) He's a so called republican because that's the side his bread's always been buttered on and the Dems probably nauseated him.

(ii) The Side on Which My Bread is Buttered [Blog title]

(iii) In this primer of power, we have all the crudities of the youngster who has as yet inadequate conceptions of the side on which his bread is buttered. ...

(iv) The side the bread is buttered on [headline]

(vi) Mar 3, 2008. if these guys step out of line I'm sure the side their bread is buttered on will become apparent. In the American retail world, ...

(vii) The side one's bread is buttered on tends to affect one's credibility.

that it must be definite:

(30) a. In his pursuit to find out which side Benji's bread is buttered on, Andy J,...
b. Why is this drivel on Massey's site? Makes one wonder who's side WSAZ's bread is buttered on!
c. I chose the super closeup to convey the fact that we don't know which side the guy's bread is buttered on. Eg. Goodie or baddie.
d. pictures of Arafat as if he was a hero when even Arafat knew which side the bread was buttered on.[23]

C. When the specifier of *bread* is a pronoun it is not necessarily bound to a higher subject.

(31) a. I guess we know which side your bread is buttered on.
b. I know what side your bread is buttered on, I'm in, I'm ONE OF YOU.
c. I know which side Haseo's bread is buttered on.
d. He had the manners and listening attitude down pat—but you know which side his bread is buttered on.
e. I'm pretty sure that we know which side Michelle's bread is buttered on.

D. The noun phrase headed by *side* need not contain a *WH*-word:[24]

[23]More examples of this type for those inclined to reject these, again selected from many others attested on the web:

(i) If this is not proof as to which side the MSM'S bread is buttered, then I don't know what is!
(ii) It is now clear, though, on which side the Global Times's bread is buttered.
(iii) LOL I think we know which side the umpire's bread was buttered!
(iv) a little checking showed which side the military's bread was buttered on and the side they'd ...
(v) Maria knows on which side the family's bread is buttered, and realizes that without the income generated by Vermeer's oils, the household would be thrown into the street.
(vi) Cameron knows which side the UK's bread is buttered on.

[24]See also footnote 20.

(32) a. Gmail allows you to use an email client, but they restrict some of the goodies to web access, because that is the side their bread is buttered on.

b. but if these guys step out of line I'm sure the side their bread is buttered on will become apparent.

E. The pattern may occur without all or any part of it constituting an embedded question—(32a) and (33), for example:

(33) a. That's the side Buckley's bread is buttered on.

b. Nvidia know that this is the side their bread is buttered on ...

c. The sage whom thus we celebrate Was bound to pray for Church and State; And piously his prayers he mutter'd, For on that side his bread was butter'd.

d. Married into the nation's most prominent Democrat family, California Gov. Arnold Schwarzenegger flopped to the GOP side that his bread is buttered on.

F. A verbal governor of the past participle *buttered* need not be the passive auxiliary *be*. The *get*-passive is also possible, although admittedly rare:

(34) a. Rep. Bachmann said. "They are incredulous about the possibility of losing their majority and they know which side their bread gets buttered on and ACORN is their friend."

b. Beck knows which side his bread gets buttered on.

c. This story still uses liberal connotations and loaded terms, though, so you can tell which side their bread gets buttered on. (punctuation added)

d. TRUE - Stafford will be back at QB and Detroit has made some good moves this off season. They know what side their bread gets buttered on.

e. It's no surprise then that they would sugar coat or down play anything which makes their benefactors look bad, they know what side their bread gets buttered on.[25]

G. Perhaps surprisingly, pied-piping tokens of this idiom are about as frequent on the web as preposition-stranding ones. In actual Google hits *on * side * bread * buttered* scores 480 versus 490 hits for *side * bread * buttered on*. A few examples of pied-piping:

(35) a. They know on which side their bread is buttered and will adapt quite quickly to what they see as the potential winning side.
b. Wendy knows on which side her bread is buttered.
c. Still, few Costa Ricans have anything bad to say about their country's popularity as a destination—perhaps simply because they know on which side their bread's buttered.
d. Salespeople know on which side their bread's buttered.

The contraction of *bread's* in the last two examples suggests that the pied-piping version of the idiom is not restricted to formal contexts.

We also find examples with the stigmatized, preposition-doubled form, as well as those with no preposition.

(i) Sometimes it needs outsiders such as these Spaniards to show them Yanks on which side the bread is buttered on.
(ii) Knowing on which side his bread was buttered on, he flew the flag for the conservative side of politics.
(iii) Pastors, knowing on which side their bread was buttered on, gave more to those that paid more and gave little to those that contributed little.

[25]The use of *get*, rather than *be*, in this idiom is relatively rare. Google yields only 50 true hits for *their bread gets buttered on* versus 498 for *their bread is buttered on*. We have not attempted to compare this ratio of roughly 1/10 to the relative frequencies of the *get*- and *be*-passives. A case could be made to count examples like those in (34) as word play or other forms of nonce extension of the grammar, thus excluding them from the data on which analysis of the construction is based. Judgment calls of this kind are seemingly unavoidable in grammatical research, even when based on corpus data.

(iv) Tesco's boss knows which side his bread is buttered.
(v) I Know what Side My Bread Is Buttered.

As suggested by an anonymous referee, the existence of such non-standard forms provides further evidence that the usual syntactic constructions are in play in creating sentences containing many, if not all, "phrasal" idioms.

The reduction in the actual size of the idiom can be taken further.[26] Neither the words *side* nor *on*, although frequently occurring with the idiom words *bread* and *buttered*, are necesary parts of the idiom.[27]

(36) a. There will be a fine fracas soon, and I must see, whatever happens, that my bread is well buttered.
b. There, as his declassified 600-page FBI file shows, his bread would be buttered by Harry Bridges' Communist-controlled International Longshore and Warehouse Union.
c. I fear that those people are basically keeping their bread well buttered by fomenting the threat of terrorism, which serves their interest as it does Beijing's.
d. But it seems that the company's bread will be buttered by users looking to get around location restrictions.
e. Think about how Ike's bread gets buttered at work. What is he rewarded for?
f. From a business perspective, is your bread best buttered at your current job or elsewhere?
g. Politicians everywhere seem to understand their bread is buttered with political donations, even if those donors are in Washington, or Miami, or Dallas, and that politician resides in Guatemala City.
h. OK, so he's a screenwriter, right. Actually, no. His bread is really buttered with voice work. He's been

[26]We are indebted to an anonymous referee for this observation.
[27]We cite numerous examples to demonstrate the robustness of the phenomenon.

doing English dubbing for Japanese anime since he was ten years old...

i. The most popular actors in American cinema know how their bread is buttered and embrace the public.
j. It's hard to blame a politician for knowing how the bread is buttered around here.
k. Teixeira knows where his bread is buttered.
l. Suffice it to say, Mrs. Clinton knows where her bread is buttered.
m. Of course, there would be some countries who would resist, having had their bread royally buttered by Blatter, but FIFA couldn't survive the resignations of Germany, Italy, Spain, England, France, USA, etc.
n. Despite having had their bread well-buttered by a series of British monarchs ... the Sultans became enamoured of German power and Prussian state organization...

1.4.2 The Analysis of *the side the bread is buttered on*

As we have just seen, the idiom often cited as *to know which side one's bread is buttered on*, or something similar, boils down to just two necesary idiom words: the noun *bread*, meaning something like 'needs or desires' and the past participle *buttered*, meaning something like 'satisfied', and two optional idiom words: *side*, meaning something like 'place', and *on*, meaning something like 'at'. The properties of these listemes interact with the general phrasal constructions of the grammar, such as the Predicational Head-Complement Construction, which licenses VPs and non-case-marking PPs, and the Head-Functor Construction, which licenses binary branching NPs (*inter alia*), to determine the syntactic privileges of occurrence of the idiom and to compose the semantics of each token.

The analysis to follow covers the most extensive use of the idiom, in which the two optional words *side* and *on* are employed. We gloss the meaning of the *side someone's bread is buttered on* idiom as something like the '**location** (*side*) at which [someone's] **needs or desires** (*bread*) are **satisfied** (*buttered*)', where the key frame (relation, predicate) is that of satisfaction or gratification and its arguments are a THEME (the 'needs') and a LOCATION. Someone who knows 'the *side* their *bread* is *buttered* on', knows the **place** where their **needs** are **satisfied**.[28] The FRAMES list of the semantically key *buttered* listeme is given in (37):

(37) $$\left[\text{FRAMES}\ \left\langle \begin{bmatrix} \textit{buttered[satisfy]-fr} & \\ \text{LOCATION} & \text{y} \\ \text{THEME} & \text{x} \end{bmatrix} \right\rangle \right]$$

The *buttered[satisfy]-fr* is a canonical frame (*c-frame*); since *buttered* is the governing lexeme of the idiom, and the phrase it projects (and to which it contributes its LID value) occurs in canonical contexts. The idiom says something about where someone's needs are satisfied, but nothing explicitly about who or what they are satisfied by. When we assert—or especially question or deny—someone's knowing the side their bread is buttered on, we may or may not have a particular benefactor in mind. We will see below that the value of the THEME feature of the *buttered[satisfy]-fr* is identified with the index of the *bread* constituent and the value of the LOCATION feature is identified with the index of the NP headed by *side*, which is also the index of the PP headed by *on*.

The syntactic analysis of the idiom consists entirely of lexical entries (listemes), exploiting the original NSW proposal that semantic and syntactic composition of idioms derive from the non-canonical nature of the words they contain in interaction with the canonical phrasal constructions of the language. The syntactic possibilities and constraints follow from the properties of the listemes for idiomatic *buttered*,

[28]We can imagine alternative semantic parses of the idiom and expect interspeaker variation in this and similar cases.

$$\begin{bmatrix} \textit{word} & \\ \text{FORM} & \langle \text{ buttered } \rangle \\ \text{ARG-ST} & \left\langle \text{X:NP}_y \begin{bmatrix}\text{LID} & \langle \textit{i-bread[needs]-fr}\rangle \\ \text{MRKG} & \textit{def}\end{bmatrix}, \text{PP}_x[\text{LID } \langle \textit{i-side[loc]-fr}\rangle] \right\rangle \\ \text{SYN} & \begin{bmatrix} \text{CAT} & \begin{bmatrix} \textit{verb} & \\ \text{LID} & \langle \boxed{1} \rangle \\ \text{VFORM} & \text{pas}\end{bmatrix} \\ \text{VAL} & \langle \text{X},\ldots\rangle \\ \text{GAP} & \langle \text{NomP}_x \rangle \end{bmatrix} \\ \text{SEM} & \begin{bmatrix}\text{IND} & \text{s} \\ \text{FRAMES} & \langle \, \boxed{1}\textit{buttered[satisfy](s,x,y)} \, \rangle\end{bmatrix}\end{bmatrix}$$

FIGURE 1 The Idiomatic Participle *buttered*

bread, on, and *side* in interaction with various phrasal constructions of English. We posit an idiomatic passive participle *buttered* 'satisfied' with two arguments: an NP headed by the idiomatic noun *bread* 'needs/desires' and a prepositional constituent that resolves either to a PP headed by an idiom preposition *on* or to the preposition *on* itself, depending on whether a given token employs the usual mechanisms of pied-piping or stranding (see Sag (2010a, 2012)). A feature structure modeling the idiomatic participle *buttered* is sketched in Figure 1.

The idiomatic preposition *on* has an object argument headed by idiomatic *side* (see (38)). As noted above, the *side* argument denotes the location where needs are satisfied (see (40)). The *on* preposition identifies its index with that of its object, and hence refers to the 'location' at which 'needs' are 'satisfied'. The NP headed by *bread* denotes the 'needs' (see (39)). The first argument of *buttered* is an NP lexically headed by *bread* and, as demonstrated in the data section, must be definitely determined by either a genitive NP or *the*. The *buttered* listeme also has a non-empty GAP list containing a nominal phrase (NP or PP) coindexed with the *on* constituent (and hence with the *side* constituent). Thus either the *on* PP or its NP *side* object will normally appear in a filler position, licensed by one or another filler-head construction. The listemes for *buttered* and *on* are thus formulated with sufficient abstraction to allow the filler phrase to resolve to either the preposition-stranded or pied-piped form ([*Remember*] *which side the bread is buttered on.* vs. [*Remember*] *on which side the bread is buttered.*) Consequently, the expressed complement of *buttered* may be either the stranded preposition *on* or nothing (assuming a traceless theory of gaps like those in Sag (2010a) or Chaves (2012)).

The LID value of *buttered[satisfy]-fr* (a *c-frame*) identifies it as a canonical lexeme. As noted, it behaves canonically externally despite participating in idiomatic expressions because it selects idiomatic forms. The FORM value of *buttered* is ⟨buttered⟩. The ARG-ST specifies two arguments. The first argument, tagged X, is required to be an NP headed by idiomatic *bread*, whose index is y, and which is marked as definite. This argument is identified in the semantics with the THEME of the *buttered[satisfy]-fr*, i.e. with the needs to be satisfied. Unless an argument (member of the ARG-ST list) of a predicate is extracted, it is identified with the corresponding element of the VAL list. Hence *buttered* is specified as $[\text{VAL} \;\; \langle X, \ldots \rangle]$.[29]

The second member of the ARG-ST list is an optional prepositional phrase whose LID identifies it as being headed by idiomatic *on* and which is indexed x. The GAP list contains a nominal phrase (that is, either an NP or a PP) coindexed with the *on* PP of the ARG-ST list. If that NomP is resolved to the whole PP (i.e. if the PP is pied-piped), the VAL list will have no member reflecting the second member of ARG-ST list. If only the NP object of *on* appears on the GAP list, then the bare preposition *on* will be stranded and

[29]This is accomplished not by redundant stipulation, but by general principles of argument realization, e.g. the Argument Realization Principle discussed in Sag et al. (2003).

so appear on the VAL list. In the version of the idiom in which there is no PP[*on*] (and *a fortiori* no *side*), there will be no PP_x entry on the ARG-ST list and the value of GAP will be the empty list.

The listeme for idiomatic *on* is given in (38). It requires an idiomatic *side*-headed NP object and has no semantics of its own, but, following a long tradition of GPSG/HPSG, identifies its index and its LID with that of its object:

(38)
$$\begin{bmatrix} \textit{trans-p-word} & \\ \text{FORM} & \langle \text{on} \rangle \\ \text{SYN} & [\text{CAT}\ [\text{LID}\ \langle Z \rangle]] \\ \text{ARG-ST} & \left\langle \text{NP}_y[\text{LID}\ \langle Z{:}\textit{i-side[loc]-fr} \rangle] \right\rangle \\ \text{SEM} & \begin{bmatrix} \text{INDEX} & y \\ \text{FRAMES} & \langle\rangle \end{bmatrix} \end{bmatrix}$$

The listemes for idiomatic *bread* and *side* are given in (39) and (40). The notation *cn-word* abbreviates *common-noun-word.*

(39)
$$\begin{bmatrix} \textit{cn-word} & \\ \text{FORM} & \langle \text{bread} \rangle \\ \text{SYN} & [\text{CAT}\ [\text{LID}\ \langle Z \rangle]] \\ \text{SEM} & \begin{bmatrix} \text{INDEX} & y \\ \text{FRAMES} & \langle Z{:}\textit{i-bread[needs]}(y) \rangle \end{bmatrix} \end{bmatrix}$$

(40)
$$\begin{bmatrix} \textit{cn-lxm} & \\ \text{FORM} & \langle \text{side} \rangle \\ \text{SYN} & [\text{CAT}\ [\text{LID}\ \langle Z \rangle]] \\ \text{SEM} & \begin{bmatrix} \text{INDEX} & \text{x} \\ \text{FRAMES} & \langle\ Z{:}\textit{i-side[loc]}(x)\ \rangle \end{bmatrix} \end{bmatrix}$$

Let us illustrate a clause built by the interaction of the

listemes constituting this idiom with the relevant phrase-building constructions of English:

(41) [He finally figured out] what side the bread is buttered on.

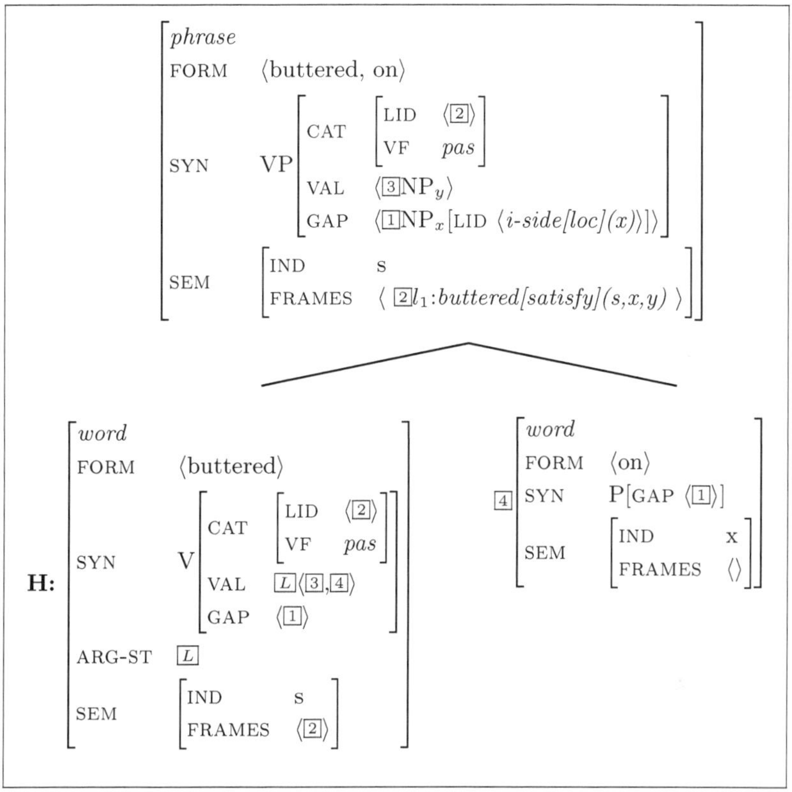

FIGURE 2 A Predicational VP Construct: *buttered on*

In Figure 2 we see that the LID of the passive participle *buttered* is identified with the content of the FRAMES value, via the tag $\boxed{2}$.[30] And, since LID is a CAT feature, it reappears as the corresponding feature of the mother phrase *buttered on*. The VALENCE list of *buttered* is identified, via the tag

[30]In the following discussion the reader familiar with neither SBCG nor HPSG may wish to consult Sag (2010a) for technical details.

[L], with its ARG-ST value, since there is no extraction or null argument instantiation for *buttered*. The VAL list contains the tags [3] and [4], the second of which tags the *on* constituent, which is the right sister to *buttered*. Since the first valent, [3], is not realized as a sister, it reappears in the VAL list of the mother, *buttered on* (uncancelled valents are passed up to an expression's mother, as in Categorial Grammar). Although there is no extraction or null instantiation of arguments of *buttered*, there is nonetheless a non-empty GAP list, since there is extraction of the object of the complement sister *on*.[31] Since a mother phrase inherits the gaps of its daughters (unless it is the mother of a filler-gap construct), the GAP value of the mother is identified with that of the lexical head. As a result, the singleton member of the GAP list of *on* is indirectly passed to the mother *buttered on* and will require the filler NP higher in the tree to be *side*-headed. *On*'s index, x, appears as the LOCATION of the *buttered[satisfy]-fr* in the FRAMES value of the mother (and head daughter).

The Predicational Head-Complement Construction combines idiomatic *buttered* and the idiomatic preposition *on* to license the gap-containing, non-finite, passive VP *buttered on*. This same construction combines the finite passive auxiliary *is* with *buttered on* to license the gap-containing, finite, passive VP *is buttered on*. The Subject-Predicate construction combines the NP *the bread* with the gap-containing VP *is buttered on* to form the gap-containing clause *the bread is buttered on*. This is summarized in the analysis tree shown in Figure 3. Finally, the Non-Subject *Wh*-Interrogative Construction (Sag 2012:167) allows the filler NP *what side* to combine with the gapped clause to license the non-gapped clause *what side the bread is buttered on*, as shown in Figure 4.

[31] This follows the analysis of Sag (2010b), where each predicate 'amalgamates' the GAP values of its arguments into its own GAP value. For an alternative compatible analysis, see Chaves (2012).

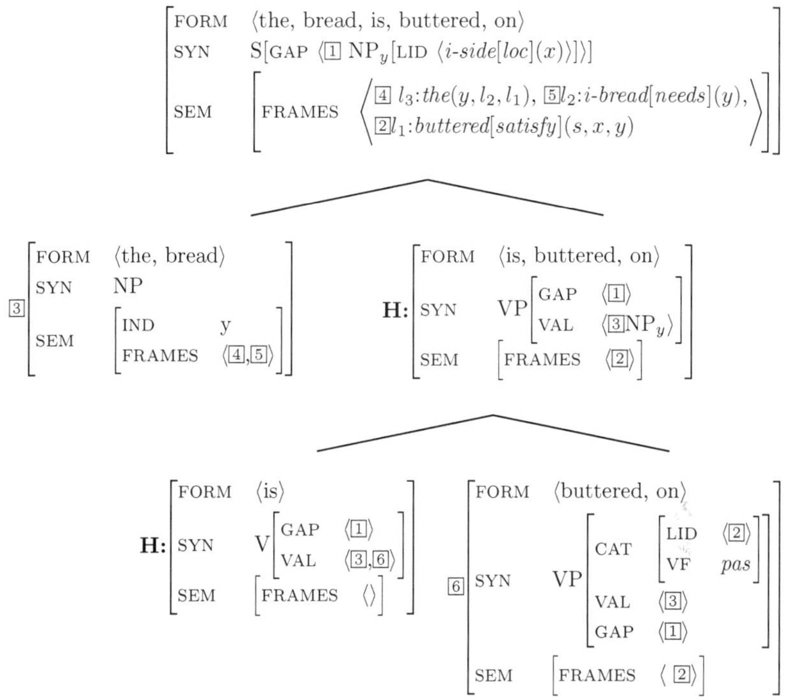

FIGURE 3 Analysis: *the bread is buttered on*

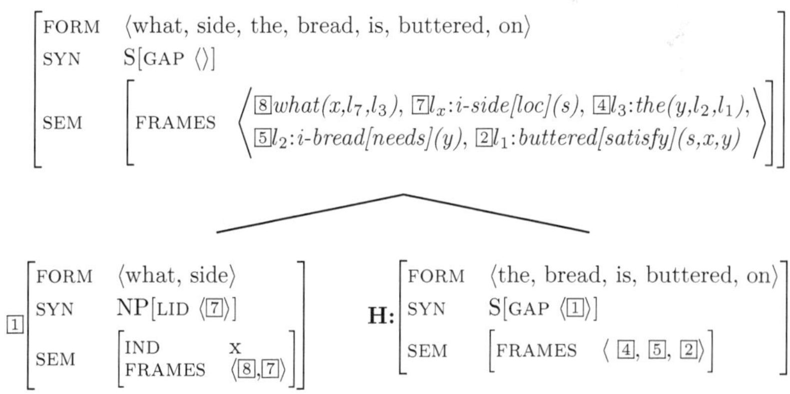

FIGURE 4 The NonSubject *Wh*-Interrogative Clause: *what side the bread is buttered on*

1.4.3 What's X Doing Y?

The MRS analysis of *wh*-interrogatives used in the previous section also provides a natural home for a treatment of the 'What's X Doing Y?' (WXDY) Construction, illustrated in (42), whose importance was first discussed by Kay and Fillmore (1999).

(42) a. What were you doing talking to that awful man?
'Why were you talking to that awful man?'
b. What is your name doing in my book? (Kay and Fillmore (1999):3)
'How come your name is in my book?'

The semantic fact of particular importance in Kay and Fillmore's discussion is the interpretation paraphrasable in terms of *why*, *how come* or *what is the reason that*, as indicated in (42).

The essential ingredients of WXDY are the following:

(43) a. an interrogative filler *what* participating in a *wh*-interrogative construction
b. a form of the copula governing *doing*
c. a gap associated with the object of the progressive participle of the verb *do*
d. a predicative XP following *doing*, forming a constituent with it
e. the impossibilty of negation, either of *be* or of *do*
f. a causal interrogative semantics
g. a pragmatic attribution of incongruity of the proposition whose cause is being questioned.

These points are illustrated by the following examples:

(44) a. I wonder what the salesman will say this house is doing without a kitchen. (invented example, (Kay and Fillmore, 1999, ex. (3)c))
b.*What does your name keep doing in my book?
c.*What will your name (be) do in my book?

d. What is he doing? (lacks WXDY semantics)
e.*What weren't you doing (not) talking to my aunt?
f.#What is he doing drunk, which everyone knew he would be?

Example (44a) is of particular importance in showing that the scope of the causal operator is not necessarily the same as the clause following the *what.* That is, though the position of *what* demarcates the top of the interrogative clause, it is the embedded structure *this house is doing without a kitchen* whose causality is to be explained by the salesman. (44a) does not mean 'I wonder why it is that the salesman will say that this house lacks a kitchen'.

WXDY finds a simple analysis within SBCG. Perhaps unsurprisingly, this analysis, like the previous ones, is purely lexical in nature. First, in order to account for the role of *be* in WXDY, we posit a listeme like the following:

(45) $\begin{bmatrix} \textit{copula-lxm} & \\ \text{ARG-ST} & \left\langle \text{X} , \begin{bmatrix} \text{VP} & \\ \text{LID} & \langle \textit{i-doing-fr} \rangle \end{bmatrix} \right\rangle \end{bmatrix}$

This listeme, which inherits all of its remaining properties from the Copula Construction (a lexical class construction), selects a subject (X) and a VP complement whose LID is the idiomatic *i-doing-frame*. Like other copula *be*-lexemes, this is an auxiliary verb with subject-raising properties. And because its FRAMES list is empty, it makes no contribution to the semantics.

The lexicon contains only one listeme whose LID is *i-doing-fr*, and hence only one lexeme that gives rise to words that can head the VP complement of the *be* in (45). This listeme, because it includes the specification [VF *prp*], will have only one kind of word realization—a present participle as sketched in (46):

(46)

$$\begin{bmatrix} \textit{word} & \\ \text{FORM} & \langle \text{doing} \rangle \\ \text{ARG-ST} & \left\langle \boxed{1}, \boxed{2}, \boxed{3}\text{XP}\begin{bmatrix} \text{VAL} & \langle \boxed{1} \rangle \\ \text{LTOP} & l \end{bmatrix} \right\rangle \\ \text{SYN} & \begin{bmatrix} \text{CAT} & \begin{bmatrix} \textit{verb} & \\ \text{LID} & \langle \textit{i-doing-fr} \rangle \\ \text{VF} & \textit{prp} \end{bmatrix} \\ \text{VAL} & \langle \boxed{1}, \boxed{3} \rangle \\ \text{GAP} & \langle \boxed{2}\text{NP}_x[\text{LID} \left\langle \textit{what-fr} \right\rangle] \end{bmatrix} \\ \text{SEM} & \begin{bmatrix} \text{INDEX} & x \\ \text{FRAMES} & \left\langle \begin{bmatrix} \textit{justification-fr} & \\ \text{EXPLICANS} & x \\ \text{EXPLICANDUM} & l \end{bmatrix} \right\rangle \end{bmatrix} \end{bmatrix}$$

The ARG-ST list of the verb in (46) contains three elements: a subject ($\boxed{1}$), a direct object ($\boxed{2}$), and a predicational phrase ($\boxed{3}$). The predicational phrase, XP, has a unique (subject) valent, which is identified with the subject valent of *doing*. The indication [LTOP l] encodes the identification of the principal frame[32] of the semantics of the predicational phrase with the EXPLICANDUM argument of *doing*. The direct object is absent from the VAL list and present on the verb's GAP list. This element is specified as [INDEX x], which identifies it with the index of the verb's semantics, and [LID ⟨*what-fr*⟩], assuring that the filler daughter will also be so specified. The relevant properties of the word *what* are specified in (47). This is the ordinary interrogative noun *what*, as indicated

[32] In a FRAMES list, the members form a virtual, singly-rooted tree via use of the LABEL feature to allow all but one frame of the list to be identified with the value of an attribute of one other member. See Sag (2012:6ff), following Copestake et al. (2005).

by its non-null WH value. The empty-set value of the REL feature indicates that *what* is not a relative word, such as, for example, *who* in *the knave who stole the tarts*. In the SEM value the *what-fr* shows *what* to be an interrogative quantifier. Its BOUND VARIABLE x is identified with the unique argument of its RESTRICTION, the *thing-fr*, as indicated by the tags l_1. (The notations *label* for the features LABEL and SCOPE of the *what-fr* indicate that these features take an unspecified value of type *label*.)

(47)
$$\begin{bmatrix} \textit{word} & \\ \text{FORM} & \left\langle \textit{what} \right\rangle \\ \text{SYN} & \begin{bmatrix} \text{CAT} & \begin{bmatrix} \textit{noun} & \\ \text{LID} & \boxed{1}\left\langle \textit{what-fr} \right\rangle \\ \text{SELECT} & \text{none} \end{bmatrix} \\ \text{WH} & \boxed{1} \\ \text{REL} & \{\} \end{bmatrix} \\ \text{SEM} & \begin{bmatrix} \text{INDEX} & \text{x} \\ \text{FRAMES} & \left\langle \begin{bmatrix} \textit{what-fr} & \\ \text{LABEL} & \text{label} \\ \text{BV} & \text{x} \\ \text{REST} & l_1 \\ \text{SCOPE} & \text{LABEL} \end{bmatrix}, \begin{bmatrix} \textit{thing-fr} & \\ \text{LABEL} & l_1 \\ \text{INST} & \text{x} \end{bmatrix} \right\rangle \end{bmatrix} \end{bmatrix}$$

Finally, by couching the semantics in terms of a *justification-frame*, we encode the pragmatic incongruity effect observed by Kay and Fillmore without further stipulation. Note that, aside from register difference, (48a) and (48b) have quite similar perlocutionary effect.[33]

[33]An anonymous referee suggests that taking the *what* here as the ordinary *what* and imputing the meaning of justification to *doing* is not the only way the semantics of the idiom could be parsed out. One could, for example, enrich the meaning of *what* to something including the force of challenge, rather like *how come*, and concomitantly bleach the meaning of *doing* of the justification notion. It would be

(48) a. What is your name doing in my book? (=42b)

b. What is the justification of your name being in my book?

In sum, the WXDY Construction is analyzed in terms of a *be* listeme that selects for a complement whose LID is *i-doing-fr*. Because words like the participle in (46) are the only kind that mention *i-doing-fr*, these are the only words available to serve as lexical heads of the VP complement of *be* in WXDY. But since words like (46) have a nonempty GAP list, they must appear at the bottom of a filler-gap dependency. Moreover, since the first member of their GAP list must have the properties of interrogative *what*, that filler-gap dependency must be a *wh*-interrogative clause (main or embedded) whose filler daughter is the word *what*. (46) also links things together to produce a semantics asking about the justification for a certain proposition, where that proposition is constructed from the subject of *do* (which is also the subject of *be*) and its final complement. A construct illustrating WXDY, a FS of type *wh-int-ns-cl*, is shown in Figure 5. The notation [IC +] encodes the fact that *What is Bo doing here?* is an independent clause. The notation INV indicates subject-auxiliary inversion. The semantics is indicated in abbreviated notation in (49b):

(49) a. What is Bo doing here?

b. $what(x, l_3, l_1)$, $l_3{:}thing(x)$, $l_1{:}justification(x, l_2)$, $l_2{:}location(Bo, here)$

c. 'What justifies Bo being here?'

disingenuous to maintain that hard choices like this can always be avoided in the analysis of idioms. Our rule of thumb has been to assign a canonical interpretation to as many words as possible.

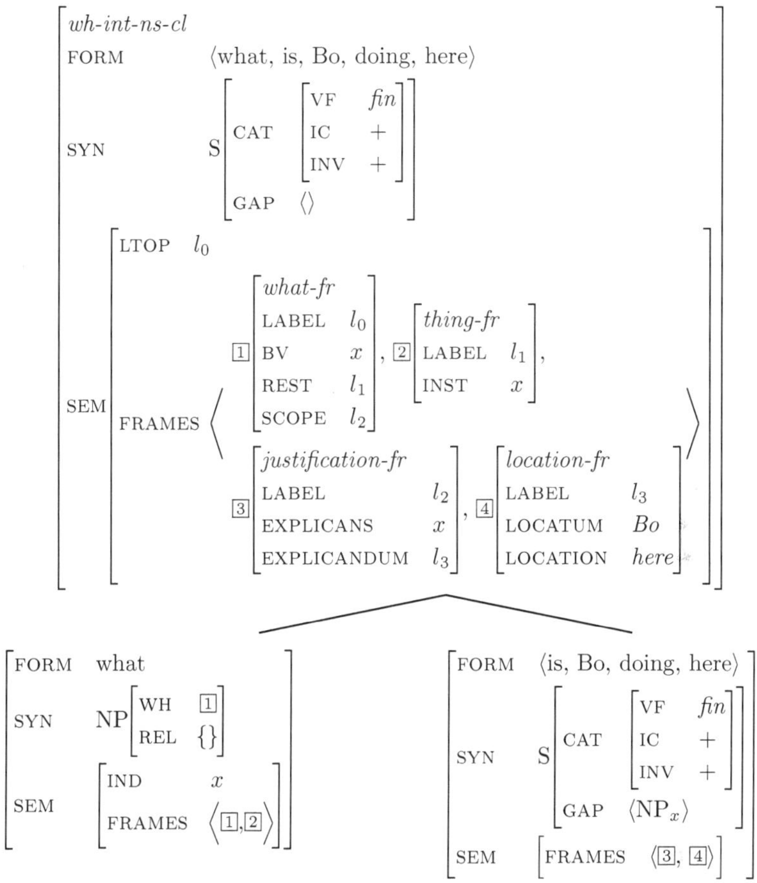

FIGURE 5 A Construct Illustrating the WXDY Phenomenon

1.5 Locality and Idiomaticity

We have not yet addressed an additional problem that arises in the idiom data. Certain idioms contain obligatory modifiers, as well as obligatory determiners. An example is (50):

(50) bark up the wrong tree.

In this idiom it is possible to insert an optional modifier between *wrong* and *tree*, as shown in (51). The possibility of such modifiers forecloses the possibility of treating the whole idiom as a 'word with spaces'.

(51) a. Barking up the wrong avocado tree in search of authentic Mexican... flavors

b. Barking up the wrong evidence tree...

c. Could we have been barking up the wrong linguistic tree all these years by over-emphasizing the importance of complexity and accuracy?

d. It isn't always possible to avoid wrong turns, but these steps may help keep you from barking up the wrong family tree.

Another example of an idiom that includes obligatory modifiers is *sing(ing) a different tune*, as exemplified in (52).

(52) a. The Sox are singing a different, quieter tune ahead of spring training.

b. However, after spotting a few emerald green dresses underneath the mistletoe last year, I may be singing a different (Christmas) tune...

c. ... today's deal from Light Touch Aesthetics for a restorative body wrap will have you singing a different holiday tune.

d. To most Americans, this school marm brandishing a switch seemed to be singing a different, even principled, tune.

The problem that facts like these raise for approaches like the HPSG analysis of Pollard and Sag (1994), or the SBCG treatment sketched in Sag (2012), is that the Head-Functor analysis of noun phrases provides no way for a common noun to require a modifier that stands in the functor relation to it. The main predicator, e.g. idiomatic *bark*, can require a PP complement headed by idiomatic *up*, and idiomatic *up* can require an object headed by idiomatic *tree*, but idiomatic *tree* cannot specify that it is modified by idiomatic *wrong*. Indeed, as Richter and Sailer (2009) have shown, this problem of nonlocal dependencies in idiomatic expressions is widespread, crossing clause boundaries in the case of many German idioms that they analyze. In the next section, we show how the same tools we apply here for treating nonlocal idiomatic dependencies in English can provide an account of the German data they discuss.

This problem relates to an issue that we mentioned in passing in section 3, where we proposed the listeme (24) (repeated here) to analyze the semantically empty lexeme *bucket* of *kick the bucket*:

(24)
$$\begin{bmatrix} \textit{cn-lxm} & \\ \text{FORM} & \langle \text{bucket} \rangle \\ \text{SYN} & \begin{bmatrix} \text{CAT} & \begin{bmatrix} \text{LID} & \langle \textit{i-bucket-fr} \rangle \end{bmatrix} \\ \text{VAL} & \langle \rangle \end{bmatrix} \\ \text{SEM} & \begin{bmatrix} \text{IND} & \textit{none} \\ \text{FRAMES} & \langle \rangle \end{bmatrix} \end{bmatrix}$$

This listeme shows an empty FRAMES list and an LID value of *i-bucket-frame*, unlike the other listemes discussed by Sag (2012), where the FRAMES list and LID value are identified. This raises the question of how to state the general principle and to allow for its exceptions. Given our system of monotonic constraints, this boils down to the question of what class of expressions (i.e. what lexical type) is subject to the identity constraint and what exceptions need to be stated.

The solution to both the problems of modifiers in idioms and obligatory modification in general requires a slight revision in the typology of lexemes. It is convenient to begin by considering the second problem mentioned, obligatory modification. The MRKG feature has until now functioned much like the LID feature, except that the latter is clearly 'passed up' from head daughter to mother, while MRKG passes up from the non-head daughter to its mother in a head-functor construct. Both features are conceived, however, as providing a partial semantic characterization of the expression they mark. Since the hierarchy representing the range of the LID feature provides a comprehensive semantic taxonomy of lexemes, there is neither formal nor empirical motivation for positing a distinct range of values for the MRKG feature. Any non-maximal classification of a lexeme, such as degree word, *deg*, or definite, *def*, will appear at some level in the frame hierarchy *degree-fr* or *definite-fr*; any maximal classification of a lexeme, such as *i-wrong-fr*, will of course also appear there. We simplify the formalism by eliminating a special set of values for the MRKG feature and identifying the MRKG value and LID value for all lexemes.[34]

Thus identifying the MRKG and LID values provides a solution to the obligatory modification problem. Under the proposed change a predicator or functor can specify in its respective ARG-ST or SELECT value a complement or head with a specified MRKG value. This MRKG value of a head can, in the relevant cases, only be acquired from combination with a functor sister bearing that MRKG value in a head-functor construct, and the MRKG value can identify that modifier uniquely if desired. A predicator or potential functor (mainly determiner or modifier) can specify, as loosely or tightly as required, a modifier of the head of the phrase it subcategorizes for or selects. For example, the idiomatic *the* of *up the wrong tree* can specify that the idiom word *tree* it selects has a MRKG value that guarantees that *tree* is modified by *wrong*. Similarly, the idiomatic *up* can subcategorize, not only for a NP whose LID value calls for idiomatic *tree* to be its head, but also that the MRKG value of the phrase it selects indicate the idiomatic *the* which in turn, as we just saw, ensures that the *tree*-headed nominal *the* selects contains the idiomatic modifier *wrong*.[35]

[34]This identification holds *only* for lexemes. We will see how the fact that phrases can, and often do, have different LID and MRKG values provides a strategic advantage. Just as there are semantically empty frames that serve to identify (projections of) semantically null idiom words like idiomatic *bucket*, so there are semantically empty frames that serve to identify certain "marker" words, such as the complementizer *that*.

[35]The idiom word *up* is syntactically a preposition, not a particle. In fact, there is a variant of the idiom, which some sources characterize as a mistake, employing the preposition *at* instead of *up*. One can't **bark the wrong tree up/at*. A referee points

We first consider how the lexemes for *the*, *wrong*, and *tree* are combined into the phrase *the wrong tree*.[36]

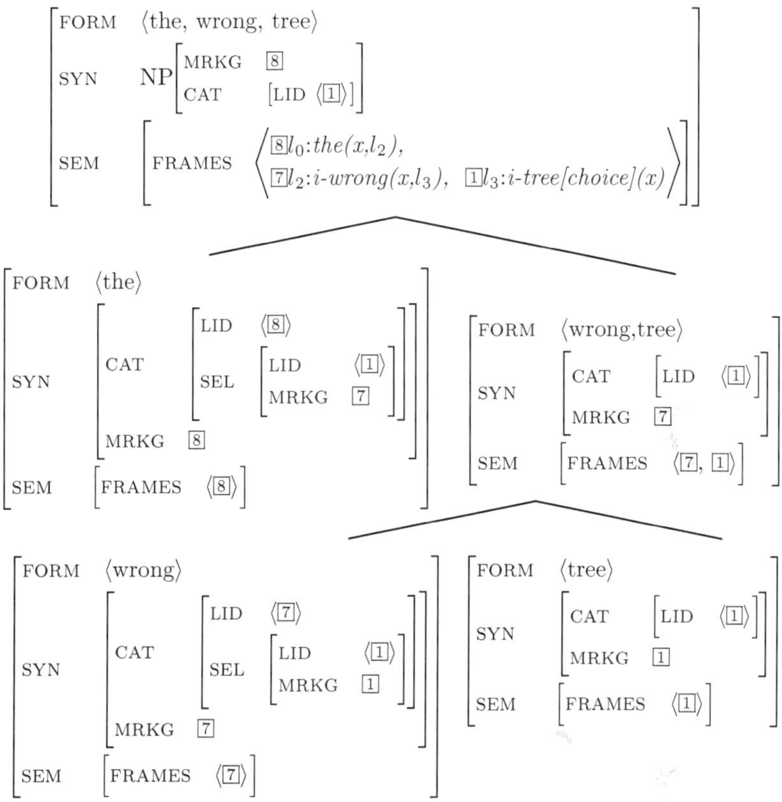

FIGURE 6 Analysis of *the wrong tree*

The terminal nodes in the analysis tree in Figure 6 display the relevant information about the lexemes *the*, *wrong*, and

out that in order to license *[very wrong] tree* – for which Google searches provide substantial support – one has to assume that intensifier *very* identifies its MARKING value with that of the AP it modifies.

[36]We assume that *bark*, *up*, *the*, *wrong*, and *tree* are all idiom words; *the* and *wrong*, however, have the same semantics as the corresponding canonical words, while differing in some syntactic properties, specifically LID and MRKG features. In particular, *the* has LID and MRKG features *the[wrong.tree]-fr*. We take the semantic breakdown of the idiom to be, roughly, *bark* 'make' *up* (simply raises the semantics of its object) *the* 'the' *wrong* 'wrong' *tree* 'choice'.

tree.[37] The SELECT value of *wrong* calls for a selectee whose LID and MRKG values both show l_3:*i-tree[choice](x)*. The word formed from the idiomatic *tree* lexeme is the only possible expression satisfying this constraint. The mother of the resulting head-functor construct is a phrase specified both as [LID⟨ l_3:*i-tree[choice](x)* ⟩] and [MRKG l_2:*i-wrong(x,*l_3*)*], the former inherited from the head daughter and the latter from the functor daughter, licensed by the Head-Functor Construction. At the next level, a syntactically idiomatic but semantically canonical lexeme *the* selects a phrase with [LID ⟨ l_3:*i-tree[choice](x)* ⟩] and [MRKG *i-wrong-fr*], again licensed by the Head-Functor Construction. The resulting (mother) phrase has constraints [LID ⟨ l_3:*i-tree[choice](x)* ⟩] and [MRKG *the[wrong.tree]-fr*]. We will see presently that a phrase bearing just these constraints satisfies a valence requirement of idiomatic *up*. We have exemplified how the proposed identification in each listeme of LID and MRKG values in listemes eliminates the otherwise troubling problem of obligatory modification.

Before continuing with the derivation of the phrase 'barking up the wrong tree', we propose a further emendation to the framework of Sag (2012). Verbal lexemes are there partially defined by the following lexical class construction (Sag 2012:112):

[37]Note that in the lexemes *the*, *wrong*, and *tree*, the LID and MRKG values are identified, while this is not the case for the phrases *wrong tree* and *the wrong tree*. In Figure 6, and elsewhere below, the quantifier *the* appears without a third argument because the phrase being modeled does not contain the quantifier's scopal phrase. For example, *the(x,*l_2*)* abbreviates *the(x,*l_2*,label)*.

(53) **Verb Lexeme Construction** ($\uparrow$*lexeme*):

$$
\textit{verb-lxm} \Rightarrow \begin{bmatrix} \text{ARG-ST} & \langle X\ , \ldots \rangle \\ \text{SYN} & \begin{bmatrix} \text{CAT} & \begin{bmatrix} \textit{verb} & \\ \text{LID} & L \\ \text{SELECT} & \textit{none} \\ \text{XARG} & X \end{bmatrix} \\ \text{MRKG} & \textit{unmk} \end{bmatrix} \\ \text{SEM} & \begin{bmatrix} \text{LTOP}^{38} & l_{0 =_q 1} \\ \text{FRAMES} & L{:}\langle ([\text{LABEL} \;\; l_1]) \rangle \end{bmatrix} \end{bmatrix}
$$

The constraints on lexemes in general with regard to identity of LID and FRAMES values are not mentioned in Sag (2012), but there are certain classes of lexemes for which this identity cannot hold, as noted above and by Sag in his discussion of *kick the bucket*. It is argued that the idiomatic lexeme *bucket* must be formulated with the empty list as the FRAMES value and yet must have an identifying LID distinct from the empty list in order for it to be identifiable by the idiomatic *kick*. Non-predicative ('case-marking') prepositions (including idiomatic ones such as *up* of *up the wrong tree*) must also be formulated with distinct LID values and FRAMES values. Similarly, infinitive predicative *be* contributes no frames to the meaning of the clauses in which it occurs, and so would also naturally be represented as [FRAMES $\langle\rangle$].

We slightly amend the lexical branch of the signature hierarchy to (a) unify the LID and MRKG values for all lexemes to account for obligatory modification and (b) properly distinguish common lexemes from empty lexemes: those with empty FRAMES lists and concomitantly distinct FRAMES and LID values.

[38] The notation [LTOP $l_0 \ldots$] indicates that the main frame of the verb will not be outscoped locally by any nonquantifier frame. See Sag (2012):94 for further discussion. Questions of quantifier scope are not at issue in this paper.

(54)

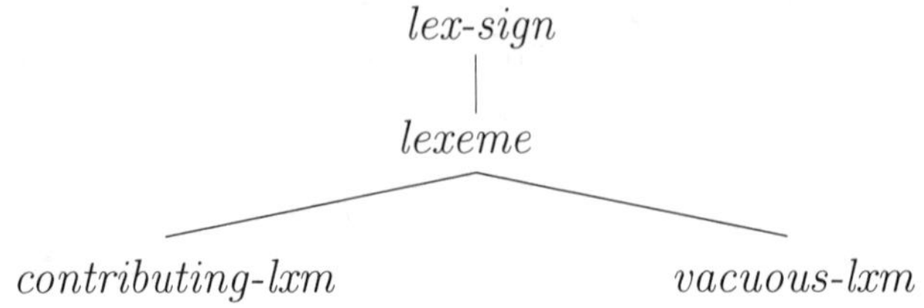

The corresponding type declarations[39] are given in (55):

(55) a. *lex-sign*: [ARG-ST *list(expression)*]

b. $$\textit{lexeme}\text{:} \left[\text{SYN} \begin{bmatrix} \text{CAT} & [\text{LID } \textit{list(frame)}] \\ \text{MRKG} & \textit{list(frame)} \end{bmatrix}\right]$$

c. $$\textit{contributing-lxm}\text{:} \begin{bmatrix} \text{SYN} & [\text{CAT } [\text{LID } L]] \\ \text{SEM} & [\text{FRAMES } L\text{:}\textit{nelist(frame)}] \end{bmatrix}$$

d. $$\textit{vacuous-lxm}\text{:} \begin{bmatrix} \text{SYN} & [\text{CAT } [\text{LID } \textit{nelist(frame)}]] \\ \text{SEM} & [\text{FRAMES } \langle\rangle] \end{bmatrix}$$

We note that in (55d) the FRAMES and LID values are not identified, as they are in (55c).

We now complete our analysis of *barking up the wrong tree*. Idiomatic *up* is of type *vacuous-lxm*. This lexeme, specified as [SEM [FRAMES ⟨⟩]], adds no frames to the semantics of the phrase it projects and it concomitantly displays an LID value, *i-up-fr*, distinct from its FRAMES value, ⟨⟩. As said before, idiomatic *up* selects a (noun) phrase with [LID ⟨*i-tree[choice]-fr*⟩] and [MRKG *the-fr*]. The listeme for idiomatic *up* is given in (56):[40]

---

[39] Type declarations, which occur in the grammar signature rather than the "constructicon," employ the format *type*: [constraint AVM]

[40] Notice that this treatment, like most lexical analyses in the SBCG/HPSG tradition, is highly modular. Further properties of the lexemes instantiating (56) follow from the interaction of other constructions, e.g. (i) and (ii):

(i) Intransitive Preposition Lexeme Construction:

$$\textit{intran-p-lxm} \Rightarrow \textit{p-lxm} \;\&\; \begin{bmatrix} \text{ARG-ST} & \langle \text{NP}_x \rangle \\ \text{SEM} & [\text{INDEX } x] \end{bmatrix}$$

(ii) Preposition Lexeme Construction:

p-lxm ⇒ [SYN [CAT *preposition*]]

(56)
$$\begin{bmatrix} \textit{vacuous-lxm \& intran-p-lxm} & \\ \text{FORM} & \langle \text{up} \rangle \\ \text{SYN} & [\text{CAT } [\text{LID } \langle \textit{i-up-fr} \rangle]] \\ \text{ARG-ST} & \left\langle \begin{bmatrix} \text{SYN} \begin{bmatrix} \text{CAT} & [\text{LID } \langle \textit{i-tree[choice]-fr} \rangle] \\ \text{MRKG} & \textit{the[wrong-tree]-fr} \end{bmatrix} \end{bmatrix} \right\rangle \end{bmatrix}$$

And this lexeme gives rise to a word that projects a saturated head-complement construct (*sat-hd-comp-cxt*) whose mother's FORM value is ⟨*up,the,wrong,tree*⟩, as shown in Figure 7. This structure uses the Saturational Head-Complement Construction (Sag 2012:188), which licenses the *up* word serving as the head daughter and the *the wrong tree* phrase as the complement daughter.

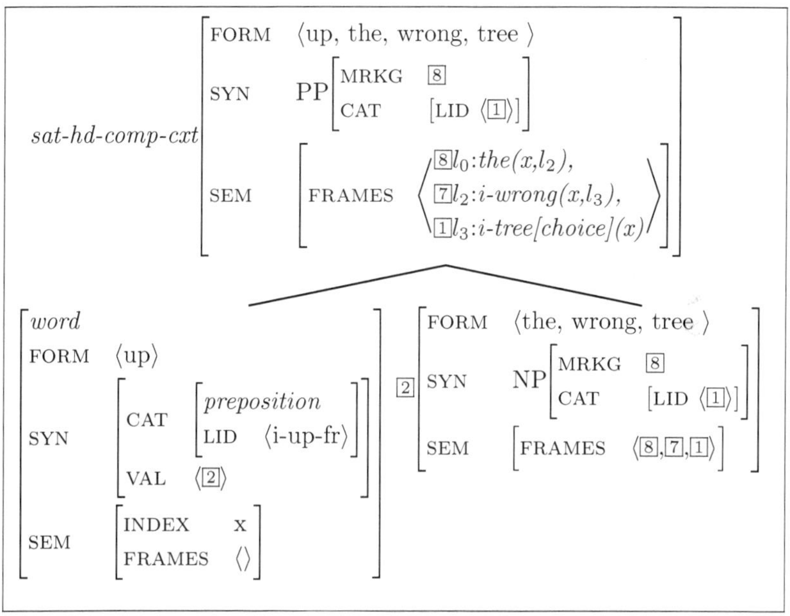

FIGURE 7 *up the wrong tree*

There is no news in the remainder of our analysis of *bark up the wrong tree*. The idiomatic listeme *bark* is formulated to contribute a frame meaning roughly 'make', to subcategorize for a subject that represents the agent of that frame and a PP, headed by idiomatic *up*, that expresses the incorrect choice made by the agent. The lexeme for idiomatic *bark* is shown in Figure 8.

$$\begin{bmatrix} \textit{prep-intran-v-lxm} & \\ \text{FORM} & \langle \text{bark} \rangle \\ \text{SYN} & \begin{bmatrix} \text{MRKG} & \boxed{1} \\ \text{CAT} & [\text{LID } \langle \boxed{1} \rangle] \\ \text{VAL} & \langle\, \text{NP}_y,\ \text{PP}_x[\text{LID } \langle \textit{i-up-fr} \rangle] \rangle \end{bmatrix} \\ \text{SEM} & \begin{bmatrix} \text{INDEX} & s \\ \text{FRAMES} & \left\langle \boxed{1} \begin{bmatrix} \textit{bark[make]-fr} & \\ \text{SIT} & \text{s} \\ \text{AGENT} & \text{y} \\ \text{THEME} & \text{x} \end{bmatrix} \right\rangle \end{bmatrix} \end{bmatrix}$$

FIGURE 8 Idiomatic bark

LID and MRKG are not the only features relevant to the analysis of nonlocal idiomatic dependenciess; XARG has a significant role to play, as well. There are many English idioms that require referential and agreement identity between a genitive within an NP and some other argument of the idiom, or which assign a semantic role to the embedded genitive. Bond et al. (2015) identify more than 500 such idioms, and provide an analysis which differs from the one to follow in imposing only semantic constraints on well-formedness, but shares the insight that the XARG value of a possessed NP enables lexical control in these idioms. Some are illustrated in (57)–(58):

(57) a. He_i lost [his_i/*her_j marbles].

b. They_i kept [their_i/*our_j cool].

(58) a. Adrenaline$_i$ made [her$_j$ hair] stand on end.
b. This$_i$ tickled [my$_j$ fancy].

As noted in Sag (2012), the presence of a prenominal genitive within an NP is encoded via a nonempty value for the feature XARG. If an object NP includes information about its prenominal genitive in its XARG value, then the listeme of a verb like *lose* (in its 'lose your cool' sense) can be formulated as in (59):[41]

(59)
$$\begin{bmatrix} \textit{strans-v-lxm} & \\ \text{FORM} & \langle \text{lose} \rangle \\ \text{ARG-ST} & \left\langle \text{NP}_x, \text{NP}_y \begin{bmatrix} \text{XARG} & [\textit{pron}]_x \\ \text{LID} & \langle \textit{i-cool[composure]-fr} \rangle \end{bmatrix} \right\rangle \\ \text{SEM} & \begin{bmatrix} \text{FRAMES} & \left\langle \begin{bmatrix} \textit{losing-fr} & \\ \text{AGENT} & x \\ \text{THEME} & y \end{bmatrix} \right\rangle \end{bmatrix} \end{bmatrix}$$

This specification requires both that the object NP contain a prenominal pronominal genitive NP and that that pronoun be coindexed with the subject of *lose* (blocking **He lost your cool* and the like).

We assume that NPs like *your cool* are built via the same Genitive Nominal Construction that is used for such NPs generally. This construction requires that the mother's XARG value be identified with the prenominal genitive NP, as in (60):

[41] Note that we use '*pron*' as a shorthand for an overt pronominal sign. By contrast, '*pro*' designates a covert pronominal.

(60)

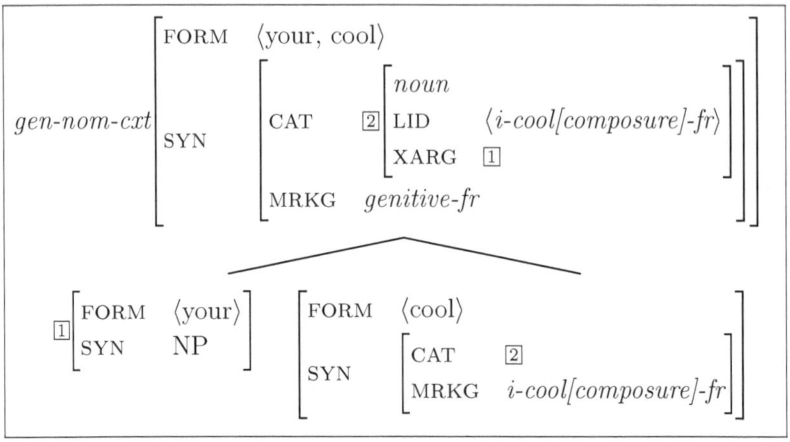

Thus, because only certain verbs, e.g. *keep*, *lose* and *blow* (in their relevant idiomatic listemes), select a direct object whose LID value is ⟨*i-cool-fr*⟩, these are the only lexical elements that can govern NPs headed by *cool* in its relevant idiomatic sense. The genitive within the *cool* NP and the subject of the governor are always coindexed. Various semantic treatments are possible. For example Sag (2012) expresses some analyses in the version of MRS used here and others in the semantics developed in Ginzburg and Sag (2000). The lexical entry in (59) assumes that *lose* is dyadic, with the direct object NP forming a second semantic argument (the THEME argument).

The phenomena just discussed are outside the analytic scope of the version of HPSG developed by Pollard and Sag (1994). As argued in Sag (2010b, 2012), these data provide considerable motivation for the analysis of verbal and nominal signs in terms of nonempty XARG specifications. Finally, note that XARG values, unlike VAL lists, do not 'shrink' in a bottom-up progression from head daughter to mother within an analysis tree. That is, no elements are 'cancelled off' an XARG list—the information about the external argument is locally visible at the top of the phrasal domain projected by the lexical head because XARG is a CAT feature and hence is regulated by head feature percolation.

One more idiom further illustrates some of the features of idioms already discussed and also provides a particularly interesting case of a bound genitive pronoun, e.g. *blow one's nose, crane one's neck, get one's comeuppance.* In the idiom illustrated in (61), the verb *keep* involves an AGENT (the keeper of the secret), a THEME (the item kept 'under one's hat', i.e. 'kept secret'), and the *under*-phrase, which specifies where the secret is kept.

(61) a. Maybe Tim kept the best stories under his hat?
b. This has never been shared before, so keep it under your hat.
c. ... so I kept it under my hat until I had enough money to shoot it myself.

We follow the online analysis proposed by The Phrase Finder, where *under one's hat* is decomposed as 'in one's head', i.e. not communicated and hence 'kept secret'.

Notice that there are variant expressions involving *keep* and *under*, e.g. *They kept it under wraps, keep it under control,* the idiomaticity of which seems less tightly bound to *keep.* Thus one finds examples like (62a,b):

(62) a. We wonder how long this story was under wraps.
b. Everything is under control.

By contrast, the idiomatic interpretation of *under one's hat* requires the presence of *keep.* The invented examples in (63) have no idiomatic interpretation:[42]

(63) a. This story is under my hat.
b. They have the information under their hat.

[42]This was apparently not always the case:

(i) The man whose estate lies under his hat need never tremble before the frowns of fortune. [*What I Remember*, by Thomas Trollope (the brother of Anthony), 1887.]

Thus our analysis of *keep under one's hat* requires a listeme like (64), where the verb *keep* selects a subject, direct object, and *under*-PP whose object must be headed by *hat*.

(64)
$$\left[\begin{array}{ll} \textit{obj-control-v-lxm} & \\ \text{FORM} & \langle \text{keep} \rangle \\ \text{ARG-ST} & \left\langle \text{NP}_x, \text{NP}_y, \text{PP}\left[\begin{array}{ll}\text{VAL} & \langle \textit{pro}_y\rangle \\ \text{LID} & \langle \textit{i-under[in]-fr(y,z)}\rangle \\ \text{XARG} & \text{pron}_x \\ \text{LTOP} & l\end{array}\right]\right\rangle \\ \text{FRAMES} & \left\langle\left[\begin{array}{ll}\textit{keep-fr} & \\ \text{SIT} & s \\ \text{AGENT} & x \\ \text{THEME} & y \\ \text{STATE} & l\end{array}\right]\right\rangle \end{array}\right]$$

The index y of the first argument of the *i-under[in]-fr* of the PP valent is identified with the index of the object NP_y of *keep* and the THEME argument of the *keep-fr*. The XARG $\textit{pron}_x$ of the PP valent is coindexed with the subject NP_x and its index x is identified with the AGENT argument of the *keep-fr*.

Since *i-under[in]-fr* is an *i-frame*, the idiomatic interpretation will be licensed only when selected by an appropriate governer. In this way, the idiomatic use of the *under*-phrase is restricted to the contexts in which it is governed by *keep*.

This idiomatic lexeme for *under* is sketched in (65):

(65)
$$\left[\begin{array}{ll} \textit{trans-p-lxm} & \\ \text{FORM} & \langle \text{under} \rangle \\ \text{SYN} & \left[\text{CAT}\left[\begin{array}{ll}\text{XARG} & \text{X} \\ \text{LID} & \langle \text{Y} \rangle\end{array}\right]\right] \\ \text{ARG-ST} & \left[\text{NP}_y,\ \text{NP}_z\left[\begin{array}{ll}\text{XARG} & \text{X: pron}_x \\ \text{LID} & \langle \textit{i-hat[head]-fr} \rangle\end{array}\right]\right] \\ \text{SEM} & \left[\text{FRAMES}\ \left\langle Y{:}\left[\begin{array}{ll}\textit{i-under[in]-fr} & \\ \text{LOCANDUM} & y \\ \text{LOCATION} & z\end{array}\right]\right\rangle\right] \end{array}\right]$$

This lexeme guarantees that idiomatic *under* governs an *i-hat*-headed NP whose pronominal genitive determiner XARG is identitifed with the XARG of the preposition itself, hence implicitly of the PP it projects, and is coindexed with the subject of *keep*, as sketched in Figure 9.

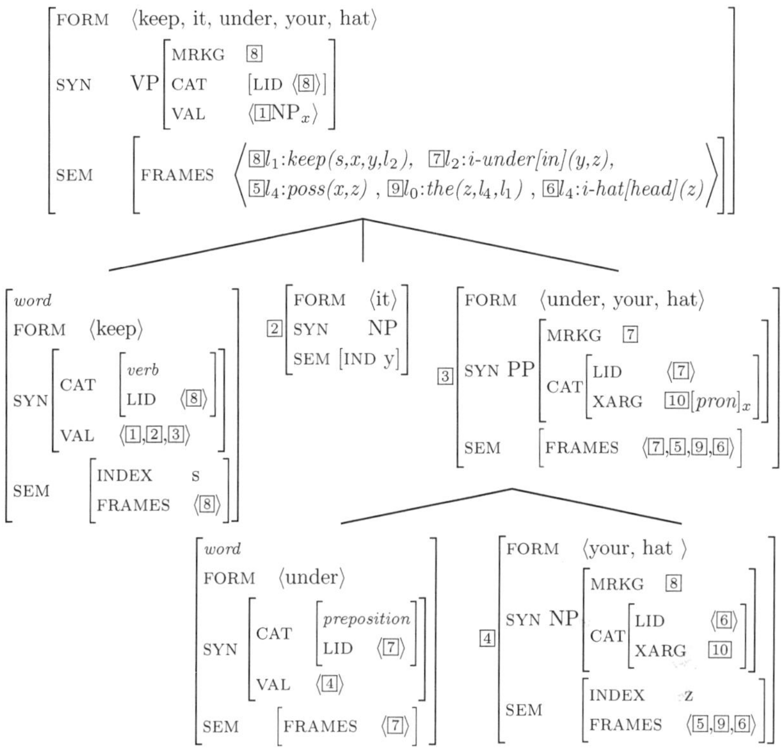

FIGURE 9 Analysis of: *keep it under your hat*

In Figure 9 the tree structure is determined by the interaction of the valence properties of the individual words and the standard combinatorial constructions of the grammar that build noun phrases, prepositional phrases, and verb phrases. The idiom itself has no phrasal properties. *Your hat* is a canonical noun phrase (determiner phrase, if you prefer); *under your hat* is a canonical prepositional phrase; and *keep it under your hat* is a canonical verb phrase. The phrase-structural relations observed are determined by the constructions that license such phrases in the grammar generally; no special phrasal machinery is necessary to license the idiom.

Regarding the composition of the semantics in Figure 9, look first at the FRAMES value of the root constituent. The *keep* frame has four arguments: s (a Davidsonian event variable), x, y, and l_2. Note that x is both the index of the subject valent of *keep* and the first argument of the possessor frame $\boxed{5}$, which identifies the index x of the subject valent and the index x of x's hat (i.e. 'head'). This identification is effected by (a) the joint action of the provision in (64) that identifies the index of the XARG of *keep*'s PP[*under*] argument with that of its subject argument and (b) the property of (65) whereby the tag X identifies the XARG of the preposition *under* (and therefore implicitly the PP *under* projects) with the XARG of its object NP[*hat*]. The y variable is introduced by the *it* constituent, which represents the information that is kept secret. Back in Figure 9, the l_2 label points to the *i-under[in]-fr*, which says that y (the secret) is in z (x's head). The *the* frame tagged $\boxed{9}$ is introduced by the *your hat* constituent $\boxed{4}$, and represents the definiteness semantics of the possessive determiner. The frame tagged $\boxed{6}$ assigns the variable z to the index of the *hat* (head) constituent.[43]

1.6 Locality

The present SBCG approach to idioms maintains strict locality.[44] It does not permit any listeme or construction to license a dependency more distant than that obtaining within a lo-

[43] With respect to the percolation of marking values, recall that marking and LID values are identical within lexemes and that they percolate from heads in head-complement structures and from functors in functor-head structures.

[44] We would like to thank Frank Richter and Manfred Sailer for discussion of some of the matters treated in this section. They are of course not responsible for such errors as we have persisted in.

cal tree. It thus conforms to the widespread observation that actual dependencies across the world's languages tend very strongly to be local, apparent exceptions such as extraction presenting in many languages evidence of comprising a series of local dependencies (see e.g., Sag 2007).[45] We conclude that a conservative approach to theory construction seeks a grammatical architecture whose general properties make local dependencies directly expressible and posits additional machinery to express genuinely non-local dependencies only in the special circumstances in which they arise, if any.

Richter & Sailer (2009 [R&S]), based on earlier work of Sailer (2003) and Soehn (2004), have developed a theory of idioms within constructional HPSG that eschews a lexical and localist approach in favor of a phrasal theory that permits idioms to establish dependencies at an arbitrary depth.[46] Although we find much of value in their treatment of a difficult grammatical question, there is one aspect of their theory that we find unnecessarily powerful. One mechanism by which R&S license such dependencies is by allowing the signs that appear on the DTRS list to contain a DTRS feature. Consequently, a phrasal sign can be defined to specify, for example, that a certain idiom word is a daughter, of a daughter, of a daughter ... of an argument of a specified idiom predicator. The R&S theory of decomposable idioms would thus permit the licensing of a *spill-the-beans*-type phrasal idiom with idiomatic listemes *spill* ('divulge') and *beans* ('secrets') that could license sentences such as (66).

[45]To be sure, there exist highly "nonconfigurational" languages, e.g., Warlpiri and other Pama-Nyungan languages, whose loosely constrained word orders require machinery not necessary for English. One example is the HPSG Linearization Theory originally proposed for German by Reape (1994), further developed by Kathol (2000) and others, and specifically adapted within a localist and constructional HPSG for Warlpiri by Donohue & Sag (1991; see also the references there).

[46]"Being able to refer to deeply embedded parts of a phrase in [an idiom of a type to be discussed below] is an important ingredient to this theory' (R&S p. 18). It is not clear to us whether R&S intend the suspension of locality to apply only to idioms or to the grammar generally. If the former, they do not specify how the restriction to idioms is to be implemented.

(66) a.*Someone spilled that I forgot to remind everyone not to divulge the beans.

b.*Kim spilled that Marion had predicted that Sandy would forget to tell Pat not to divulge the beans.

That is, the R&S theory would permit there to be an idiomatic lexeme *beans* whose entry in the lexicon would specify that *beans* is dominated at an arbitrary depth by an idiomatic *spill* whose ARG-ST requires only a sentential complement. Of course, the R&S theory would permit the lexicon to refrain from including such items but it would not forbid it. A theory such as the one we have presented, which does not permit the licensing of dependencies of arbitrary depth, captures the generalization that sentences like (66) do not occur.

R&S's abandonment of locality is not casual. They find it to be necessitated by certain facts. The particular data which R&S argue require dependencies of arbitrary depth consist in a number of German idioms in which it appears that coreference is required between a matrix subject and a non-subject constituent of a complement clause. Examples are given in (67), in which the constituent marked X is interpreted as coreferent with the matrix subject.

(67)

a. (nicht) wissen, wo X_{dat} der Kopf steht
not know where X_{DO} the head stands
('have a lot of stress') (R&S 1b)

b. glauben, X_{acc} tritt ein Pferd
believe X_{DO} kicks a horse
('be very surprised') (R&S 1c)

R&S question the adequacy of a theory of the kind proposed here—as briefly sketched in Sag (2012 [cited by R&S in a preprint version dated 2007])—based on the observation that Sag (2012) specifies that the external argument of a predicator is its subject. Consequently non-subject constituents such as those indicated with X in (67) are not visible to the matrix subject. If SBCG allows only subjects to serve as external arguments and the interpretation of coreference between matrix subject and complement non-subject in (67) is dictated by the grammar rather than the result of a pragmatic process, then the SBCG approach cannot account for the facts of (67). R&S suggest that the SBCG approach might be saved by allowing the ARG-ST to float to the top of a phrase, which would make embedded arguments visible to the matrix subject at the cost of abandoning locality. They continue, however, by presenting facts that they consider to pose a problem for even the anti-locality solution just proposed. Interestingly their evidence for challenging that (to our mind undesirable) solution suggests one of two possible defenses of the strictly localist, SBCG approach. R&S cite the English idiom illustrated in (68). In this case, "X is embedded in a locative modifier. Unless locative modifiers are on the ARG-ST list, the locality assumptions of SBCG do not seem to leave the necessary kind of structure accessible to enforce coreference between X and the matrix subject" (R&S p.19).

(68) look as if butter wouldn't melt [in X's mouth] ('look completely innocent') R&S (32)

But is the word *look* part of this idiom? The examples in (69) could be multiplied.

(69) a. This horror novella depicts the fictional life of; [sic] Ethel; a sweet-looking little old lady, who **seems** as if butter wouldn't melt in her mouth...

b. Now Sun is almost 5 and he's just about the cheekiest monkey out there, and Shine is 2 and a half and most of the time **appears** as if butter wouldn't melt in her mouth.

c. ... a brat who pulls all kinds of mischief and then **acts** as if butter wouldn't melt in his mouth.

d. ... where she sits and sulks for several minutes before returning to the bedroom to **pretend** that butter wouldn't melt in her mouth.

e. Look at that innocent expression. Butter wouldn't melt in his mouth!
f. You lie like butter wouldn't melt in your mouth, Edward.
g. Justin Bieber—Once upon a time butter wouldn't melt in little Justin's mouth. Now internationally famous for being a weapons-grade petulant brat...
h. ...he was baited by bullies who made him destroy furniture or school property then pretend he instigated it. Butter wouldn't melt in their mouth.

In section 4 we cited analogous evidence that—contrary to what one finds frequently claimed—there is no matrix verb in the *side-bread-buttered-on* idiom. Similarly, the idiom illustrated in (68) and (69) is better analyzed as involving the words *butter, wouldn't, melt,* and *mouth,* but not any particular clausal-complement-taking verb, as most clearly demonstrated in (69e,f,g,h). Thomas Wasow has suggested (pc) that idioms of clausal form may carry a pragmatic requirement that one of the constituents therein is contextually bound. In the case of (69h), the contextual antecedent is evidently the bullies. In (69g) there is no controlled pronoun. In (69e,g, and h) there is no higher verb. In (69e) the pragmatically recoverable antecedent is the person the addressee is asked to look at.

Another English analogue to the German idioms that appear to require coreference between a matrix verb and a nonsubject argument of its complement might be the idiom illustrated in (70).

(70) My friend didn't know what hit him when I poured a bucket of water over his head.

It is common for putatively authoritative sources to include the matrix verb *know* in the idiom. For example, the Cambridge Dictionaries Online gives the idiom as "not know what has hit you." Wictionary lists it as "not know what hit (one)," and the Free Dictionary by Farlex (online) gives it as "not know what hit you." However, the idiom *what hit s.b.* occurs both as a complement to many predicators other than 'know', and freestanding.

(71) a. National Affairs: What Hit Him?... What had happened to Harold Stassen in the Nebraska primary?

b. Editorial: Obama still trying to figure out what hit him.

c. "The people are full of anguish, like they don't understand what hit them," Solar TV News reporter David Santos recounted.

d. Ace cueist Pankaj Advani looked uncomfortable in an all-India level final, making faces, raising eyebrows, trying to make out what hit him ...

e. An excellent multiplayer weapon when used with the gauss - most players can't tell what hit them!

f. With the right medical attention, and proper drugging, Lady CBC will not remember what hit her.

g. We were filming a scene where the Indians attack the fort when I suddenly developed a splitting headache. I can't imagine what hit me.

h. Even today, despite numerous works on the crisis—some of them excellent –most Americans remain perplexed by what hit them.

We are thus led to imagine the possibility in the case of (67b), for example, that the idiom might be restricted to X_{acc} *tritt ein Pferd* plus a pragmatic condition "that it can only be used in contexts describing the mental state of the referent of the accusative pronoun" (Thomas Wasow pc). We envision the possibility that—for English at least—there may be no idioms that grammatically require coreference of a matrix argument with a non-subject of a complement clause and hence no empirical motivation for a formulation that abandons locality. We tentatively suggest that something of the sort could also be true of German. The first defense of the lexical approach is therefore the suggestion that possibly there are no idioms which require coindexation of a non-subject argument of a complement clause with an argument of a governing verb, the apparent counterexamples containing instead a pragmatic requirement that a pronominal non-subject argument of a complement clause be bound by a contextually given antecedent—which often happens to be an argument (usually the subject) of the matrix predicate. We have not made a full study of the relevant facts of either German or English (or any other language) and so do not propose this possibility as more than a suggestion for future research.

To summarize this section, we have suggested that there may exist a pragmatic alternative to R&S's interpretation of certain German idioms as syntactically requiring coreference of a matrix subject and a complement non-subject. The coreference observed may instead represent a pragmatic property (conventional implicature) of these idiomatic constructions.

Although we disagree with R&S with respect to the matters focused on most closely in this section, we are entirely in sympathy with their (otherwise) successful effort to incorporate into an explicit theory of grammar a theory of idioms that takes account of the extensive and complex facts regarding partial productivity and partial compositionality that idioms present.

1.7 Idiom Words Governed by Non-Idiom Predicators

Nunberg et al. (1994) cite McCawley (1981) as pointing out that sentences like (72) and (73) jointly create a problem for the claim that the existence of idioms provides an argument for the existence of transformations. We are not concerned here with arguments for or against transformations but rather with whether examples like these pose a problem for the present lexical approach to idioms.

(72) Pat pulled [the strings [that got Chris the job]]. (=NSW (33)a)

(73) [The strings [that Pat pulled]] got Chris the job. (=NSW (33)b)

Example (72) does not cause a problem for the approach to idioms advanced here, because the idiom word *strings* is not governed by a non-idiom predicator.[47]

Example (73), however, does present a problem for the current analysis because in this case the nominal phrase headed by *i-strings* is an argument of the canonical predicator *got.* Speaking informally, *pulled* in the relative clause seems somehow to license the token of *i-strings* that is governed in the main clause by *got.* The construction in (74) licenses nominal phrases which, although headed by idiom words, can nonetheless serve as arguments of canonical predicators, for example, *the strings that Pat pulled* in (73).[48]

(74) **Canonical Idiomatically-Headed Nominal Construction (↑*noun-lxm*)**

$$canon\text{-}idiom\text{-}hd\text{-}nom\text{-}cxt \Rightarrow \begin{bmatrix} noun \\ \text{MTR} \begin{bmatrix} noun \\ \text{SYN}[\text{CAT}\ [\text{LID}\ \langle c\text{-}frame\rangle]] \end{bmatrix} \\ \text{DTRS} \left\langle \text{X:}\begin{bmatrix} noun \\ \text{SYN}[\text{CAT}[\text{LID}\langle i\text{-}frame\rangle]] \end{bmatrix}, \begin{bmatrix} rel\text{-}cl \\ \text{SYN}[\text{CAT}[\text{SELECT}\ X]] \end{bmatrix} \right\rangle \end{bmatrix}$$

The construction in (74) simply codes the fact that a noun

---

[47]Although (72) and (73) are invented examples, attested ones are easy to find. Compare (i) to (72) and (ii) to (73).

(i)... the "big city" bankers who, many people were convinced, pulled the strings that manipulated the political system as well as the economy.

(ii)... the daughter was not aware of the strings that were being pulled for her.

[48]And *the strings that were being pulled for her* in (ii) of the preceding note.

or nominal phrase with [LID *i-frame*] can, when modified by a relative clause, head a nominal phrase with [LID *c-frame*] and thus serve as an argument for a canonical predicator, as in (73). If this isolated fact can be found in future research to follow from something more general, that development will of course be welcome. Meanwhile, a constructional approach such as SBCG, while always seeking the smallest number of the most general constructions the facts permit, provides a theoretical vehicle to account for isolated facts of this kind without departing from explicit representation.

1.8 Conclusion

We have outlined a lexical theory of phrasal idioms. A pervasive property of flexible idioms is that the words that appear in citation forms unmodified are often modified in actual use. This modification is theoretically crucial because it shows that the modified words are not merely words phonologically but also semantically and syntactically. In the following examples, we have confined ourselves to internal modification (ignoring external modifiers like *proverbial, metaphorical, literal, figurative,* etc. and epithets like *danged* or *confounded.*) In the (75) examples idiomatic *cat* is modified; in the (76) examples idiomatic *bag* is modified. We present what may seem like an excessive number of (attested) examples to illustrate the point that ordinary modification of idiom words is commonplace. Modifiability of idiom words demonstrates that they are real words with real meanings, which have to be combined to produce meaningful phrases and sentences by the same grammatical machinery that combines the meanings of ordinary words.

(75) a. I'll bet there might even be more than a few wealthy Palm Beachers who also have not let the **financial** cat out of the bag to everyone in their family.

b. Now, however, it has to be fleshed out, and in that respect you have not let the **whole** cat out of the bag.

c. We're one day closer to Capcom Cup and it's definitely time to let the **final** cat out of the bag with the Super Street Fighter 4 AE brackets.
d. Heather said that Blossom almost let the **entire** cat out of the bag today... read on if you want a glimpse of what is coming.
e. Hamid Karzai has let the **Pentagon's** cat out of the bag—to the displeasure of the Obama Administration.
f. So, without further ado, it brings me great pleasure to finally let the (**first**) cat out of the bag and announce today, the Fritz & Fräulein Collection will be featured and sold at Tommy Hilfiger's beautiful new flagship store,...
g. "Might as well let the **other** cat out of the bag," he said: ...
h. Solo let **the Olympic's** cat out of the bag when she narrated her experience to the press.
i. Don't let the **last** cat out of the bag.
j. Now, however, it has to be fleshed out, and in that respect you have not let the **whole** cat out of the bag.
k. Well the liberal Austin bloggers let the **political** cat out of the bag.
l. Georgia, always the truth bringer of the family, let the **cinematic** cat out of the bag, when she allowed that the picture was not such an ordeal as it would have been had their lives been filmed for the entire year they spent on the island....

(76) a. Time to let the cat out of the **Instagram** bag... I'm pregnant!
b. Who let the cat out of the **Bloomingdales** bag?
c. Kandi Burruss may have let the cat out of the **Bravo** bag last night during "Watch What Happens Live."

d. Someone let the cat out of the **Duluth Pack** bag a week early.
e. …a fetching real estate purveyor down in Miami Beach who kindly let the cat out of the **celebrity real estate** bag about six-time Grammy-winning singer/songwriter Billy Joel…
f. So, Mary Burke has finally let the cat out of the **cellophane** bag by formally announcing her candidacy for governor.
g. …and this week the folks at Zillow let the cat out of the **real estate** bag …
h. Yup, I let the cat out of the **family** bag. Probably the whole reason I am straightforward…
i. Now that director Wes Ball has let the cat out of the **concept art** bag,
j. Perhaps sensing that he'd let the cat out of the **plot** bag a little early, King then told Cronenberg and the audience that he wasn't completely committed to the new novel …
k. Good morning everyone! Time to let the cat out of the **internet** bag.
l. A little less surprising now you've let the cat out of the **fur-trim, diamante embellished clutch** bag, but we suppose it's the thought that counts.
m. But a guy in Philadelphia (not Mississippi, Pennsylvania this time) let the cat out of the **voter suppression** bag:…
n. But some believe it is because some major problems are on the way and NASA does not want other Scientists to let the cat out of the **cosmic** bag to [sic] soon.

The modifiability of idiom words argues for a lexical theory of idioms. Idiom words are real words; they share the morphological and phonological properties of their literal counterparts through multiple inheritance and contribute their own idiomatic meanings. Often these meanings have been motivated historically by metaphors or metonymies of varying degrees of currency. Idiom words are combined with ordinary words and phrases into the phrases and sentences of the grammar by the familiar combinatorial constructions; no special combinatorial machinery is required for idioms. Once idiom words are defined and idiom predicators appropriately distinguished from canonical predicators, nothing further is needed. The ordinary combinatorial constructions that are required for the regular grammar suffice. We suggest that in the past insufficient attention has been paid to the description of idioms within explicit theories of grammar, and we have attempted to do so here within the approach of Sign-Based Construction Grammar.

In particular, we have shown that SBCG can provide an analysis in which the occurrence of an idiom word is predicted to be precisely the limited range of environments in which it is observed to occur and that such prediction can be achieved in a formal approach that abjures movement, empty categories, and dependencies of arbitrary depth.

Our theory of idioms is lexicalist because we find that syntactically flexible idioms are semantically compositional: their meanings are put together from the meanings of special idiom words according to the same processes—combinatorial constructions—that put together the meanings of ordinary phrases and sentences. A corollary of this finding is that syntactically inflexible idioms are inflexible precisely because (some of) the words of which they are composed, being meaningless, fail to meet the semantic requirements of the constructions that would provide their flexibility. A welcome result of the commitment to a lexical approach is that little has had to be added to existing theory to account for the data of idioms.

2

Partial Inversion in English

Paul Kay and Laura A. Michaelis

Introduction

Canonically, a finite clause in English has a single constituent that serves as subject. This constituent precedes the finite verb in non-inverted clauses such as simple declarative sentences, follows the finite verb in inverted clauses such as matrix questions, agrees in person and number with the finite verb and with a tag subject when a tag is present, and undergoes raising (Postal 2004). Five non-canonical constructions violate these generalizations and in the literature have called into question the identity of the subject constituent. In each of these five constructions the finite verb agrees with a following constituent despite the fact—among others—that the constituent preceding the verb exhibits subject behaviors of the kind identified by Keenan (1976). An example demonstrating the raising property is shown in (1).[1]

(1) Out of the woodwork during their show seemed to emerge all of these really big meat-head type guys and they started moshing hard.

Such cases involve what might be viewed as competition between preverbal and postverbal constituents for the sta-

[1] All positive numbered examples were retrieved from Google searches at the time of drafting, except as otherwise noted.

tus of traditional subject: while in (1) the PP argument acts like the syntactically privileged argument of *emerge* for the purposes of raising[2], the NP argument is the only obligatory argument of *emerge* and the one that in finite contexts determines its inflection. This situation is reminiscent of Keenan's (1976) proposal that the behavioral and coding properties that coalesce in canonical subject cases are separable and may accrue to distinct arguments in a given clause (see also Van Valin and LaPolla 1997: ch.6). While the postverbal nominal argument has the coding properties characteristic of subjects (showing nominative case-marking, controlling verb agreement), the preverbal setting argument has the requisite behavioral properties (including undergoing raising). We refer to this situation, and the constructions that participate in it, as Partial Inversion. Regarding such cases, especially the ones we term Oblique Inversion (OI, often referred to as Locative or Stylistic Inversion[3]) and Existential *there* (E-*there*), there is an extensive literature, often involving arguments about whether the preverbal constituent is to be regarded as subject, and, if so, in what sense (including Bresnan (1994), Postal (2004), Kim (2003), Culicover and Levine (2001), Bruening (2010), Schachter (1992), Webelhuth (2011), and Salzmann (2013), for Oblique Inversion). The five maximal constructions[4] we will be concerned with are Oblique Inversion (OI), Presentational *there* (P-*there*), Deictic Inversion (DI), Existential *there* (E-*there*), and Reversed Specificational *be* (RS-*be*), illustrated in (2)–(6).[5]

[2]We argue below, however, that in (1) and similar examples the clause-initial argument is constrained by both raising and extraction.

[3]We follow Postal (2004) in rejecting the term Locative Inversion in light of attested examples, to be discussed in Section 4, in which the preverbal constituent does not express a location.

[4]Maximal constructions license the types that occupy terminal nodes in a multiple-inheritance hierarchy of typed feature structures, to be discussed later. Non-maximal constructions express cross-constructional generalizations.

[5]SBCG is a declarative, constraint-based framework. We retain the term "inversion," despite its association with procedural approaches, for the sake of continuity with traditional terminology. Similarly, with "raising" and others.

(2) **Oblique Inversion** [OI] (aka Locative Inversion, Stylistic Inversion)

a. But then emerged suddenly a new fear.

b. From despair arose the greatest nation.

c. [On the river the moon produced a comforting glow] and in the distance shown rays of lightning ...

d. [Down at the harbor there is a teal-green clubhouse for socializing and parties.] Beside it sparkles the community pool. (Vanity Fair, August 2001)

(3) **Presentational *there*** [P-*there*]

a. There will arise someday a pharoah [sic] that does not know Joseph.

b. With humans there emerged the incredibly enlarged forebrain . . .

c. But there began a series of upheavals, he says, "directed chiefly towards the northern hemisphere almost exclusively,"...

d. There then developed games of being chased and caught and from time to time he wanted me to pick him up in my arms like a baby, ...

(4) **Deictic Inversion** [DI]

a. Here come the robot lawyers.

b. There goes the bus ...

c. There's my Dad with a bunch of cowboys ...

d. Here came the waitress. She had on a mini-skirt, high heels, see-through blouse with padded brassiere.

(5) **Existential *There*** [E-*there*]

a. Is there really an elephant in the garden?

b. There are likely to be problems with the finale.

c. There remain three issues to be addressed.

d. There exist two possible solutions.

(6) **Reversed Specificational *be*** [*BE*]

a. My biggest worry are the injury risks.

b. ... your best bet are places where the shoreline drops off quickly...

c. My worst nightmare were the soups she would make for dinner.

d. But the problem were the raiders outside the town...

We distinguish these agreement patterns from others in which a post-verbal constituent embodies all of its clause's subject properties, as in auxiliary-initial clauses (7a), quotative inversion (7b)[6], or predicate pre-posing (7c).

(7) a. Never has he looked so happy. May you triumph! Are you home?

b. "I love you too," said my mother.

c. Also intact were the auditory pathways and the motor pathways to the speech organs.

While the examples in (7), like those in (2)–(6), illustrate postverbal agreement, they do not exemplify partial inversion because they lack distribution of subject properties over more than one constituent.

In each of the five partial-inversion cases, the finite verb agrees with a post-verbal constituent, which receives discourse-pragmatic focus. This constituent is not necessarily the immediate postverbal constituent, as illustrated by examples (3a) and (5a). By considering all five cases of partial inversion together, we will attempt to demonstrate that the question of which constituent is the subject is not a fruitful one. Rather,

[6] A reviewer suggests that quotative inversion as in (7b) shares some properties with partial inversions and might be classified with them. In line with current thinking (see, e.g., Matos 2013), we see quotative clauses (i.e. the clause whose subject NP expresses the source of the quote and whose verb is a speech-act verb, e.g., *she said*) as parenthetical expressions, because they have the same initial, medial and final placement possibilities as epistemic adverbs like *probably* (Jackendoff 1972:98-100). In recent work, Jackendoff (2023) argues that parenthetical expressions are not in fact components of syntax. He proposes instead that a parenthetical is a constituent in the prosodic representation of its host, and that it is "related to its host in discourse structure." As parenthetical clauses, final quotative clauses, inverted and non-inverted, are structurally dissimilar to the partial-inversion patterns we consider in this paper, in which the pre-verbal expression is often a complement of the derived verb.

we propose, in Sign-Based Construction Grammar (SBCG, Sag 2010, 2012, Kay and Sag 2012, Michaelis 2012, Chaves 2014, Van Eynde 2015), a uniform analysis, which captures formally the properties that the five patterns have in common, uses no special-purpose machinery to describe either the inflectional properties of the quirky-agreement patterns or their constituent structure, and accounts economically for the distribution of properties of canonical subjects across the various constituents of the five constructions. In addition, we will argue for certain discourse-pragmatic and aspectual properties of the constructions in this family, as they are revealed by corpus searches. For example, we contest the prevailing view that the PP 'subject' of OI necessarily denotes a topic or 'discourse old' referent (contra Bresnan (1994), Birner and Ward (1998), Webelhuth 2011, and Salzmann 2013). We note further that a verb appearing in the OI pattern need not be intrinsically locative-selecting and moreover that the preposed element in OI is not necessarily referential. Further, E-*there* clauses (illustrated in (5)) and specificational-*be* clauses that are not reversed like the ones in (6) need not exhibit post-verbal inflection. We hope to demonstrate the parsimonious character of a monostratal, lexicalist, constraint-based, approach over approaches admitting of inaudible constituents (Postal 2004, Bruening 2010), movement (see Salzmann (2013) for references to earlier treatments in the GB/Minimalism tradition), or of several parrallel dimensions of structure (e.g. Bresnan 1994). Our analysis is strictly lexical in that no special phrasal construction is required to license any of the examples (2)–(6) that is not also required to license clauses exhibiting canonical subjects and canonical agreement. All of the non-prototypical properties of partial inversion clauses are projected from the lexicon. Finally, on a methodological note, we encounter and clarify several instances in which theoretical analyses have been built on intuitive grammaticality judgments for which the web furnishes inescapable counterevidence.

The remainder of this chapter is structured as follows. Section 1 sets out the basic data regarding the properties shared and not shared among the five maximal constructions of the split-subject family. Section 2 gives a brief and informal introduction to Sign-Based Construction Grammar. Section 3 sketches an SBCG treatment of agreement. Section 4 introduces the Split Subject Construction, which encapsulates the unity of the partial inversion phenomenon by specifying what the five types of partial inversion have in common. Section 5 discusses Oblique Inversion (aka Locative Inversion, Stylistic Inversion). Section 6 treats Presentational-*there*. Section 7 is devoted to Deictic Inversion. Section 8 treats Existential-*there*. Section 9 considers Reversed Specificational *be*. Section 10 presents our conclusions. The Appendix sketches an SBCG approach to inflection, as it relates specifically to subject-verb agreement in English and briefly considers long distance agreement in English as it relates to Split Subject structures.

2.1 Uniformity and diversity in the split subject family of constructions: the basic data

Since all of the properties common to the five members of the split-subject family of constructions and many of the properties distinguishing them from each other are exhibited by the Oblique Inversion Construction, it is convenient to introduce those properties by considering examples of OI.

2.1.1 Oblique Inversion

2.1.1.1 *Non-canonical agreement*: In a finite declarative clause (FDC) an OI verb agrees with its post-verbal argument.

See examples (2).

2.1.1.2 *Raising*: The argument that appears preverbally in an OI FDC may be interpretable as the subject of a raising verb.

(8) a. From out of nowhere seemed to come the deep, resonant voice that interrupted their satanic devotion.
b. Out of the woodwork during their show seemed to emerge all of these really big meat-head type guys... (ex. 1 repeated)[7]

Culicover and Levine (2001) [C&L] propose that there are really two distinct stylistic inversion constructions. In Light Inversion, the verb is unaccusative, the postverbal constituent lacks weight in the sense "correspond[ing] exactly to the one that is relevant to Heavy NP Shift" (C&L: 284), and raising is impossible. We discuss this two-construction hypothesis in section 5.3. With regard to the possibility of raising in OI, it is true that attested examples with relatively heavy postverbal constituents in an FDC, like (8a,b) are easier to find than examples with light final constituents and unaccusative verbs, such as those in (9). Nevertheless, examples of the latter type are attested.

(9) a. After getting our chicken fix, we wandered around Covent Garden having one of those inevitable post-uni, 'what the hell now?' conversations – when out of nowhere seemed to come a sign.
b. And then seemed to appear from nowhere this little cutie.
c. Out of nowhere seemed to appear a ghostly dove.
d. Out of nowhere seemed to appear the Wilcock/Fulford etc. crowd.
e. Then, out of nowhere seemed to come a golden opportunity.[8]

---

[7] A reviewer questions whether OI really permits raising, claiming that the inverted preverbal argument doesn't raise and presenting the allegedly ungrammatical example **Did out of this impasse seem to come existentialism*. The examples in (8) and (9) show that OI is in fact compatible with raising of the setting argument.

[8] We follow C&L in positing that "'movement along a path' is ... typical of

f. Then out of the blue appeared a small branch although there was not a tree in sight.
g. Out of the blue appeared a police van and from the front passenger seat ...

2.1.1.3 *Focus*: The post-verbal argument in an OI FDC is in focus; the preverbal argument may or may not be a topic.

For example, in (2d) *it* is clearly topical, while in (2c) the distance is clearly not topical.

2.1.1.4 *Lexical constraint on the verb*: The verbal constituent in an FDC is intransitive, although not necessarily unaccusative.

Bresnan (1994) and Rappaport Hovav & Levin (2008), among others, have claimed that OI (aka Locative Inversion) is restricted to unaccusative verbs. This hypothesis is rejected by Birner (1984), Birner and Ward (1998), Kim (2003), and C&L, among others. Our own observations agree with those of the latter group: both unaccusative and unergative verbs participate in OI. The limitation of OI to intransitive (including passive) verbs, although not strictly to any subclass of intransitives, might be viewed as a grammatical entrenchment of the statistically dominant discourse pattern sometimes designated Preferred Argument Structure (Du Bois 1987, Dubois et al. 2003, Durie 1988), which holds that a clause normally contains only one referential and non-anaphoric constituent conveying focused, new information. A transitive verb, although it typically has a focal postverbal argument/direct object (Michaelis and Francis 2007), cannot simultaneously satisfy both the PAS and the OI templates because its subject is not an oblique expression. The restriction to some subtype of intransitives holds for all five species of the split-subject genus, suggesting that all five members

the unaccusative construction" (p. 295, note 12), and further "that such an interpretation can be associated with any verb that can be plausibly used to denote a property of movement along a path," as C&L exemplify in (i).
(i) Into the room stumbled/wobbled/stormed/blustered/skidded Fred.

of the split-subject family are similarly motivated as specifically dedicated to the presentation of focused (typically new) discourse participants, motivating the exclusion of transitive verbs.[9]

The preceding four constraints apply to all five split-subject constructions. The following six constraints apply to a proper subset of split-subject constructions, in four of the six cases a majority.

2.1.1.5 ***Subject-auxiliary inversion* (SAI): The argument that appears preverbally in an FDC appears immediately postverbally in an inverted clause, such as polar question or constituent question.**

(10) a. Did out of this impasse come existentialism, a belief that man could define his temperament and impose meaning on the world?

b. From whence will come any help?

---

[9]C&L present some invented examples of OI containing direct objects, which they view as grammatical although awkward (2001:308, (i) = C&L's (57)).

(i) a. In the backyard were quietly sunning themselves a group of the largest iguanas that had ever [been] seen in Ohio.

b. The economist predicted that at that precise moment would turn the corner the economics of half a dozen South American nations.

c. In the laboratory were dying their various horrible deaths the more than ten thousand fruit flies that Dr. Zapp had collected in his garden over the summer.

d. Outside in the still upright hangar were heaving deep sighs of relief the few remaining pilots who had not been chosen to fly in the worst hurricane since hurricanes had names.

Although C&L observe, based on the possibility of passivization, that the apparent direct objects in (i) – for example, *the corner* in the idiomatic VP *turn the corner* in (i)b – are indeed internal syntactic arguments of the verb, they also observe that these direct objects are non-referring and carry no thematic role. We agree that at least some of the examples in (i), which are predicted to be simply grammatical by the C&L analysis, are at least marginally acceptable. We also agree with the characterization of them as awkward and we underscore C&L's observation that the direct objects in these sentences are non-thematic and non-referential. However, we do not interpret these observations as support for an analysis of OI that rejects the generally accepted intransitivity constraint on OI verbs. Rather we take them to illustrate an innovative, semi-grammatical stretching of OI (as defined here on intransitive verb inputs). Four observations support this interpretation: (1) the fact that such examples require special prosody, including a major prosodic juncture preceding the final NP (C&L 2001: 293, Peter Culicover p.c.), (2) the morpho-lexical heaviness of the final constituent (which C&L also observe), (3) the exclusive focus on the final constituent in OI, and (4) the non-referential and non-thematic status of the direct objects.

The existing literature on OI seems for the most part to assume that OI is a clausal construction and does not consider the SAI clausal pattern, for example, as potentially coexisting with OI. The fact that four of the five split-subject patterns co-occur with SAI provides one source of evidence among several[10] for the lexical nature of the split-subject phenomenon.

2.1.1.6 *Negation*: An OI clause may apparently be negated, perhaps only under special pragmatic circumstances

It has generally been held that sentential negation of OI is ungrammatical in English (e.g., Aissen 1975:9, Levine 1989: 1015, Bresnan 1994: 88). That is not strictly correct, as the following examples show.

(11) a. No, opposite him was not sitting a strange woman in his girl's body; it was his girl, herself, no one else.
b. Although clinical parameters seemed to describe a sicker population in ICD implanted patients, from neuropsychological tests did not emerge any significant differences.
c. And in all the land were no women found so fair as the daughters of Job.
d. To him has never come any external revelation.
e. To your soul, has never come any thought of the beautiful, the lofty, the good!
f. In front of him was not standing a black-dressed lady any more [sic] but a tall gentleman with a turban on his head...
g. The door swung wide open and before me was not standing a zombie, but a man in dark clothes and a hat which read, "FBI".

---

[10]For example, *it-cleft*:

(a) But it was a German Carolingian who had last claimed a very disunited Italy and it was from among the German duchies that arose a king, Otto the Great (936-973) ...

(b) However, it was out of the left wing that came the whole post-modernist, reality-is-a-shared-social-construction view.

h. ... it looks like the vampire woman injected blood into the human and it caused something to happen, now before him did not stand a human, ...

2.1.1.7 ***Lexical constraint on* FDC*-preverbal constituent*: The preverbal constituent in an OI FDC is not lexically constrained.**

Although this constraint obviously applies to both *there* constructions and to Deictic Inversion, it does not apply to OI. In fact, various claims in the literature notwithstanding, the FDC preverbal constituent in OI is constrained neither to be a PP (12) nor to denote a location (13).

(12) a. Slowly and gradually appeared the form of the Lady of the Mist.

b. At first all went well, and then suddenly arose the mysterious complaint that I was *persona non grata* with the British Council.

c. Their voices, from clearest soprano to richest bass, blended in low concordances, until, gradually, came words, like figures forming in mist.

d. Seeding begins. Then came a downpour.

e. But suddenly arose a new entity, The Dragons.

f. Then slowly arose bodies dented with their own life-jackets, the cork of which was in some cases torn away.

g. Today begins a two-day series taken from a short, 800-word sermon.

h. Now began a dispute.

Bresnan (1994) and Webelhuth (2011) among others take it to be an essential part of the OI pattern that the initial constituent in an FDC denote a physical location. According to Webelhuth (2011:92), OI, like deictic inversion, “draw[s] the hearer’s attention to the object expressed by the postverbal NP via the region it is contained in.” It is apparent, however, that OI does not require the preverbal element to display locative semantics, and it is for this reason that Postal (2004) and Bruening (2010), among others, oppose Bresnan's semantic characterization of OI and the label "Locative Inversion", bringing to bear invented examples structurally similar to the attested ones in (13).

(13) a. A motion to call a convention was rejected by a large majority and in its stead was adopted a resolution authorizing special town meetings...
b. For that reason was adopted a special Law on Protection from Domestic Violence...
c. From this can be deduced the fact that the roots of Δ in R are asymptotically equal to those of Δ_1.
d. With this pen was written all of the events that would occur from then, til eternity.
e. Against this has been objected the inconvenience of a protracted session.
f. It is a solemn question, Stephen, because on it may depend the salvation of your eternal soul.
g. To those two gods correspond the goddesses Ishtar and Isis.

2.1.1.8 ***The Anti-complementizer Effect*** **(ACE; aka** ***that*****-trace). OI is one of the two maximal partial-inversion constructions to exhibit the "*that*-trace" phenomenon, the other being P-*there*.**

Bresnan (1994) gives the invented examples (14). Attested examples appear in (15).

(14) a. It's in these villages that we all believe (*that) __ can be found the best examples of this cuisine. (= Bresnan's 68)
b. It's this cuisine that we all believe (*that) __ can be found in these villages. (= Bresnan's 70)

(15) a. Only then, I believe, (*that) will emerge a new narrative on trade.
b. What favourable news we have from East Tennessee & Virginia, from which I cannot but think, (*that)

will arise a division and strife amongst the people of the North.

Culicover (1993:98) observed[11] that the ACE can be neutralized by insertion of an adverbial phrase after *that*, especially when the postposed argument is relatively heavy. The phenomenon is evidenced in both a canonical relative clause, as shown in (16a) versus (16b), and an OI relative clause, as shown in (16c) versus (16d).

(16) a. *Robin met the man who Leslie said that was the mayor of the city. (Culicover 1993:98)
b. Robin met the man who Leslie said that for all intents and purposes was the mayor of the city. (Culicover 1993:98)
c. *On which table were you wondering whether had been put the books that you had bought? (Culicover 1993:104)
d. On which table were you wondering whether under certain circumstances might have been put the books that you had bought? (Culicover 1993:104)

2.1.1.9 *The Complementizer Effect* (CE). Just as the ACE is reversed when subject extraction is from a canonical relative clause – in which case *that* is required (17b) – so *that* is required with OI subject relative clauses (17d).

(17) a. It was a fateful decision that left its mark on the Netherlands.
b. *It was a fateful decision left its mark on the Netherlands.
c. ... but it was only in the 14th-15th century that was found evidence of quarries and transport of the blocks of Ceppo...
d. *... but it was only in the 14th-15th century was found evidence of quarries and transport of the blocks of Ceppo...

[11] As cited by Postal (2004), among others.

2.1.1.10 ***Question Tag.*** **OI may be the only maximal partial inversion type that does not permit a question tag.**

We have not found a practical strategy to settle the matter by corpus search and our intuitions are unclear. If the postverbal constituent in an OI FDC is definite, there arises the question whether it might felicitously control a question tag. Consider adding such a tag to (2b), as in (18). To the extent that sentences like (18) are acceptable they suggest a subject property of the postverbal constituent in OI.

(18) ?From despair arose the greatest nation, didn't it? (Attested only without the tag)

2.1.2 Presentational *there*

2.1.2.1 ***Non-canonical Agreement.*** **In a P-*there* FDC, the Agreement Source (AS), that is, the constituent with which the finite verb agrees, does not appear in canonical subject (preverbal) position.**

(19) In the month of July, 1767, about seven in the evening, there were sitting in the kitchen Thomas Wheeler, postilion, Ann Hall, my own woman, Sarah, a waiting-woman to Mrs. Mary Pointz, and Dame Lacy.

2.1.2.2 ***Raising.*** **The expletive *there* that introduces a P-*there* FDC undergoes raising.**

(20) And from this consciousness that they had attempted to conquer an unconquerable thing there seemed to arise a feeling that they had been betrayed.

2.1.2.3 ***Focus.*** **The postverbal constituent is focused in a P-*there* FDC.**

(21) Only one window showed a light behind them; in it there stood a lamp,. . .

2.1.2.4 ***Lexical Constraint(s) on the verb*****: The verb in P-*there*, as in the OI construction, is limited to intransitives.**

In arguing against Postal's (e.g. 2004) hypothesis that a OI FDC has an expletive subject, Bresnan offers several invented examples intended to show that there are OI clauses which have no P-*there* counterpart. Bresnan's examples (76), with her judgments, are repeated in (22).

(22) a. Into the room (*there) ran Mother.
b. Out of it (*there) steps Archie Campbell. (Birner 1992:43)
c. About a half an hour later in (*there) walk these two guys.
d. Home (*there) came John.
e. Leaning against the wall (*there) stood a/the raggedy old man

However, apparently comparable examples with *there* present are readily attested.

(23) a. One of them had been smashed, and out of it there ran a stream of golden coins...
b. And presently the blossom opened, and out of it there stepped the loveliest fairy in the whole world.
c. But he told the servant to let them in, and as the door opened in there strode a company of strong and handsome young men.
d. ... the door opened, so softly, and in there came a little body in simple white night garb, with a quaint old-fashioned nightcap on, candle in hand.
e. Beside him, leaning against the wall, there stood a man of dark complexion, who fixed his glowing eyes upon him.
f. To our home there often came servants of Christ – plain, godly men, who seemed to me to carry with them the atmosphere of eternity.

The hypothesis of Bresnan among others (see Bresnan 1994. fn. 39, p.99) of a semantic limitation of P-*there*, mainly to non-directionals, is hard to sustain in light of facts like those of (23). We find evidence of no semantic limitation on P-*there* verbs. However, as far as we can determine Bresnan is correct in proposing a discourse-pragmatic constraint on P-*there*, distinguishing it from OI – namely, that in a P-*there* FDC, the postverbal NP constituent must not only have a focal referent but also one that is discourse new.[12] It appears plausible that the examples in (22), with *there* present, sound odd in isolation precisely because necessary discourse context is absent: in isolated examples like these, heavier postverbal constituents are easier to construe as having discourse-new referents, and thus tend to seem more acceptable than lighter ones.

2.1.2.5 *SAI.* P-there is compatible with SAI, for example with negative preposing in (24).

(24) Not in vain is there still standing a wailing wall.

2.1.2.6 *Negation.* P-there is compatible with negation.

(25) Unfortunately, ... there didn't develop any sort of centre of excellence within the Department.

2.1.2.7 *Lexical constraint(s) on arguments.* The preverbal constituent in a P-*there* FDC is lexically fixed as expletive *there*.

(26) Out of it there/*here/*it ran a stream of golden coins. (Cf. (23a))

2.1.2.8 *ACE.* When a P-*there* clause appears as a complement to a verb like *believe* and *there* is extracted, e.g., topicalized, the complementizer *that* may not appear, as illustrated in (27a); compare a subject WH question (27b).

(27) a. ... and there I suggest (*that) is the flaw in his method. (Attested without *that*)
b. What does Emdin suggest (*that) is the flaw in most teacher education programs? (Attested without *that*)

[12] We take Bresnan to propose such a constraint when she observes that P-*there* tokens with proper names as postverbal NPs, as in her (78b): *In the closet (*there) still sat Fido*, show decreased acceptability insofar as the use of such NPs "implies familiarity to speaker and hearer" (1994: 100).

2.1.2.9 ***CE.*** **The constraint that requires the complementizer to be present in a subject relative clause is not relevant to P-*there* because an expletive, e.g. *there*, cannot be modified.**

*It is there (that) will come a time when it matters.

2.1.2.10 ***Question Tag.*** **Unlike OI, a P-*there* FDC accepts a tag whose subject is controlled by the preverbal constituent. Compare (28) to (3).**

(28) a. No, but there will come a time for that, won't there?
b. But there began a series of upheavals, didn't there? (Attested without tag)
c. Now, there came a time, didn't there, during your conversations with Mr. Goosen when he asked you, ...?

2.1.3 Deictic Inversion

2.1.3.1 ***Non-canonical Agreement.*** **In a DI FDC, the AS does not appear in canonical subject (preverbal) position. The negative judgments in (29) are based on standard present-day English.**

(29) a. Here come/*comes the robot lawyers.
b. Well, there go/*goes all my hopes and dreams.

2.1.3.2 ***Raising.*** **The locatives *there* or *here* that introduce a DI FDC undergo raising.**

(30) Here seemed to come the proof...

2.1.3.3 ***Focus.*** **The postverbal constituent is focused in a DI FDC.**

(31) Here came the waitress. She had on a mini-skirt, ... [= (4d) and (124a)].

2.1.3.4 ***Lexical Constraint(s) on Verb.*** **The verb in DI is limited to the pair *come* and *go*, whose common semantics we refer to, for want of a standard term, as 'axial'.**

(32) *Here approached/arrives/arrived/appeared/showed up the waitress.

2.1.3.5 *SAI.* DI is not compatible with SAI.

(33) a. *Does here come our bus?
b. *Which bus does here come?
c. *Never will here come our bus.

2.1.3.6 *Negation.* DI is not consistent with negation.

(34) *Here (still) doesn't come our bus.

2.1.3.7 *Lexical Constraint(s) on Argument(s).* The preverbal constituent in a P-*there* FDC is lexically fixed, as locative *here* or *there*.

(35) Here/*From Chicago/*Right now/*Around the corner comes our bus.

2.1.3.8 *ACE.* The ACE does not apply to DI because subject extraction from a DI complement clause is impossible regardless of presence or absence of the complementizer.

(36) a. *It's here that I believe __ (that) comes our bus.
b. *It's there that she just said __ (that) goes the last bus.

2.1.3.9 *CE.* The CE does not apply to DI clauses because DI clauses do not appear as relative clauses.

(37) a. *The bus (that) here comes is late.
b. *Our bus, (that) here comes, is late.

2.1.3.10 *Question Tag.* DI clauses seem sometimes able to bear a question tag, but apparently only anteceded by the postverbal NP.

(38) a. uh-oh, there goes all the suspense$_i$, doesn't it$_i$?
b. So, there goes that theory$_i$, doesn't it$_i$?
c. Well, there go our chances$_i$, ?don't they/*doesn't it. (attested only without tag)

2.1.4 Existential *there*

2.1.4.1 *Non-canonical Agreement.* In formal genres of English, both written and spoken, the verb in an E-*there* FDC agrees only with the postverbal NP. (This constraint does not apply in other registers and dialects.)

(39) There were/*was several people up there.

2.1.4.2 *Raising.* Existential *there* is compatible with raising.

(40) a. There seems to be a problem.
b. There appear to be some discrepancies in how black and white students experience education.

2.1.4.3 *Focus.* The postverbal constituent in an E-*there* FDC is in focus.

(41) There was a man in a tutu at the Supreme Court and he stole the show.

2.1.4.4 *Lexical Constraint(s) on the Verb.* The verb of an Existential *there* clause is [drumroll... rimshot] a verb of existence. Certainly *be*, and arguably also *exist* and *remain* also qualify, although neither of the latter share precisely the privileges of occurrence of existential *be*.

2.1.4.5 *SAI.* An E-*there* clause is compatible with SAI.

(42) Is there an elephant in the room?[13]

2.1.4.6 *Negation.* An E-there clause can be negated.

(43) a. There isn't any God.
b. There aren't many sure things in life, ...
c. This is what happens when there isn't the option to

[13]We have no ready explanation for the following distinction, noted by a reviewer: while extraction of the postverbal argument in E-*there* is possible, insofar as a secondary predicate follows the gap site, the other partial-inversion patterns do not appear to permit extraction of the postverbal argument:

(i) What is there ∅ to eat? (E-*there*)
(ii) ??I know what temple on the Acropolis once stood ∅. (OI)
(iii) *They are asking what bus here comes ∅. (DI)

A possible search for a functional motivation might start from the observation that E-*there* is the only one of the maximal split-subject constructions that is not always strictly presentational.

boot players for betrayals in certain infection game-types in MCC matchmaking.

Keenan (2003) excludes from the category of existential sentence certain subtypes of apparent existentials that allow definite postverbal constituents and which fail to maintain their sense under polar question or negation. He poses the hypothetical dialog in (44).

(44) A: How do I get to UCLA from here?
B: Well there's always the bus, but it doesn't run very often.

And says of it, "*Is there always the bus?* (and *There isn't always the bus*) are unnatural in such contexts, so questioning (and negating) do not preserve the naturalness of DPs like *the bus* in such sentences (Anna Szabolcsi, p.c.) ..." (Keenan 2003: 187, footnote). We will consider and insist on inclusion of these so-called 'list' or 'reminder' cases of apparent existentials in section 8.

2.1.4.7 ***Constraint(s) on Arguments.*** **Expletive *there* is required in an E-*there* clause.**

2.1.4.8 ***ACE.*** **The ACE is observable in E-*there* sentences:**

(45) There they said (*that) are many stars.

2.1.4.9 ***CE.*** **The CE cannot be observed in existential sentences because expletive *there* cannot head a relative clause or serve as the focus in a cleft sentence:**

(46) *It is there (that) is an issue.

2.1.4.10 ***Tag.*** **An E-*there* FDC can support a question tag.**

(47) There are three Eldar gods, aren't there?

2.1.5 Reversed Specificational *be*

We follow the analysis of specificational copula clauses according to which the preverbal constituent is a topical predicate and the postverbal constituent is that predicate's focused argument (Mikkelsen 2005, 2004a,b, 2002, Heycock and Kroch 2002, among others). "Reversed" specificational clauses, in the present terminology, are specificational clauses in which the copula agrees with the postverbal constituent. So far we have only encountered cases in which the agreement is plural, e.g. (48a), and no examples like (48b).

(48) a. My biggest worry are the injury risks.
b. *My biggest worries is the injury risk.

2.1.5.1 ***Agreement.*** **As just noted, in an RS-*be* clause, agreement of the copula is with the postverbal constituent.**

2.1.5.2 ***Raising.*** **Raising is possible in an RS-*be* clause.**

(49) a. The biggest problem appear to be the increased costs associated with the production and logistics of biomass assurance.
b. ... in this case we do not record x_0 since the problem appear to be the side effects.
c. The main issue seem to be the accusim suppercharg-ers.
d. The main issue seem to be the nylon straps...

2.1.5.3 ***Focus.*** **Obligatory focus on the postverbal constituent in ordinary specificational clauses has been observed often (Mikkelsen 2002 and references cited there).**

This holds true for reversed specificational clauses as well. Contrastive focus on the subject of predicational clauses, such as (50a) is evident in (50b). In the parallel specificational examples of (51), this is not the case. The initial constituent of an RS-*be* clause cannot be contrastively stressed to indicate focus. (All of the examples in (50), (51), and (52) are invented.)

(50) A: The locusts were our biggest problem.
B: Wrong, the APHIDS were our biggest problem.

(51) A: Our biggest problem were the locusts.
B: #Wrong, a MINOR problem were the locusts. (Our biggest problem were the aphids.)

2.1.5.4 *Constraint(s) on the verb.* The copula *be* is by definition required in RS-*be* clauses.

2.1.5.5 *SAI*

Like standard specificational *be*[14] RS-*be* can be realized in inverted clauses, such as polar questions. Invented examples (52a,b) present polar questions based on the attested declaratives (6a,b).

(52) a. Are our biggest worry really the injury risks?
b. Aren't my best bet still the places where the shoreline drops off quickly?

2.1.5.6 *Negation.* RS-*be* is compatible with negation.

(53) The problem aren't puns per-se, it's when people abuse them without rhyme or reason to derail a conversation.

2.1.5.7 *Constraint(s) on argument.* RS-*be* places no absolute constraint on either argument, but a reversed specificational clause's preverbal constituent, although topical, is non-referential.

One of Mikkeksen's tests of referentiality involves the anaphoric pronoun in a tag; singular human antecedents require *he* or *she*. The non-referentiality of the subject of an ordinary specificational clause is illustrated in an example like (54). Sentence (54a) is specificational; its subject is predicational and so can't antecede *she*. Sentence (54b) is predicational; its subject is referential and can't antecede *it*.

(54) a. The lead actress in that movie is Ingrid Bergman, isn't it?/*isn't she? (Mikkelsen's ex. (9))
b. Ingrid Bergman is the lead actress in that movie *isn't it/isn't she? (Mikkelsen's ex. (10))

Reversed specificationals manifest the same predicational/ referential distinction but in a slightly different way. In reversed specificationals the postverbal constituent appears to

[14]Mikkelsen (2002) points out that within the Minimalist framework an analysis of specificational clauses is possible that does not require a special specificational *be*. The present lexical analysis does indeed posit a specificational *be*; it does not, however, need – as Mikkelsen acknowledges – to posit discourse-sensitive (uninterpretable) *syntactic* features such as TOPIC and FOCUS.

possess enough 'subjecthood' to serve as a pronominal antecedent, resulting in two potential anaphoric agreement patterns, as in (55a). By contrast, in an ordinary specificational clause, as in (55b), only the preverbal constituent is a potential antecdent.

(55) a. But finally, the "winning couple" were John and Astrid, weren't they?/wasn't it? (attested without tag).

b. But finally, John and Astrid were the "winning couple", weren't they?/*wasn't it? (invented example).

2.1.5.8 ***ACE.*** **It appears that complement specificational clauses, whether or not 'reversed', resist subject extraction. So ACE is not relevant to them.**

(56) a. *It's the winning couple that Pat believes that was/were John and Astrid.

b. *It's the winning couple that Pat believes was/were John and Astrid.

c. *The winning couple, Pat believes (that) was/were John and Astrid.

An additional source of evidence in favor of viewing the preverbal expression as the XARG of RS-*be* comes from tag-questions: in RS-*be* sentences, it is the preverbal NP, rather than the postverbal (agreeing) NP, that predominantly controls the reference of the subject pronoun in a tag. In an online (Qualtrics) survey, 195 respondents were asked to choose the appropriate tag for each of the following five RS-*be* sentences.

(57) a. The only thing we get paid for are the aluminum cans, [isn't it?/aren't they?]

b. The major issue were the people handling the application, [wasn't it?/weren't they?]

c. Your primary concern are the additional charges, [isn't it?/aren't they?]

d. Your first sight were those two huge bare feet, [wasn't it?/weren't they?]

e. The problem is the people who don't vote, [isn't it?/aren't they?]

Respondents were given the choice of adding either tag, neither tag, or both tags. Only a handful (23) selected the both-tag option, while almost a third (294) of the total (902) responses favored the neither-tag option. The majority 585 (65%) chose one or the other of the two single-tag positions, pre- or post-verbal. Of these, 498 (85%) chose preverbal NP control of the tag, while (87) (15%) chose postverbal control. Although there were clearly aspects of this task that respondents were not comfortable with, the degree of respondents' preference for preverbal control is unlikely to be due to chance. If we consider each single-tag response as the result of an independent binomial trial with the null hypothesis probability of preverbal control as .5, the probability of obtaining 498 or more preverbal control responses in 585 independent binomial trials is, to five decimal places, zero. We conclude that there is strong evidence for attributing a subject property to the preverbal NP in SE-*be*, despite the fact that agreement is with the postverbal NP. This outcome would not be predicted if the only factor considered were the relative referentiality of the two NPs and discourse roles were not also considered (Mikkelsen 2002).

2.1.5.9 *CE*. Specificational clauses which are also restrictive relative clauses do not appear to occur, possibly because of conflicting information-structure functions of the two clause types. So the constraint which requires the complementizer *that* to introduce subject relative clauses does not apply to RS-*be*.

(58) a. *I have always admired the leading actress in Casablanca (that) was Ingrid Bergman.

b. *We congratulated the winning couple (that) were John and Astrid.

2.1.5.10 *Tag.* Agreement-reversed specificational clauses accept question tags, as previously discussed and is further evidenced by (55a) and the acceptable version of (55b).

Table 1 presents a summary of the facts of this section.

Constraint Construction	Agreement	Raising	Focus	Verb Constraint	Inversion	Negation	Argument Constraint	ACE	CE	Tag
1. OI	✓	✓	✓	intrans	✓	✓	✗	✓	✓	?
2. P-*there*	✓	✓	✓	intrans	✓	✓	✓	✓	NA	✓
3. DI	✓	✓	✓	axial	✗	✗	✓	NA	NA	✓
4. E-*there*	✓	✓	✓	exist	✓	✓	✓	✓	NA	✓
5. RS-*be*	✓	✓	✓	*be*	✓	✓	✗	NA	NA	✓
Legend	1	2	3	4	5	6	7	8	9	10

TABLE 1 Applicability of constraints to maximal split-subject constructions

Legend

1. Agreement: In an FDC, the verb agrees with the postverbal constituent.
2. Raising: The argument that appears in subject position in a simple declarative clause is interpretable as subject of a raising verb.
3. Focus: The postverbal argument in an FDC is in focus.
4. Verb Constraint: The verb is constrained as indicated, either as simply intransitive or more narrowly.
5. Inversion: The argument that occurs postverbally in an FDC also does so in an SAI clause such as WH-question.
6. Negation: Negation is compatible with the licensed clause.
7. Argument constraint: One or more arguments are lexically constrained by the verb.
8. ACE: The "Anti-Complementizer" ('*that*-trace') effect holds for the construction in question.
9. CE: The 'Complementizer Constraint', requiring the complementizer that in subject relative clauses, holds for the construction in question.
10. Tag: A question tag is compatible with the licensed clause.

✓: A licensed clause is subject to the constraint.
✗: The constraint is applicable to the licensed clause but not compatible with it.
NA : The constraint is not applicable to the licensed clause.

Agreement, Raising, and Focus are observable effects of all five maximal split-subject constructions. Limitation to intransitive verbs is also common to all five, with DI and E-*there* imposing further semantic restrictions. Each of the remaining six constraints is relevant to a majority of the maximal constructions.

2.2 Sign-Based Construction Grammar

SBCG[15] assumes that a language consists principally in a non-finite set of signs. Signs are modeled as functional feature structures (FSs) assigning values to the features PHONOLOGY (PHON), morphological form (FORM), ARGUMENT STRUCTURE (ARG-ST), SYNTAX (SYN), SEMANTICS (SEM), and CONTEXT (CNTXT). SBCG recognizes a second type of model object: a *construct*, which models a local tree as a functional feature structure with two features: a MOTHER (MTR) feature, whose value is a sign, and a DAUGHTERS (DTRS) feature, whose value is a non-empty list of signs.[16] As is common in constraint-based approaches, a strict distinction is maintained between elements of the language model, e.g., signs and constructs, and elements of the grammar which licenses them: listemes and constructions. A listeme licenses a lexeme or, in the case of non-compositional idioms, a phrase. Constructions are of two types, lexical class constructions, which, in combination with listemes, define classes of lexemes, and combinatorial constructions, which define classes of constructs, local trees. A lexical rule in SBCG is a combinatorial construction with a lexical mother and a single lexical daughter. The Split Subject (SS) Construction, which we take up in section 3, is a lexical rule, a non-branching local tree, whose input (DTRS) and output (MTR) are lexemes. It plays a major role in the analysis of partial inversion.

The feature structures that constitute the language model

[15]For a more detailed introduction to SBCG, see Sag (2012). This section is based in significant part on Kay & Michaelis (2019) and Kay, Sag & Flickinger (this volume).

[16]Since signs do not contain a DTRS feature and since constructs are limited to local trees whose daughters are signs, all non-local dependencies are encoded in SBCG as a sequence of local dependencies. A tree that spans more than two levels of structure may be used to illustrate the successive embedding of constructs that constitutes the analysis of the licensing of the root sign but does not correspond to any model object in SBCG. This aspect of the theory constitutes an explicit claim about the predominantly local nature of dependencies in human languages (See, for example, Sag 2007).

are elements of a multiple inheritance hierarchy of types. Subtypes of sign include *lexeme*, *word*, and *phrase* (see Sag (2012:178) for detail). Each sign has a FORM feature, whose value is a morphological representation of the expression, notated here in standard English orthography. The other features of the sign are PHON(OLOGY), ARG-ST (argument structure; for lexical signs only), SYN(TAX), SEM(ANTICS), and CONTEXT.[17] The value of SYN is a feature structure that specifies the features CAT(EGORY), VAL(ENCE), and MRKG (MARKING).[18] CAT values are feature structures assigned to various word-class types (*noun*, *verb*, etc.), and specify values for the features appropriate to that type, including Lexical Identity (LID), whose value is a list of *frames*.[19] The MARKING (MRKG) value of a lexical sign (only) is identified with its LID value.[20] LID values are percolated from heads, making the identity of the lexical head available at the phrasal level; MRKG values are percolated from *functors* (specifiers or modifiers). Thus in an NP or N′ the identity of both the head (via the LID value) and the modifier or specifier (via MRKG value) are visible to potential governing predicators.

The value of the ARG-ST feature is a list of the signs that are the arguments – syntactic and semantic – of a predicating lexeme or word, in order of increasing obliqueness, or decreasing accessibility (subject, direct object,...). Members of the ARG-ST list reappear in the list value of the VAL feature, except when extracted or given null realization (Chaves et al. submitted). The ARG-ST feature is limited to lexical signs, that is lexemes and words. Unlike the VAL feature, it does not appear in phrasal signs. This limitation provides one aspect of the highly local nature of SBCG.

[17]The PHONOLOGY feature is not relevant to the material of the present chapter and is not included in our diagrams.

[18]Since, the MARKING feature does not play a role in the present analysis, that feature is often omitted in the diagrams.

[19]Typically this is a singleton list. See Sag (2012:84ff.) for greater detail.

[20]For readers familiar with HPSG, the LID feature subsumes the function of the PFORM feature and accomplishes the analogous work for lexical heads of all categories.

The external argument is the argument that may be raised, controlled, etc. When a lexeme has an external argument (XARG), it is the first element on the ARG-ST list. The XARG feature in effect allows a predicator that selects a given type of phrasal sign to 'see' the first argument of the verb within that phrase. The XARG feature plays a key role in the analysis of idioms (Kay, Sag & Flickinger (this volume), Kay & Michaelis 2019). In an English finite and non-inverted clause, the XARG is the subject. Possible values of XARG are *sign* and *none*. If a noun phrase has an XARG, it is a genitive determiner.

The signs that may occur in an ARG-ST list are subtyped as either overt or covert. The VAL(ENCE) feature provides a list of the overt signs, which are realized as sisters of a lexical head, or in the case of subject, as sister to the verb phrase. The GAP feature provides a list of the overt signs that are extracted, that is, realized as the filler constituent of a filler-gap construct. The VAL and GAP lists exhaust the overt signs of an ARG-ST list. Covert signs, implicit arguments, do not play a role in the present chapter (see Chaves et al. (submitted) for discussion of covert signs).

The VAL list of a word shrinks as successive phrases headed by the word are projected. Expressions like NPs, PPs, APs, and clauses have the empty list as their VAL value: they are 'saturated', in the sense that they contain constituents corresponding to all of the predicator's arguments that are neither realized as fillers in a filler-gap construct nor interpreted sans realization (Chaves et al. submitted).

A second property of the SBCG architecture that enforces locality is that only constructs, but not signs, have a DTRS feature. Since the members of the list constituting the value of the ARG-ST feature are signs and since a sign does not have a DTRS feature, it is possible for a predicator to specify properties only of its daughters, not of its 'granddaughters'. Long-distance dependencies are encoded as a sequence of local dependencies, via the GAP (formerly SLASH) feature, in the tradition of GPSG and HPSG.

The value of SEM includes specifications for the features INDEX and FRAMES. We assume an indefinitely large number of referential indices. The FRAMES feature takes a list of *frames*, elementary predications[21], as its value. A frame can serve as an argument of another frame and the totality of frames in a given frames list form a directed, non-cyclic, singly-rooted graph (informally, a tree) mediated by the "argument of" relation. The feature LABEL indicates an "argument of" relation; if *frame* A is an argument of *frame* B the value of the LABEL feature of A is the value of a feature of B. LABELS are indicated. The LTOP feature indicates the root of the tree of embedding relations of a FRAMES list. By "grabbing" the LTOP value one can "pick up" the whole FRAMES list. As we proceed we will introduce more features in the context of their use in particular constructions. As a preliminary, we sketch an SBCG approach to agreement.

2.3 Agreement

Without elaborating a full theory of agreement,[22] we follow the general approach of Pollard and Sag (1994:60-99) (P&S) in proposing that the inflectional properties of English finite verbs reflect certain interpretive properties of one privileged argument. These properties are part of the referential index of that argument, and the nature of these properties is determined in considerable part by what is relevant in the context in which the act of reference takes place, rather than exclusively by denotational properties of the argument per se. The two are usually, but not invariably, correlated, although sometimes, as in the case of arbitrary gender, the properties

[21]In the present study these lists are all singleton (See Sag 2012). SBCG frames are formally equivalent to the RELS of Minimal Recursion Semantics (MRS), in, e.g., Copestake et al. (2005). We adopt here a simplified form of MRS, making no use of the mechanisms for keeping track of relative scoping relations among quantifiers. We make limited use of the LABEL feature.

[22]For a fully developed theory of agreement within a closely related, constraint-based approach, see Wechsler and Zlatić (2000, 2003) (W&Z). ee also Kathol (1997) and Wechsler (2011).

determining agreement are purely conventional. P&S give examples that illustrate the manner in which context of use may determine such properties — as in the reference transfer cases first noted by Nunberg (1977). P&S also suggest an analogy between the agreement-relevant features of indices and the reference markers of Discourse Representation Theory, based on the way the two function in the tracking of referents in a sustained discourse. For example, in (59a) the plural verb *are* reveals that the food (hash browns) is the discourse object being tracked, whereas in (59b) the singular verb *is* reveals that the referent being tracked is the diner.

(59) a. The hash browns at table nine are/*is getting cold. [P&S (18), p.69)

b. The hash browns at table nine is/*are getting angry.

We follow W&Z and Kathol (1999), who assign an AGREEMENT (and/or CONCORD) feature to targets of agreement in order to account for a wide range of phenomena. For example, verbs can show person and number agreement when there is no argument to furnish the index features. Kathol illustrates the point, indicating that in German impersonal passives there is third person singular agreement inflection on the verb although there is no overt subject argument, as in (60). Latin shows similar facts in (61).

(60)

An	jenem	Abend	wurde	viel	gelacht.
during	that	evening	was:3sg	much	laughed

'There was much laughter that evening.' [Kathol 1999 (15) p.10[23]]

(61)

Ad	virtutem	venitur	per	ipsam
to	virtue	come:3sg:pass	through	herself

'One comes to virtue through virtue itself' (Seneca, *Epistulae Morales* 89.8.10) [Napoli 2013 (6) p. 375]

English finite verbs show third singular agreement with

[23]Page reference is to the online version, at `http://citeseerx.ist.psu.edu/viewdoc/download?doi=10.1.1.49.1289&rep=rep1&type=pdf`.

sentential and prepositional subjects. We follow P&S in assigning [PER 3] and [NUM *sg*] to the INDEX values of expletive *it* and expletive *there*, and also to the INDEX values of PP's and S's.

Although P&S neither restrict their attention to English agreement nor overlook some of the complex agreement phenomena of English, Kathol (1999) and W&Z establish that more feature machinery than that provided by the INDEX agreement process of P&S is required to capture the details of agreement in a wider range of cases, including conflicts between constituent internal and cross-constituent agreement and conflicts between grammatical gender and natural gender. We do not here attempt to present a general theory of agreement, but only posit the minimal agreement machinery necessary to capture the less complex facts of English canonical and non-canonical verbal agreement.[24]

Sag (2012) does not discuss agreement. Sag (2012:112) presents the construction in (62) for constraining verbal lexemes, which we expand slightly in (63) in order to show an AGR(EEMENT) feature.

(62) **Verb Lexeme Construction** ($\uparrow$*lexeme*) (preliminary, simplified, after Sag 2012:181)

$$\mathit{verb\text{-}lexeme} \Rightarrow \begin{bmatrix} \text{ARG-ST}\ \langle X, \ldots \rangle & \\ \text{SYN} & \begin{bmatrix} \text{CAT} & \begin{bmatrix} \mathit{verb} & \\ \text{LID} & L \\ \text{SELECT} & \mathit{none} \\ \text{XARG} & X \end{bmatrix} \\ \text{MRKG} & \mathit{unmrk} \end{bmatrix} \\ \text{SEM} & \begin{bmatrix} \text{FRAMES} & L \end{bmatrix} \end{bmatrix}$$

The representation in (62) may be read as follows. A sign of

[24]In particular, we do not take up W&Z's arguments that both an AGREEMENT feature and a separate CONCORD feature are necessary to deal with the complex agreement phenomena of a language like Serbian/Croatian.

the type *verb-lexeme* inherits the constraints of the type *lexeme*, '(↑*lexeme*)', and is constrained by the feature structure description in the AVM following '⇒'. In (62) the value of the ARG-ST feature is a list whose first member is represented by the tag *X*. The value of the SYN feature is a feature structure description showing the CAT features.[25] The CAT value indicates the type *verb*. The LID value is the list tag *L*, which can be seen below as the value of the FRAMES feature of the SEM value. The SELECT feature is shown for completeness, but plays no active role in verbs. The XARG value *X* identifies this item with the first element of the ARG-ST list. The MARKING (MRKG) feature is also shown for completeness.

(63) **Verb Lexeme Construction** (↑*lexeme*) (modified)

$$
\textit{verb-lxm} \Rightarrow \begin{bmatrix}
\text{ARG-ST} & \langle X, \ldots \rangle \\
\text{SYN} & \begin{bmatrix}
\text{CAT} & \begin{bmatrix} \textit{verb} & \\ \text{LID} & L \\ \text{SELECT} & \textit{none} \\ \text{XARG} & X \end{bmatrix} \\
\text{MRKG} & \textit{unmrk} \\
\text{AGR} & \begin{bmatrix} \text{PER} & \textit{per} \\ \text{NUM} & \textit{num} \end{bmatrix}
\end{bmatrix} \\
\text{SEM} & \begin{bmatrix} \text{FRAMES} & L \end{bmatrix}
\end{bmatrix}
$$

Canonically, the English finite verb agrees with the external argument (XARG). As noted, the XARG is the only argument of a lexical head visible from outside the phrase projected by that head and serves as the subject in a subject-predicate clause. We further constrain the Verb Lexeme Construction as the Canonical Verb Lexeme Construction to reflect this fact.

[25]Certain features, such as VAL, WH, and REL, which play a role in filler-gap structures, need not be shown because they are inherited from *lexeme*, which is a subtype of *syntax-object*, whose features are determined in the grammar signature. (Sag 2012:72-73)

(64) **Canonical Verb Lexeme Construction**
($\uparrow$*verb-lexeme*)

$$\textit{canon-v-lxm} \Rightarrow \left[\text{SYN}\left[\begin{array}{ll}\text{CAT} & \left[\text{XARG}\left[\text{SEM}\left[\text{INDEX}\begin{bmatrix}\text{PER} & X\\ \text{NUM} & Y\end{bmatrix}\right]\right]\right]\\ \text{AGR} & \begin{bmatrix}\text{PER} & X\\ \text{NUM} & Y\end{bmatrix}\end{array}\right]\right]$$

This lexical-class construction ensures that a canonical English verb lexeme identifies the agreement information of the verb with that of the INDEX of its XARG. The inflectional constructions that are sensitive to AGR values specify *word* mothers that are [VF *fin(ite)*] and identify the SYN values of mother and daughter; morphological and phonological reflexes of agreement only occur on finite verbs in English. In other languages agreement in participles is widespread and in infinitives not uncommon.[26] The two immediate subtypes of *verb-lexeme* posited in Sag (2012) are *transitive-verb-lexeme* and *intransitive-verb-lexeme*; *canonical-verb-lexeme* is cross-classified with each of these to produce immediate subtypes of *canonical-transitive-verb-lexeme* and *canonical-intransitive-verb-lexeme*, as shown in (65).

(65)

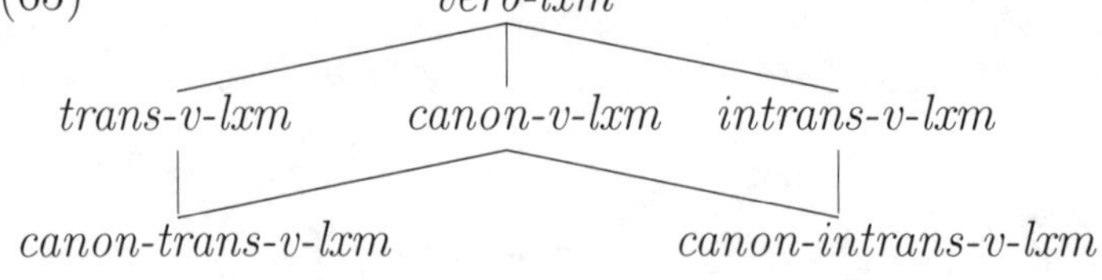

While agreement with the XARG is the canonical choice in English, it is not the only choice, as we have seen in (2)–(6). A derivational construction that assigns the role of agree-

[26]E.g., in Portuguese, Galician, Medieval Old Neapolitanmu, and Sardinian (Ledgeway 1998), Hungarian (Tóth 2000), Hindi-Urdu (Bhatt 2005), and several Caucasian languages (Haspelmath 1999, Polinsky & Potsdam 2001).

ment source (AS) to a non-XARG is needed to account for non-canonical agreement. That construction is the Split Subject Construction. The SS Construction provides the unity to our analysis of the superficially disparate phenomena of English partial inversion. The *split-subject-intransitive-verb-lexeme* type, licensed by the mother of the SS Construction, inherits *intrans-v-lxm*, but not *canon-intrans-v-lxm*, yielding the type hierarchy in (66).

(66)

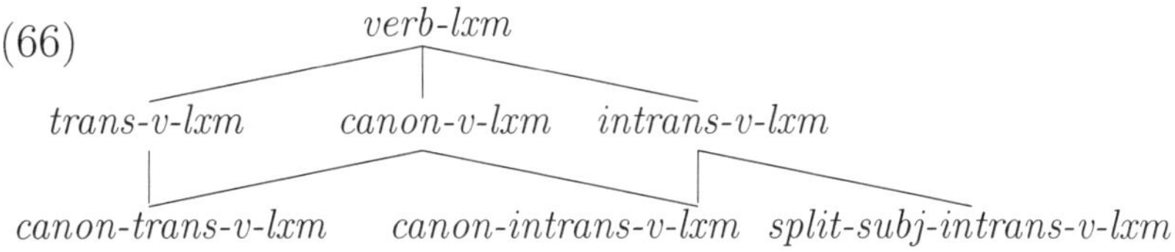

2.4 The Split Subject Construction

The Split-Subject Construction (69) licenses a unary branching structure, a mother with a unique daughter. Constructions of this kind implement the concept of lexical rule (Müller & Wechsler 2014). SS is also a derivational construction, that is, one which specifies a DTRS list – in this case singleton – containing lexical signs (words or lexemes) and a lexeme mother (Sag 2012:119 ff.). The single daughter of SS is of the type *canonical-intransitive-v-lexeme*; the mother is of the type *split-subject-intransitive-v-lexeme* (*s-s-intrans-v-lxm*).

In SS the mother's XARG is distinct from the daughter's. The XARG of the mother of a split-subject expression may or may not be an argument of the daughter. This point has particular bearing on the analysis of OI. While Bresnan (1994) and Kim (2003) assert that the initial constituent in OI must be an argument of the lexical verb, this appears not to be the case. Bresnan (1994) (ex.13) presents the constructed data in (67), the point being that *Among the guests* is an argument of *sitting* but not of *knitting*.

(67) a. Among the guests was sitting my friend Rose.
b. *Among the guests was knitting my friend Rose.

Compare to (16b) the attested example in (68).

(68) And there, in the midst of the swirl, was smiling Sam Waksal – a reedy, charming bachelor biotech entrepreneur ...[27]

Attested examples of fronted constituents in OI that are not complements of the lexical verb are common:[28]

(69) a. In the bed was sleeping a young woman with long, dark hair.
b. ... and in the distance glowed the lights of a small town.
c. From the mast flapped the banner of King Aurelius and of Braime.
d. ... and in the distance glowed a dim unnatural light
e. On the horizon shimmered the mirage.
f. Under the tree were playing a group of dirty children.
g. Nearby grazed some horses...
h. In Maria's sticky hand melted a chocolate-chip ice-cream cone. (Birner and Ward 1998: 193)
i. And in this lacey leafage fluttered a number of grey birds with black and white stripes and long tails. (Levin and Rappaport Hovav 1995: 226)

[27]A referee suggested that (68) is not an example of OI. That is, *smiling* is not a present participle in an OI clause but an adjectival modifier within an NP and the copula is the main verb of a presentational clause. However, the context makes clear that *smiling* is indeed a present participle in a VP *was smiling*, heading a finite OI sentence. The text continues: "That night Waksal had particular reason to celebrate: not only was the party a perfect amalgam of all that he had aspired to – big money and serious science spiced with celebrity and society – but 2001 had been the defining year for his long-struggling business." [https://www.vanityfair.com/news/2002/06/imclone-cancer-drug-sam-waksal]. There is no hint that "smiling Sam Waksal" is a sobriquet of some 'kind. Incidentally, if "Smiling Sam Waksal" was being used as a name, "Smiling" would normally appear capitalized.

[28]Salzmann (2013) notes similar examples of fronted elements that are not arguments of the OI verb. He points out that these facts are inconsistent with standard analyses in the GB/MP tradition, in which the fronted constituent originally occupies Spec,TP, and also with argument-structure analyses like Bresnan's, in which the fronted element must be included in the inherent argument structure of the verb.

j. Down at the harbor there is a teal-green clubhouse for socializing and parties. Beside it sparkles the community pool. (Vanity Fair, August, 2001)

k. Beside it glowed the delicate apricot, whose scent was like a woman's perfume.

l. Inside it buzzed a flying insect, furry-bodied and gray.

In the mother of a split-subject-construct, the AS is not the XARG; it is an internal argument and is identified with the XARG of the daughter. In creating an external argument that is not the agreement source, SS effectively splits canonical subject properties between the 'new' and 'old' XARGS. The lexeme types that directly license OI, P-*there*, DI, E-*there*, and RS-*be* are all subtypes of *s-s-intrans-v-lxm*.

In a finite OI, P-*there*, DI, E-*there*, or RS-*be* clause, the verb is inflected in accordance with the PER(son) and NUM(ber) values of the eventual post-verbal (internal but nevertheless agreement-triggering) argument by an inflectional construction that is sensitive to these values and to the V(ERB)F(ORM) and TENSE values of the verb. An example of such an inflectional construction is presented in the Appendix.

(70) **The Split-Subject Construction** (↑*derivational-cxt*)

$$
\textit{split-sbj-inv-vb} \Rightarrow \left[\begin{array}{ll}
\text{MTR } Z! & \left[\begin{array}{ll} \multicolumn{2}{l}{\textit{split-subj-i-v-lxm}} \\ \text{ARG-ST} & \langle Y{:}\text{XP}_j, X, \ldots\rangle \\ \text{SYN} & \left[\text{CAT} \left[\begin{array}{ll}\text{XARG} & Y\\ \text{AGR} & \left[\begin{array}{ll}\text{PER} & U\\ \text{NUM} & V\end{array}\right]\end{array}\right]\right] \\ \text{CONTEXT} & \left[\text{INFO-ROLE}\left[\text{FOCUS } i\right]\right]\end{array}\right] \\
\text{DTRS} & \left\langle Z{:}\left[\begin{array}{ll}\multicolumn{2}{l}{\textit{canonical-i-v-lxm}}\\ \text{ARG-ST} & \langle X{:}\text{NP}_{i[PER\ U, NUM\ V]}, \ldots\rangle \\ \text{SYN} & \left[\text{CAT}\left[\text{XARG } X\right]\right]\end{array}\right]\right\rangle
\end{array}\right]
$$

The notation (↑*derivational-cxt*) indicates that the *split-subject-construct* type is a subtype of *derivational-construct*. The mother's type is *split-subject-inverted-verb-lexeme*. The tag *X* identifies the daughter's external argument with the second (internal) argument in the mother's ARG-ST list. The similar but non-identical composite feature-structure tags, '*Z:*' on the unique daughter and '*Z!*' on the mother, indicate that the two feature structure descriptions are the same in all respects in which they are not explicitly shown to differ. (See Sag (2012:125,fn.71) for further discussion of this notation.) In the present instance, we note that the construction in (70) does not affect the semantics of the verb undergoing the rule. The ARG-ST list of the mother differs from that of the daughter in containing an external argument *Y* that is distinct from the external argument *X* of the daughter. Recall from the discussion above that the XARG of the mother may or may not be an argument of the daughter. The agreement source, tagged *X*, of the mother is the XARG of the daughter and not the XARG of the mother.

SS is a discourse-pragmatically specialized construction: it requires the internal argument of an *s-s-i-v-lxm* to fill the role of focus. The internal argument *X* is realized as the postverbal NP in a simple declarative clause headed by a split-subject verb. In the terms of Birner (1996:90) and Huddleston and Pullum (2002:1370) [CGEL], the postverbal argument is not necessarily discourse new but is never discourse older than the argument realizing the XARG. Similarly, we follow Lambrecht (1994) (see also Lambrecht and Michaelis 1998) in viewing focus as a discourse relation rather than a simple discourse status. In the relational treatment, a focal argument constitutes a relatively unpredicted argument in a predication. An argument is unpredicted to the degree that it is to be construed as identifying the denotatum of a variable in a discourse-presupposed open proposition, as in categorical or narrow-focus predications, e.g., CONGRESS is to blame. An argument may also be relatively unpredicted when both it and the predicator that selects it are discourse new; such is the case in some thetic, or sentence-focus statements, e.g., Your SHOE's untied. While typically SS statements are employed in sentence-focus utterances, in that neither the relation denoted by the verb nor the postverbal argument are discourse-presupposed, the postverbal argument is focal whether the property denoted by the SS verb can readily be construed as a contextually given, as in the case of sitting guests in (67a) or not contextually given, as in the case of smiling guests in (68).

As we have defined it, SS does not depend on, nor indeed reliably correlate with, CASE. In general, there is no necessary correlation between verbal inflection and nominative case in English. While nominative pronominal arguments are attested in what Borer (2005:256) calls V1 contexts in English, e.g. (71), such tokens have an archaic flavor, and this pattern is far less prevalent than that in which the pronominal argument is accusative (72):

(71) a. There in the crowds stood I...
b. July 4th is for boys playing baseball and in 1962 here stood I, a Youth of Endless Summers patiently waiting for the perfect pitch.
c. Only a fool goes to fight an army alone, yet here stand we Christians on the battlefield.
d. There are they who say they believe there is no God.

(72) a. There in the doorway stands me, a wide framed 6'2" mexican dude.
b. And there goes me again posting random stuff along the way.
c. But there sat the mackerel and there sat us and for five minutes neither the fish nor the actors moved.
d. Save for God's grace (and a few worldly breaks), there go us.

Borer observes that V1 constructions across languages "have presented a problem for theories of nominative case assignment and agreement" (ibid), noting that the nominative case pattern of (71) (rather than, say, the accusative pattern of (72)) is unpredicted unless, for example, one assumes "LF movement to nominative position" or some similar mechanism. Beyond being ad hoc the advantage of any such strategy is unclear; it fails to predict the alternative accusative case pattern in (72). Likewise those theories that do predict non-nominative post-verbal arguments like those in (72), through structural accusative or inherent partitive case assignment (as in Belletti 1988), run afoul of the facts of (71). We thus agree with Borer's assessment that a universal (by which we understand non-construction-particular) approach to case assignment in such patterns is not feasible.[29]

Summing up, the Split Subject Construction is a derivational construction with a unique lexeme daughter. It licenses a mother of type *split-subject-intransitive-verb-lexeme*. The verbs that head VPs and clauses like those of (2)–(6) instantiate the type *split-subject-intransitive-verb-lexeme*. The Split Subject Construction does the job of creating, on the basis of a canonical intransitive verb, a non-canonical version of that verb in which the external argument and the AS are dissociated. Having accounted, by means of the Split Subject Construction, for the properties that unite the class of partial-inversion lexemes, we now turn to the five distinct classes of partial-inversion lexemes listed in the introduction: Oblique Inversion (section 5), Presentational *there* (section 6), Deictic Inversion (section 7), Existential *there* (Section 8) and Reversed Specificational *be* (Section 9).

[29]Examples like (72) show that finite inflection does not entail nominative case-marking. Typological findings like those of Nikolaeva (2014) indicate that the converse is also true: the presence of a nominative argument does not entail finite inflection. Constructions described by Nikolaeva include the Latin narrative infinitive, a main-clause construction in which an infinitival predicate is paired with a nominative subject argument (e.g., *Graucus primo distinguere et dividere* 'Graucus first distinguished and divided (them)').

2.5 Oblique Inversion (OI)

We have seen above a number of examples of OI. All have been monoclausal, with the preposed constituent immediately preceding the finite verb. Early examples of OI were given in Aissen & Hankamer (1972:502), shown in (73).

(73) a. Under this verb is embedded the S containing the cyclic subject.
 b. To these causes are attributed most of the financial catastrophes of the decade.
 c. To the social director fell the task of finding accommodations for all the visiting icthyologists.

OI interacts with a range of filler-gap constructions in a way that renders any particular phrasal representation impossible, as shown in (74).

(74) a. These are phrases, riffs, from which I hope will emerge in time a full composition, an eschatological aesthetic of music. (relative clause)
 b. Here I will attempt a reconsideration of the evidence, out of which I hope will come a conclusive resolution to the problem. (relative clause)
 c. From whence will come any help? (matrix *wh*-question)
 d. Where could arise a basil liqueur if not in Liguria? (matrix *wh*-question)
 e. If so, when might have existed the European ydioma tripharium which is supposed to be their common mother-tongue? (matrix *wh*-question)
 f. During May 68 he and my father were arrested four times. I know from where comes my dislike for police officers. (embedded *wh*-question)
 g. Scholars will debate from whence emerged the virus which so debilitated American social and intellectual elites' cognitive abilities that it went from savior to suicide in the 75 years following its World War II triumphs. (embedded *wh*-question)

h. Did out of this impass [sic] come existentialism, a belief that man could define his temperament and impose meaning on the world? (polar interrogative)[30]
i. Rather, it was from the contradistinctive complexity of her tresses that arose such allure. (*it*-cleft)
j. However, it was out of the left wing that came the whole post-modernist, reality-is-a-shared-social-construction view ... (*it*-cleft)
k. From their depths seemed to arise an eerie sound which continued to grow and grow—screaming in her ears: the cries of the dying. (Raising)
l. From out of nowhere seemed to come the deep, resonate voice that interrupted their satanic evocation. (Raising)

The existence of matrix *wh*-questions like (74c-e) cause us to question Bruening's (2010) claim that OI is incompatible with those contexts in which 'do support' occurs, i.e., in which an auxiliary is required as head of the VP containing the postverbal argument. More generally, these examples reveal that the setting ('locative') expression can occupy a variety of syntactic positions. Accordingly, they suggest that — whatever one's theory of cleft, filler-gap or raising structures – OI cannot be equated with its canonical declarative instantiation, in which the setting expression immediately precedes a VP headed by the finite verb for which it serves as argument or adjunct. It is for this reason that we reject the assumption, implicit in some analyses of OI, that OI is

[30]This sentence provides a counterexample to the analysis of OI presented below, which specifies that the external argument is necessarily realized in a filler position. Example (74h) was declared by an anonymous referee not to be English. It was, however, written by a professional writer of English. As of February 2023 it is available at `https://tonymckibbin.com/article/robert-redford.html`. In a previous draft of this chapter, we proposed on the basis of this example and the appearance of raising that the OI XARG may be realized in subject position. Given the unique status of observation (74h) and the substantial evidence and argument in the literature (especially Postal 2004) that the external argument in OI is necessarily extracted, our proposed analysis of OI represents the XARG in an OI verb as a member of the GAP list. Raising and extraction of the external argument are, of course, compatible in general (e.g. *Who do you think is expected to win?*).

a sentence pattern or phrasal configuration. Rather, in accordance with Bresnan (1994), we view OI as the output of a lexical rule (in SBCG a subtype of derivational construction). On this account, the only phrasal information OI lexemes contain is that they will be realized in some kind of filler-gap structure. Below we will present examples of SBCG derivations that show how lexical and phrasal constructions jointly license OI clauses.

The examples in (74), particularly those containing *wh*-questions and clefts, vitiate the widely made claim that the setting expression in OI always denotes a topic (Bresnan 1994, Birner and Ward 1998, Webelhuth 2011, Salzmann 2013). In *wh*-questions, as in (74c-g), the filler expression represents a narrow focus: such questions, like narrow-focus declarative sentences, concern the value of a variable denoted by the *wh*-expression (Engdahl 2006, Lambrecht and Michaelis 1998, inter alia). In example (74c), the identity of the 'source' argument is unknown; such sentences are not countenanced in a functional account of OI like that of Webelhuth (2011), in which the construction instructs the hearer to add an entity to a "conceptually accessible" spatial schema. A similar point can be made with respect to clefts: in cleft sentences, the post-copular expression again constitutes a narrow focus — the value of the variable in a presupposed open proposition (Hedberg 2000, Lambrecht 2001). For example, (74j) might be said to presuppose that the post-modernist view arose from some source. Such sentences supply the value of the location variable rather than presupposing the identifiability of that location. Also, example (74l) poses a problem for a topic-based account of OI: the expression *from out of nowhere* does not denote a mutually known or previously established location, let alone a topical one. Thus, while we follow functional theorists of OI in asserting that the construction serves an information packaging function, we do not view it as placing discourse-pragmatic constraints on the setting expression. Instead, these facts show OI to be a focus-marking construction, constraining only the postverbal argument.[31]

Throughout the foregoing discussion, we have equivocated regarding the appropriate characterization of the setting constituent in OI. Bresnan (1994:75) (ex. 5) presents the examples in (75) as evidence that the fronted element in OI (her Locative Inversion) need not be a PP.

(75) a. Crashing through the woods came a wild boar. [Birner, personal communication [to Bresnan] 1990, attributed to Georgia Green originally]

b. Coiled on the floor lay a one-hundred-and-fifty-foot length of braided nylon climbing rope three-eighths of an inch thick. [Birner 1992:58]

Bresnan stresses the fact that these examples contain a locative phrase. The locative argument is for her a necessary component of an OI predication, since the OI sentence is seen as saying something about a location – that it has some entity within it. It is in this sense that OI is seen as an exponent of presentational focus:

> In presentational focus, a scene is set and a referent is introduced on the scene to become the new focus of attention. In the core cases, a scene is naturally expressed as a location, and the referent as something of which location is predicated—hence, a theme. (Bresnan 1994: 90)

Webelhuth (2011:92) offers a similar account of OI, arguing that it, like "deictic inversion" (also our DI), "draw[s] the hearer's attention to the object expressed by the postverbal

[31] We remind the reader that, as discussed earlier, OI sentences (and partial-inversion predications in general) can be seen to contain a focal postverbal argument whether the particular OI sentence is construed as an argument-focus sentence (wherein the relation denoted by the verb is part of the presupposition) or a sentence-focus sentence, in which both verb and postverbal argument are construed as focal. Sentence (i) illustrates an argument-focus OI sentence: the verb *be* is outside the focal scope, inasmuch as the sentence appears to presuppose the open proposition 'x is next on the docket'. Sentence (ii), however, could not plausibly be said to presuppose 'x was ticking on one wall'; it is therefore most plausibly treated as sentence-focus.

(i) Next on the docket was the Hunter 31.

(ii) On one wall ticked a clock without a case.

NP via the region it is contained in". It is apparent, however, that OI does not require the preverbal element to display locative semantics, and it is for this reason that Postal (2004) and Bruening (2010), among others, oppose Bresnan's semantic characterization of OI. They bring to bear several non-locative examples from Lawler (1977) similar to the attested examples in (76):

(76) a. A motion to call a convention was rejected by a large majority and in its stead was adopted a resolution authorizing special town meetings...
b. For that reason was adopted a special Law on Protection from Domestic Violence...
c. From this can be deduced the fact that the roots of A in R are asymptotically equal to those of A1.
d. With this pen was written all of the events that would occur from then, til eternity.
e. Against this has been objected the inconvenience of a protracted session.
f. It is a solemn question, Stephen, because on it may depend the salvation of your eternal soul.
g. To those two gods correspond the goddesses Ishtar and Isis.

The examples in (76) suggest something of the range of semantic roles that the preverbal element may fill — including a reason (76b), a logical premise (76c), an instrument (76d), and a standard of comparison (76g). In none of these examples does the preverbal element denote a location, metaphorically or otherwise.

Taking such data to preclude a semantic constraint, Postal and Bruening propose a syntactic characterization of the initial element of OI: it is a PP. Our finding is that neither a syntactic definition of the constraint on the initial element nor a semantic one agrees with the following observations. As shown in (77) and (78), adverbial and apparently nominal phrases[32] can occupy the preverbal slot in OI.

(77) a. ... and they spurred and lashed their horses and came upon the maiden; she, perceiving this, quickly plucked a hair from the crown of her head and flung it from her, and suddenly arose a mighty forest. . .

b. Slowly and gradually appeared the form of the Lady of the Mist.

c. Although small at first the light began to grow and grow, until suddenly emerged a beautiful, iridescent white dragon which embodied life.

d. Their voices, from clearest soprano to richest bass, blended in low concordances, until, gradually, came words, like figures forming in mist.

(78) a. But the next day arrived the real army . . .

b. That morning arrived the last candidate, who did not appear in the program book . . .

c. The next day arrived a deputation of braves from the Cheyenne or Shienne nation...

d. That day began a series of questions better left unanswered.

e. That day began a twelve-year spiritual journey for me.

f. . . . but the next morning appeared a dozen German intelligence agents . . .

g. In both storms a tongue of ionization, Tol, appeared over North America . . . but the following day appeared a phenomenon similar to the Tol.

It appears that there is also no syntactic constraint on the XARG in OI beyond the fact that it must be realized as a filler in a filler-gap clause. An interpretive aspect of OI entails that the initial element of OI serve as a "setting" for a presentational act. The most usual setting is, no doubt, a

[32]These phrases have sometimes been viewed as internally nominal but externally prepositional.

place, physical or metaphorical: hence the useful but inaccurate label Locative Inversion. However, a temporal designation can do as well as a locative one. At a more abstract level, a setting phrase in OI can be any phrase that directs the attention of the addressee in a way that facilitates the act of presenting to the addressee's thus-focused attention the denotatum of the postverbal phrase. Hence, adverbs like *suddenly* or *gradually* and NPs that denote points or intervals of time, like those in (78), can serve as setting phrases in OI. OI thus resembles what Langacker (1993) refers to as a reference-point construction: reference point clauses are said to provide a point of access within a conceptual network that includes both a setting expression and the entity or state of affairs of interest. In OI clauses the conceptual starting point may be the location, the time or, in the case of sentence-focus OI clauses, the manner in which an event unfolds (e.g., slowly, suddenly, gradually); or it may consist merely in reference to some contextually available proposition or fact, as illustrated by the expressions *in its stead*, *for that reason*, or *from this* in (76). We represent the reference-point function of OI with a *reference-point-frame* considered as part of the obligatory interpretive context of an OI utterance. The Oblique Inversion Construction is given in (79).

Since OI defines a subtype of *split-subject-construct*, the AVM appearing to the right of the double-shafted arrow in (79) represents the additional constraints obeyed by an *oblique-inversion-construct* beyond those defining a *split-subject-construct.*[33] The mother of an *oblique-inversion-cxt* is of the type *oblique-inversion-lexeme.* OI also adds to a *split-subj-cxt* the constraint that the mother's XARG must be realized as a filler phrase (GAP $\langle Y \rangle$). The mother's internal argument NP_i (the daughter's XARG) appears on the mother's VAL list since it cannot be extracted (e.g., **What*

[33]In fact, some of the information shown in (79) is redundant with (70), either because showing it is necessary in order to display non-redundant information or for the reader's convenience.

out of the bushes jumped?); it also controls agreement in the mother ([AGR *W*] being present in both mother's and daughter's CAT values.)

(79) **Oblique Inversion Construction** (↑*split-subj-cxt*)

$$\textit{oblique-inv-cxt} \Rightarrow \begin{bmatrix} \text{MTR} & \begin{bmatrix} \textit{obl-inv-lxm} & \\ \text{ARG-ST} & \langle Y{:}\text{XP}_j, X{:}\text{NP}_i \rangle \\ \text{SYN} & \begin{bmatrix} \text{CAT} & \begin{bmatrix} \text{VFORM} & \textit{fin} \\ \text{IC} & + \\ \text{INV} & + \\ \text{XARG} & Y \\ \text{AGR} & W \end{bmatrix} \\ \text{VAL} & X \\ \text{GAP} & Y \end{bmatrix} \\ \text{SEM} & U \\ \text{CNTXT} & \begin{bmatrix} \text{DISCOURSE-ROLES} & \begin{bmatrix}\text{FOCUS} & i\end{bmatrix} \\ \text{BACKGROUND} & \langle \textit{ref-point-fr(j,k)} \rangle \end{bmatrix} \end{bmatrix} \\ \text{DTRS} & \left\langle \begin{bmatrix} \text{SYN} & \begin{bmatrix}\text{CAT} & \begin{bmatrix}\text{AGR} & W\end{bmatrix}\end{bmatrix} \\ \text{SEM} & U{:}\begin{bmatrix}\text{INDEX} & k\end{bmatrix} \end{bmatrix} \right\rangle \end{bmatrix}$$

The mother's CAT value shows further that an *oblique-inversion-lexeme* must head a finite (VFORM *fin*), inverted (INV +), independent (IC +) clause. The mother's XARG (NP$_j$) can be seen in the CONTEXT|BACKGROUND to provide a reference point in a *reference-point–frame* for the presented eventuality (*reference-point–frame(j,k)*). For example, in *Out of the bushes jumped a rabbit*, the extracted XARG *Out of the bushes* expresses a property of the eventuality denoted by *jumped a rabbit.* Similarly, in (2b), repeated as (80), the PP *from despair* is the extracted XARG and *arose the greatest nation* denotes the eventuality for which *From despair* provides a reference point.

(80) From despair arose the greatest nation.

In OI, as in the other four maximal, partial-inversion constructions, the constraint information regarding agreement, as well as that regarding the focus status of the postverbal argument, is inherited from *split-subject-cxt*, (70). However, nothing in *split-subject-cxt* or in the OI construction (79) requires the external argument of the mother lexeme to belong to the ARG-ST list of the daughter lexeme. As a result, the present account accommodates examples like those in (76)–(78), in which the XARG of the OI verb is not a selected argument of the corresponding lexical entry. Recall that the OI verbs in these examples include such non-locative-selecting, intransitive verbs as *smile, sparkle, melt, flutter* and *flap*. These examples are hard to reconcile with Bresnan's (1994) version of OI as resulting from the interaction of universal principles that determine how the arguments of a specifically locational verb are syntactically realized. On that account, "locative inversion arises when location is predicated of a theme argument which is presentationally focused, causing the locative to be mapped to the subject and the theme to an unaccusative object in accordance with the LFG mapping theory" (Bresnan 1994: 92).[34] But we have seen, along with others (at least as early as Lawler 1977), that the grammatical pattern in question is not restricted to the semantics of location, so it cannot be explained in terms of a rule or rules that realize grammatically the semantics of location. The present account treats OI simply as a valence-augmenting device with a specific presentational function.

As illustrated by the construct shown in (81), an *oblique-inversion-verb-lexeme*, in this case the OI version of the lexeme *arise*, is licensed by the OI construction shown in (79),

[34]Bresnan (1994:91) acknowledges "penumbra cases" like *Through the window was shooting a sniper.* In such cases, she argues, "we [can] think of presentational focus as overlaying a theme-locative predication [...] on the lexical argument structure of the verb". It is difficult, however, to know exactly what is intended by "overlaying". The weight of the attested examples in (76), (77), and (78) suggests, rather, that while the reference point constituent is often a location in tokens of the construction in (79), locational meaning does not enter into its semantics.

including the properties inherited from *split-subject* (70).

(81)

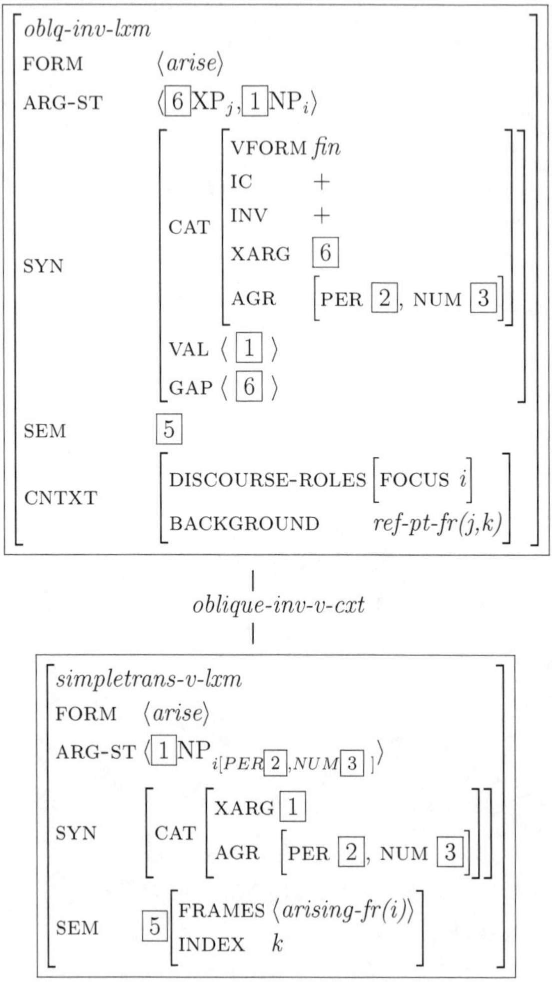

Derivation of the *oblique-inversion-lexeme arise*

Since the construct pictured in (81) is licensed by the construction shown in (79), there is a mother sign and a single daughter sign. Each sign representation is enclosed in a box. Tags are indicated by boxed numerals in feature structure representations.[35] The daughter lexeme has a single argu-

[35]These conventions are adopted to avoid confusion of diagrams of model objects

ment NP_i whose index is the argument of an *arising-fr*. In the daughter, it is the first (and only) member of the ARG-ST list, hence by convention the XARG. In the mother, this sign 'becomes' the internal argument $\boxed{1}$ but remains the agreement source. NP_i is also the information-structure FOCUS. A different 'new' XARG $\boxed{6}$ appears; it appears on the GAP list and furnishes a contextual reference point for the main predication [INDEX *k*].

The syntactic skeleton of the derivation in (86) illustrates in outline form the way the sentence *Down came snowflakes* is licensed by the Oblique Inversion Construction (79), the Preterit Construction (82), the Predicational Head-Complement Construction (83), and the XARG-*filler-head-clause* (85).

(82) **Preterit Construction** (↑*inflectional-cxt*) (adapted from Sag (2012) (57) p.116)

$$
preterit\text{-}cxt \Rightarrow \begin{bmatrix} \text{MTR} & \begin{bmatrix} \text{FORM} & \langle \mathbf{F}_{pret}(X)\rangle \\ \text{SYN} & Y{:}\begin{bmatrix}\text{CAT} & \begin{bmatrix}\text{VF} & fin\end{bmatrix}\end{bmatrix} \\ \text{SEM} & \begin{bmatrix} \text{INDEX} & s \\ \text{FRAMES} & L \oplus \left\langle \begin{bmatrix} some\text{-}fr & \\ \text{BV} & s \\ \text{REST} & l\end{bmatrix}, \begin{bmatrix} past\text{-}fr & \\ \text{LABEL} & l \\ \text{ARG} & s \end{bmatrix} \right\rangle \end{bmatrix} \end{bmatrix} \\ \text{DTRS} & \left\langle \begin{bmatrix} \text{FORM} & \langle X\rangle \\ \text{ARG-ST} & \langle \text{NP},...\rangle \\ \text{SYN} & Y \\ \text{SEM} & \begin{bmatrix}\text{INDEX} & s \\ \text{FRAMES} & L\end{bmatrix}\end{bmatrix} \right\rangle \end{bmatrix}
$$

(feature structures) or which contain model objects, such as derivation trees, like (81), with diagrams of constructions (which are descriptions of classes of model objects). The example ignores tense.

The Preterit Construction is an Inflectional Construction. In (82), the notation in the mother's FORM value says that the preterit form of a verb whose base form is X is the image of X under the morphological function that yields the preterit form of every verb (in English, in which past-tense forms do not vary by person or number). The Appendix discusses morphological functions briefly; see Sag (2012:113-114) for more detail. The combination of the notations [REST l] in the *some-frame* and [LABEL l] in the *past-fr* indicates that the *past-fr* is the restriction on the bound variable s in the *some-frame*.

The Predicational Head-Complement Construction of Sag (2012) (83) licenses a subtype of *headed-cxt*. The mother of a *predicational-head-complement-construct* may be a VP, PP, AP, or N′ ($\bar{N}$). In a *pred-hd-comp-cxt* the non-XARG valents of a lexical head are constrained to be sisters to that head. Construction (83) says that in a *pred-head-comp-cxt* the head daughter is a word whose valents consist of its XARG Y and a non-empty list L. The daughters of the construct type consist of the head daughter and the phrases (or words) constituting the list L. The mother's SYN value, $X!$, is the same as the head daughter's SYN value, X:, except that the members of L are absent from the VAL list of the mother.

(83) **Predicational Head-Complement Construction** (↑*headed-cxt*) (Sag 2012:112)

$$\textit{pred-hd-comp-cxt} \Rightarrow \begin{bmatrix} \text{MTR} & \begin{bmatrix}\text{SYN } X \,!\, \begin{bmatrix}\text{VAL } \langle Y \rangle\end{bmatrix}\end{bmatrix} \\ \text{DTRS} & \langle Z \rangle \oplus L\text{:}\textit{nelist} \\ \text{HD-DTR } Z\text{:} & \begin{bmatrix} \textit{word} & \\ \text{SYN} & X\text{:}\begin{bmatrix}\text{CAT} \begin{bmatrix}\text{XARG } Y\end{bmatrix} \\ \text{VAL } \langle Y \rangle \oplus L\end{bmatrix}\end{bmatrix}\end{bmatrix}$$

However, the construction in (83) has a flaw; it makes subject extraction impossible by specifying the daughter's XARG Y as a valent of the mother, which forecloses extraction of this sign (Rui Chaves p.c.). A revised version that remedies this flaw is given in (84) (Chaves, Kay, and Michaelis submitted). In the revised construction (84) the parentheses around the tag Y in the first member of the daughter's valence list indicate optionality. Thus, the XARG, Y, may or may not appear in the VAL list and so may appear alternatively on the GAP list and be realized in a filler position. The remainder of the daughters VAL list, L_2, is prevented from containing the XARG; as notated by *list* $(\neg Y)$, in which the parenthesis does not express optionality but rather that the list is constrained not to contain Y.

(84) **Predicational Head-Complement Construction** (↑*headed-cxt*) [revised]

$$\textit{pred-hd-comp-cxt} \Rightarrow \begin{bmatrix} \text{MTR} & \begin{bmatrix} \text{SYN } X \text{ ! } \begin{bmatrix} \text{VAL } L_1 \end{bmatrix} \end{bmatrix} \\ \text{DTRS} & \langle Z \rangle \oplus L_2{:}\textit{nelist} \\ \text{HD-DTR } Z{:} & \begin{bmatrix} \textit{word} & \\ \text{SYN} & \begin{bmatrix} \text{CAT} \begin{bmatrix} \text{XARG } Y \end{bmatrix} \\ \text{VAL } L_1{:}\langle (Y) \rangle \oplus \\ \quad L_2{:}\ \textit{list}\ (\neg Y) \end{bmatrix} \end{bmatrix} \end{bmatrix}$$

Clauses headed by an OI verb are licensed on the basis of their lexical head by the type declaration[36] in (85).

(85) $$\textit{xarg-filler-hd-inv-clause}{:} \begin{bmatrix} \textit{clause} \\ \text{HD-DTR } \textit{obl-inv-v-word} \end{bmatrix}$$

[36] Expression (85) is an example of a type declaration. This type of constraint statement is found in the grammar signature and is indicated by the colon (:) rather than the double-shafted arrow (⇒). The distinction between type declaration and construction can sometimes be a matter of choice (Sag 2012:72-73), but for the most part, type declarations may be considered informally as helping define the primary materials of the grammar out of which the constructions are fashioned.

(86)

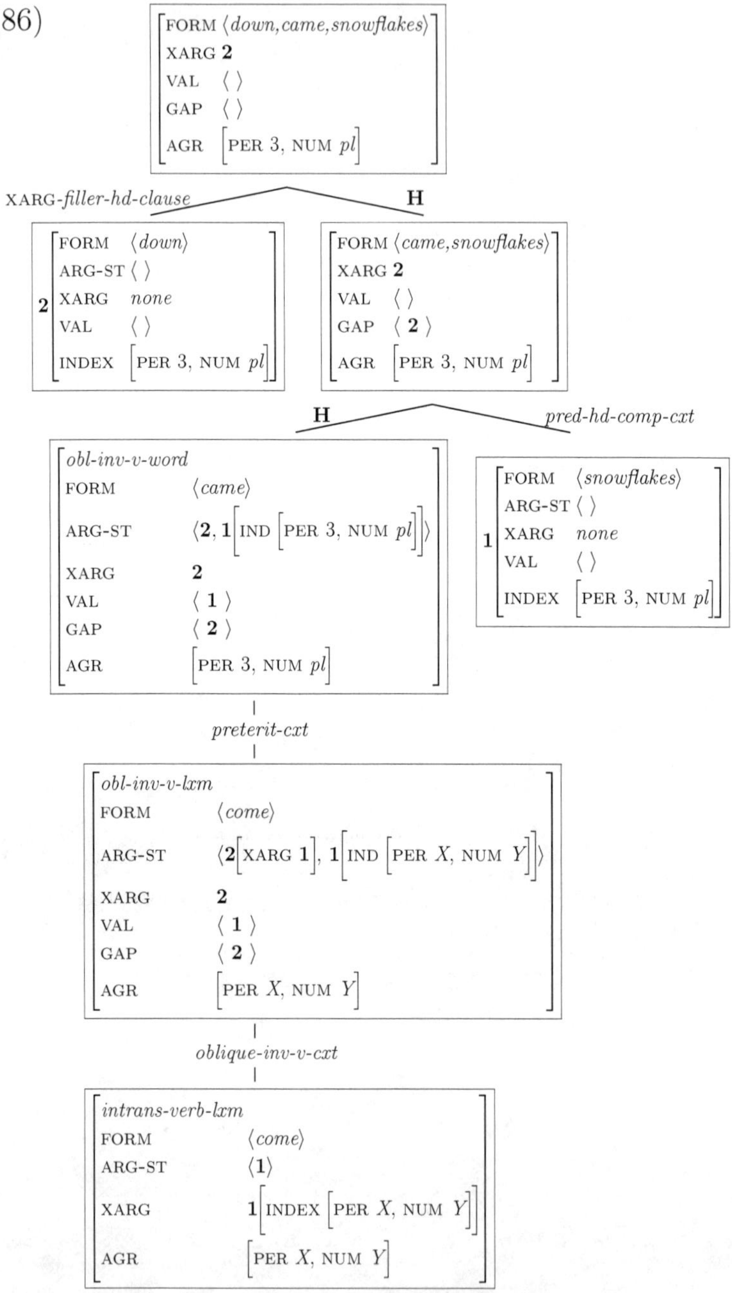

Derivation of *Down came snowflakes*

The derivation tree in (86) represents the licensing of the syntactic skeleton of the sentence *Down fell snowflakes*, which realizes the simultaneous satisfaction of the constructions we have just sketched. As we have noticed, OI places the oblique argument on the GAP list, which means it must be realized as the filler constituent in a filler-gap construct.[37]

The bottom box in (86) represents schematically the canonical intransitive verb lexeme *come*. Its unique argument is the XARG **1**. The AGR features are identified with the corresponding features of the index of the XARG. Looking upward, this *canon-intrans-v-lxm* is the unique daughter of an *oblique-inv-v-cxt*, licensed by the Oblique Inversion Construction (79). The mother of the *oblique-inv-cxt*, of type *oblique-inv-v-lxm*, differs from the canonical *intrans-i-v-lxm* daughter in adding an argument, **2**, which serves as the 'new' XARG. The VAL list of the mother contains both the added XARG **2** and the daughter's XARG **1**, now no longer the XARG. The AGR features are not identified with those of the new XARG, but remain identified with those of **1**, which is an internal argument in the mother. The form value ⟨*come*⟩ is unchanged from that of the daughter. The *oblique-i-v-lxm come* is in turn the unique daughter of a *preterit-cxt*, licensed by the Preterit (inflectional) Construction (82). The mother of the *preterit-cxt* is an *oblique-inv-v-word* whose ARG-ST, XARG, and VAL are the same as those of its lexeme daughter. (Although not shown in the figure, the semantics is augmented with a *past-fr*, and the VFORM value is *finite*, while the daughter's is *base*.) The mother's FORM value is ⟨*came*⟩. The AGR features have been resolved to [PER 3] and [NUM *pl*], which makes it possible for *came* to head a VP whose nominal complement's INDEX has those values. The *oblique-inv-v-word came* is in turn the head daughter (H) of a *predicational-head-complement-construct* licensed

[37] In the derivation tree (86) tags (indicating identity) are given as bold Arabic numerals rather than boxed numerals to minimize clutter. Non-terminal portions of feature paths are suppressed for the same reason.

by construction (83), in this case licensing a VP. The non-head daughter of the VP displays [FORM ⟨*snowflakes*⟩] and is tagged **1**, thus identified with the internal argument of *came*. The INDEX values of [PER 3, NUM *pl*] are identified with the AGR values of the *oblique-i-v-word*. In the mother of the VP ([FORM ⟨*came,snowflakes*⟩]) the VAL list is reduced to the XARG **2**. The latter sign is in turn the head of an *xarg-head-inverted-clause*, in which the gapped XARG is realized in a filler position. Agreement is determined by the XARG of the original simple intransitive lexeme. The intransitive PP *down* is in the position occupied by canonical fillers. Its tag, **2**, is absent from the VAL list of the mother, *Down came snowflakes*, of the *pred-hd-comp-cxt*. The VAL and GAP lists of *Down came snowflakes* are empty.

2.5.1 Subject properties and their discontents

Bresnan (1994) presents several arguments for attributing subject properties to the fronted constituent in OI (her LI). They are all relevant in one way or another to our analysis, but care must be exercised because not all of Bresnan's arguments apply to our analysis directly. For Bresnan, the fronted element is the functional subject (the syntactically "underlying" subject that comes with the lexical entry), but it is not found in subject position in a simple, declarative OI clause. Rather, as in several previous analyses of OI (e.g. Postal 2004, among many), Bresnan's preverbal PP does not appear in the position occupied by canonical subjects, but rather is "base-generated in topicalized position as sister of S in the c-structure" (1994: 104). As implied above in our discussion of the Split Subject Construction, in the present analysis the preverbal constituent in OI is also extracted. The most comprehensive array of arguments countering Bresnan's claims about (functional) subject status has been offered by Postal (2004) and further elaborated by Bruening (2010). In assessing the relevance of Bresnan's observations to our own analysis we will consider the counterarguments of Postal and

Bruening, among others. Our position is not that the fronted PP is *the* subject; it is rather that the fronted PP has some subject properties, a principal one of which is the status of external argument, analogous to Bresnan's functional subject.[38]

2.5.1.1 Raising

As illustrated in examples (74k,l), in OI the XARG may undergo Raising. For Bresnan, this is appropriate for the functional subject because Raising is a lexical process. Postal points out that the raising facts are equally compatible with the null-expletive-subject analysis: it can hold that it is the null expletive that raises and that the fronted PP is just an ordinary fronted PP. SBCG does not countenance either empty constituents or movement. It implements essentially the same analysis of Raising in OI as Bresnan's because, as seen above, Split-Subject, and hence OI, make the mother's XARG distinct from the daughter's XARG and thus the former is the argument that is targeted in raising matrix verbs.

2.5.1.2 The Anticomplementizer ("that-trace") effect

Bresnan and Postal-Breuning agree that OI displays the anticomplementizer ("that-trace") effect (hereafter ACE). Noting that Bresnan (1977:186) was the first to notice the phenomenon, Bruening (2010:51) cites the following examples from Culicover and Levine (2001).

(87) a. That bunch of gorillas, Terry claims (*that) t walked into the room. (Culicover & Levine 2001:285, ex.4)

b. Into the room Terry claims (*that) t walked a bunch of gorillas. (Culicover & Levine 2001:285, ex.3a)

[38]This claim is not, broadly speaking, in direct conflict with Postal's position, as he accepts that the preverbal phrase in OI displays some subject properties. He also argues that this phrase displays more non-subject properties than subject properties, a claim that we do not attempt to adjudicate. But we do not accept Postal's analysis, which relies not only on the notion of a phonetically empty expletive constituent but also on the proprietary notion "quace", which, very roughly, is the case associated with a given structural position canonically, but – crucially – not invariably (Postal 2004: 61).

Bresnan appeals to the traditional doctrine that this effect is a result of subject extraction to argue that the preverbal constituent in a simple OI clause is the functional subject. Postal (2004) and Bruening (2010) argue that the ACE is not about subject extraction, per se, but about something more general. Postal notes that the ACE applies to apparently subjectless *as* parentheticals like those in (88), as shown in (89).

(88) a. Lasers can, as is obvious, cut through stone walls. (Postal's 51a, p.32)
  b. Lasers can, as was proved by Mike, cut through stone walls. (Postal's 51b, p.32)

(89) a. Ted was cheated, as I assumed (*that) was obvious. (Postal's 69a, p. 36)
  b. Ted was cheated, as I thought (*that) had been proved by Michelle. (Postal's 69b, p. 36)

Postal's proffered proof that there is a null expletive subject in parenthetical clauses such as (88) and (89) is based on the observation that certain verbs such as *feel, hold, say, suppose*, and *think* when passivized do not allow sentential subjects, as illustrated in (90) (= Postal's 56. p.33).

(90) a. Everyone intelligent feels/holds/says/supposes/thinks that gold is rare.
  b.*That gold is rare is felt/held/said/supposed/thought by everyone intelligent.
  c. It is felt/held/said/supposed/thought by everyone intelligent that gold is rare.

Since the passive forms of these verbs occur in subjectless *as* parentheticals like (91), it cannot be that *as* is the subject of such clauses but must correspond to an extraposed clause, as in (92).

(91) Gold is not, as is deeply felt/widely held/sometimes said/usually supposed/generally thought, extremely rare. (Postal's 57, p. 33)

(92) Lasers cannot, as it had previously seemed to everyone, cut through stone walls. (Postal's 53b, p.32)

Since subjectless *as* parentheticals are subject to the ACE and since subjectless *as* parentheticals are demonstrated by facts like those in (90) not to exhibit subject extraction, ACE must not be a result of subject extraction.

Postal (2004) provides several other observations and arguments in favor of the initial phrase in an OI clause being in a filler and not the subject position. (Examples (93a–f) below correspond to Postal's (2004:19) examples (7a–f).)

(93) a. On the wall were standing two large blackbirds.
b. On the wall seemed to be standing two large blackbirds.
c. On the wall I believe to have been standing two large blackbirds.
d. On the wall are believed to have been standing two large blackbirds.
e. *I believed on the wall to have been standing two large blackbirds.
f. *It is impossible for on the wall to have been standing two large blackbirds.

> For, as partially noted in Lawler (1977:234-235), this array of facts is what would be expected under the view ... [that] in each grammatical case, the X-PP [i.e. the initial oblique] can be analyzed as being in an ordinary extraction position. Notably, ... [(93)e, f], where this is not the case, are ungrammatical, which can be attributed to the well-known incompatibility of infinitival clauses with domain internal extraction. (Postal 2004:19)

Summing up, whether or not the ACE effect is truly dependent on subject position, since the SBCG analysis places the oblique argument in filler position, we cannot claim a subject property for the oblique argument based on its structural position in a simple, declarative clause. However, the SBCG analysis, according to which the oblique argument is the extracted external argument, runs parallel to that of Bresnan, which makes the locative argument of OI the functional subject. Since the SBCG concept of XARG is in many ways equivalent to that of LFG functional subject (raising, control, SAI structures, etc.), initial 1 in the Relational Grammar tradition, and similarly in other grammatical approaches, that argument can be viewed informally as an "underlying" subject. In this respect, we see the facts considered in this section as conferring a subject property on the OI oblique argument.

2.5.1.3 The Complementizer Effect (CE)

While arguing that the preponderance of evidence points in the direction of a null expletive subject in OI – a theoretical possibility not available in SBCG[39] – Postal nevertheless offers a pattern that provides evidence for another subject property of the fronted constituent in OI. Postal (2004:21) terms the "complementizer effect" the long-noted fact that in relative clauses the ACE is in effect reversed, requiring, rather than barring, the presence of *that.* He points out that this effect holds for OI, supporting the hypothesis that the fronted expression in OI exhibits subject properties, as shown in (94) (Postal 2004:21, ex.15; Bruening 2010:53, ex.42).

(94) a. It was those towns that/∅ he studied.
b. It was those towns that/*∅ were studied.

[39] Bresnan suggests that, even if one grants the cross-language possibility of null expletive subjects, in several relevant regards English patterns with Germanic languages that lack null expletive subjects:

> A third problem [with the null expletive subject analysis of OI] is that the hypothesis of a null expletive subject in English is typologically implausible. No other properties of English point to the presence of such null 'pro' subjects.
> (i) Null expletive subjects in Romance languages are a consequence of pro-drop (see Jaeggli & Safir 1989 for a review), but English is not a pro-drop language.
> (ii) Among those Germanic languages for which null expletives have been hypothesized, such as German (Safir 1985a), Dutch (Maling & Zaenen 1978, Perlmutter & Zaenen 1984), Icelandic and Faroese (Platzack 1987), expletive subjects are optional or lacking with extrapositions, existentials, and impersonal passives. But in English, expletive subjects are obligatory in these cases.
> (iii) In the same Germanic languages, the subject is not fixed in a single structural position; but in English it is.
> (iv) In the same languages, subject extractions are not restricted by the presence of an adjacent complementizer; but in English they are.
> In all these respects, English typologically resembles the Germanic languages without null expletive subjects, such as Swedish and Norwegian (Bresnan 1994:102).

c. It was those towns that/∅ she talked about.
d. It was in those towns that/∅ she learned the best techniques for drying fruit.
e. It was in those towns that/*∅ were learned the best techniques for drying fruit.

Bruening, however, presents judgments by which he seeks to undermine the CE for OI. He writes (2010:53):

> Something else seems to be going on here, however. Locative-inversion sentences still require an overt *that* even when something other than the fronted PP has been extracted.
>
> (44) a. It was last year *(that) from that great conflict arose a new humanity.
> b. It was by sword *(that) for that perverted cause were slain thousands of innocents.
> c. It was only from the elders *(that) in those towns could be learned an impressive array of fruit-drying techniques.
>
> Here the fronted PP is not the one that has been extracted, but *that* is still required. Contrast non-locative-inversion counterparts of these sentences, where *that* can be omitted.
>
> (45) a. It was last year (that) a new humanity arose from that great conflict.
> b. It was by sword (that) thousands of innocents were slain for that
> c. It was only from the elders (that) an impressive array of fruit-drying techniques could be learned in those towns.
>
> ... what is important is that *that* must be pronounced in relative clauses involving locative inversion, whether or not it is the PP that is extracted. The complementizer effect, therefore, does NOT indicate that the fronted PP is the subject (emphasis in original).

We agree that the *that*-less versions in Bruening's (44) suffer somewhat in acceptability relative to the alternative versions with *that*, though perhaps not so much as to receive a star of absolute ungrammaticality. Nor do we find a relative preference for *that* being present entirely lacking in Bruening's examples (45).[40] In any case Bruening concludes that the most

[40] Bruening notes further that similar sentences with *there* also exhibit the property of requiring *that*, as shown in (i) (= Bruening 2010:53. ex. 46).

(i) a. It was last year *(that) from that great conflict there arose a new humanity.

likely generalization is that "there is some other constraint that requires *that* in locative inversion" (p 53). However, consideration of a wider range of data suggests that the relative preference for overt *that* in his examples (44) and (45) is probably not about OI (locative inversion) but rather about the presence of an extracted PP focus preceding a PP subject in a cleft sentence. For example, when the doubled PPs result from extraction of an adjunct PP, not from OI but from a PP-subject sentence like those in (95), we see in (96) and (97) about the same preference for overt *that* as in the OI cases of Bruening's (44).

(95) a. By the kitchen window is the best place to cool your pie. (invented)
  b. Before the monthly meeting would be a good time to distribute the leaflet. (invented)

(96) a. ??It's in the morning by the kitchen window is the best place to cool your pie.
  b. It's in the morning that by the kitchen window is the best place to cool your pie. (invented)

(97) a. ??It's not until next year before the annual meeting would be an ideal time to distribute the leaflet.
  b. It's not until next year that before the annual meeting would be an ideal time to distribute the leaflet. (invented)

The (a) versions of (96) and (97) sound to us no more acceptable than Bruening's OI examples in his (44). The pattern may not be restricted to pairs of PPs.

(98) a. ??It's not just when Mom's away behind the sofa is the best place to hide.
  b. It's not just when Mom's away that behind the sofa is the best place to hide. (invented)

---

b. It was by sword *(that) for that perverted cause there were slain thousands of innocents.

We see that the somewhat loose requirement that *that* occur between extracted PP focus constituents and PP subjects in clefts is not conditioned by OI specifically. Rather, it appears that Bruening's relatively unacceptable OI examples with multiple PPs – intended to undermine Postal's claim that the strong acceptability contrasts in (94) support the hypothesis of a subject property for OI – are not degraded in acceptability because they contain OI clauses. Rather they are somewhat degraded in acceptability because they have extracted PP foci immediately preceding the PP-subjects of clefts.[41] We conclude that Postal's proposal that the CE provides evidence for a subject property of OI stands unchallenged.

2.5.1.4 The parallelism constraint

Bresnan argues that the parallelism constraint (PC) on across-the-board extraction (XAB) operates in OI, showing that the fronted setting expression in OI is the subject. Bresnan's examples of the PC in simple cases (1994:98, ex. 71-72)[42] are given in (99). According to Bresnan, the PC requires that if the highest subject is extracted from one conjunct it must be extracted from all. This condition is satisfied in all of the cases of (99) except (c). In particular it is satisfied in (d).

(99) a. She's someone that __ loves cooking and __ hates jogging.
b. She's someone that cooking amuses __ and jogging bores __.
c. *She's someone that cooking amuses __ and __ hates jogging.
d. She's someone that cooking amuses __ and I expect __ will hate jogging.

[41] Which in turn is likely due to some more general considerations regarding ease of processing, than a strictly grammatical failure.

[42] Cited by Bruening as ex.47, p.54.

The application of the PC to OI is illustrated by Bresnan in (100) (1994:98, ex. 73-74).[43]

(100) a. That's the old graveyard, in which __ is buried a pirate and __ is likely to be buried a treasure. (SUBJ-SUBJ)

b. That's the old graveyard, in which workers are digging __ and a treasure is likely to be buried __. (NONSUBJ-NONSUBJ)

c. ??That's the old graveyard, in which workers are digging __ and __ is likely to be buried a treasure. (NONSUBJ-SUBJ)

d. That's the old graveyard, in which workers are digging __ and they say __ is buried a treasure. (NONSUBJ-EMBEDDED SUBJ)

Interestingly, Postal defends the subject relevance of the PC and implies that it supports subject properties of the fronted constituent in OI, while Bruening, who follows Postal's null expletive analysis of OI, nonetheless rejects the hypothesis that the PC applies to subjects per se. He consequently denies that the PC supports subject properties of the OI setting element.

Postal presents the examples in (101) (2004:35, ex.66).

(101) a. Such pistols are, as was obvious and Frank just demonstrated, quite deadly.

b. Such pistols are, as Frank just demonstrated and was obvious anyway, quite deadly

c. Such pistols are, as has long been suspected and Frank just demonstrated, quite deadly.

Postal finds all three examples unexceptionable, as do we. He notes that, "only under the null expletive analysis of [*as* parentheticals] advocated here, consistency with the Parallelism Constraint is *maintained*, as extraction from both conjuncts involves non-subjects in all cases" (1944:35, emphasis

[43]Cited by Bruening as ex.48, p.54.

in original). Although the examples in question involve *as* parentheticals and not OI structures, the implication that Postal supports the PC as operating on subjects is patent (although he denies resolutely that the fronted phrases in OI are canonical subjects).

Bruening, while accepting Postal's null expletive analysis of *as* parentheticals in connection with the ACE, implicitly rejects Postal's support of the PC based on that analysis because of further facts. Pointing to previous analyses of the PC (including Gazdar 1981, Falk 1983, and Woolford 1987), Bruening suggests the narrower version of the PC in (102).

(102) THE PARALLELISM CONSTRAINT: In across-the-board extraction, if one gap is the highest constituent within its conjunct, all other gaps must be as well. (Bruening 2010:(53), p.55)

However, even this more restricted version of the Parallelism Constraint fails against readily established facts. The following examples, all of which illustrate an adversative relation between the conjuncts, violate the constraint barring simple subject/non-subject asymmetries in XAB extraction.

(103) a. The things she so desperately craved __ and __ had been sorely lacking in her life.

b. The only other thing that I wanted __ and __ wasn't available on the Icon was the real-time temperature reading (as it warms up).

c. If this argument is correct, the economic approach provides a unified framework for understanding behavior that has long been sought by __ and __ eluded Bentham, Comte, Marx, and others.

d. Believing gave me exactly what I needed __ and __ had been sorely lacking as a teenager trapped in a history of familial abuse: ...

e. Regeneration Waltz recreates a sense of the rest and recovery that was sought after __ and yet __ eluded so many veterans.

f. well my guy friend who I like __ and __ doesn't like me never does that.
g. This was something I really wanted __ and __ wasn't available during my first purchasing spree.
h. And now here I am, sitting next to the girl that I like __but __ hates me.
i. I thought that it was a creature that Disney tried to hide __ but __ escaped and attacked someone ...
j. The missing thing that came to my assistance in Bob's office was my saviour, a present to take to the grave. Something I had always wanted __ but __ had eluded me.

Such examples are not restricted to adversative conjunct pairs. The following examples show a supportive or mutually reinforcing relation between the conjuncts.

(104) a. One comedienne that I seem to like __ and __ amuses me (even if I don't laugh out loud) is Sarah Millican...
b. While I'm working on the music posts, those songs plus other things I can't find embeds for plus just random stuff that I like __ and __ amuses me goes into Volume Zero.
c. Almost every country on Earth has vacancies for traveling teachers, but wouldn't it be better to be based in a place that you like __ and __ likes you back?
d. ... so don't expect to live in a country that you hate __ and __ hates you freely.
e. What can I do to get this guy that I like __ and __ likes me back to commit to going out on a date?
f. Look who I saw __ and __ saw me this morning!
g. well my guy friend who I like __ and __ doesn't like me never does that.
h. Body Snatchers was one of the first movies I saw __ and __ scared me half to death.

i. George Romero's "Night of the Living Dead," (which this writer might add was the only zombie movie I saw __ and __ scared me to death!)...

j. Those who were given caffeine but thought they received decaf reported lower levels of withdrawal symptoms – levels nearly equal to those experienced by the group that was promised __ and __ received caffeine.

Similar examples with *or* are also attested.

(105) a. It means I avoid crowded panicky shops which isn't something I like __ or __ likes me.

b. Celest would remind them that it is better to go through a breakup than be with someone who either you hate __or __ hates you.

The bearing of the PC on the matter of subject properties of the oblique argument in OI is nil because there is no PC.

2.5.1.5 *Do* support

Bresnan (1994:102f) observes that *do* support is not required when OI is questioned, citing this fact as a further subject property of the initial element in OI.

(106) a. On which wall hung a portrait of the artist? (Bresnan 1994:102, ex. 85a)

b. *On which wall did hang a portrait of the artist? (Bresnan 1994:102, ex. 85b)

This behavior contrasts with that of P-*there* in comparable circumstances.

(107) a. Which portrait of the artist hung on the wall? (Bresnan 1994:102, ex.86a)

b. *Which portrait of the artist did hang on the wall? (Bresnan 1994:102, ex.86b)

c. *On which wall there hung a portrait of the artist? (Bresnan 1994:102, ex.87a)

d. On which wall did there hang a portrait of the artist? (Bresnan 1994:102, ex.87b)

Postal objects on the grounds that in the same questioned OI contexts emphatic *do* is also ruled out, weakening the argument from support *do* as negatively associated with subject extraction.

(108) a. On which wall HUNG a portrait of the artist? (Postal 2004:41, ex. 87a)
b. *On which wall (must we conclude) DID hang a portrait of the artist? (Postal 2004:41, ex.87a)

However, it is less than clear that the single invented example (108b) proffered by Postal is empirically representative. The attested examples in (109) do not reveal any obvious reason to suspect their pertinence.

(109) a. But in that case, from which language did come the ones we could not understand?
b. Out of what urban practice does emerge today's image of Sarajevo?
c. I would have a question for you: from which AEF set did come the crew bags?
d. Following this humbling experience ... there was a brief frenzy of measuring ... concert halls, from which did emerge a set of serviceable rules as to how to get it right. Or, at least, not terribly wrong.

Bruening takes the Postal argument further, claiming that emphatic *do* is impossible in OI generally.

(110) a. On the wall hung a portrait of the artist. (Bruening 2010:56, ex.60a)
b. *On the wall DID hang a portrait of the artist. (Bruening 2010:56, ex.60b)
c. On the wall there DID hang a portrait of the artist. (Bruening 2010:56, ex.60c)

However, these judgments also fail to match observed usage.

(111) a. Out of these controversies, however, did arise a better knowledge of the true meaning of religion...

b. But out of the crisis did come cooperatives...
c. Nevertheless, out of the perusal of these letters does emerge a picture of a period: little side lights on its literary ethics, on the tastes of the times...
d. Out of the upheaval did eventually emerge a fairer, better society.
e. and there was a brief frenzy of measuring the shapes and sounds of concert halls, from which did emerge a set of serviceable rules as to how to get it right.
f. Out of this milieu did emerge a distinctive voice in film, that of Margaret Tait.
g. But from the ashes did emerge a lone mage.
h. but from that study did emerge some very favorable response data, ...
i. As you mentioned, many of the wild horse breeds died out, but from where did they emerge in the first place?

We conclude that Bresnan's claim that the absence of *do* support in OI questions is empirically justified and supports her claim of a subject property for the setting phrase in OI.

2.5.2 Summary of arguments for and against subject properties of the setting constituent in OI.

With respect to raising, the SBCG analysis (in the HPSG tradition) treats raising as an argument-structure-internal relation between the index of the XARG of a predicator and the index of the external argument of its verbal complement. Since raising and subject extraction are compatible, the assignment of the XARG to the GAP list does not prevent its satisfying raising. With regard to the ACE ("that trace") effect, we agree with the conclusion of Postal and Bruening that the ACE is about something more general than subject extraction per se and so not relevant to the question of subject properties. Third, in the case of the "Complementizer Effect" we reject Bruening's argument: that a fairly loose requirement that an OI relative clause must be introduced by *that* when it is preceded by a PP undermines Postal's claim that the CE supports a subject property for the initial PP of a OI clause. The argument fails, in our view, because it appears more likely that the (weak) requirement for *that* in the relevant examples is due, not to the fact that the relative clause is constrained by OI, but because a PP directly preceding a relative clause beginning with a PP *ipso facto* degrades acceptability, possibly reflecting relative difficulty of processing. Fourth, with regard to the Parallelism Constraint on XAB extraction, we find the facts to be significantly more complex than those presented by Bruening. However, in the end we agree with his conclusion that they provide little evidence of a subject property of the preverbal phrase in OI, since the existence of a Parallelism Constraint as a grammatical fact appears quite dubious. Fifth, we consider the objections raised by Postal and Bruening to Bresnan's claim that absence of *do* support in OI questions argues for a subject property of the PP. We find these objections to be based on intuitive judgments that do not conform to observed usage and conclude that the *do* support facts argue in favor of a subject property.

2.6 Presentational *there*

P-*there* tokens may contain an initial setting expression, as in (112a), or may lack one, as in (112b):

(112) a. In the background there loomed the Two Plus Four Agreement.
b. The word was out and there began a year-long wait list to enter the program.

As noted in section 1.2, we agree with Bresnan (1994:99) that the presence of *there* renders the sentences in (113) (Bresnan's (76a,b), repeated from (22) above), unacceptable. But the attested examples in (114), repeated from (23) above, give us reason to doubt that the operative constraint concerns directed motion.

(113) a. Into the room (*there) ran mother.

b. Out of it (*there) steps Archie Campbell. (Birner 1992:43)

(114) a. out of it there ran a stream of golden coins...

b. ... in there strode a company of strong and handsome young men.

The examples in (114) show that P-*there* sentences can in fact be used to express directed-motion events. We attribute the pattern in (113) to a discourse-pragmatic constraint noted by Bresnan herself (1994:100): in a P-*there* sentence the focal NP may not have a topical, mutually familiar or recoverable referent.

Presentational *there* clauses contrast most noticeably with DI clauses in that the latter contain locative *there* whereas P-*there* sentences contain expletive *there*. P-*there* clauses contrast noticeably with E-*there* clauses in allowing a wide range of verbs (not just *be* plus a small handful of other verbs of existence), and in freely allowing definite postverbal NPs, as in (115).

(115) a. ... it was from this combination that there grew the contemplative school of Zen Buddhism.

b. Meanwhile, in the doorway there stood the master,...

The listeme for expletive *there* is shown in (116).

(116) Listeme for Expletive *there*

$$\left[\begin{array}{ll} \textit{lexeme} & \\ \text{FORM} & \langle \textit{there} \rangle \\ \text{SYN} & \left[\begin{array}{ll} \text{CAT} & \left[\begin{array}{ll} \textit{noun} & \\ \text{LID} & \langle \textit{there[expletive]-fr} \rangle \end{array}\right] \end{array}\right] \\ \text{SEM} & \left[\begin{array}{ll} \text{INDEX} & \textit{there}\left[\begin{array}{ll} \text{PER} & 3 \\ \text{NUM} & \textit{num} \end{array}\right] \\ \text{FRAMES} & \langle\ \rangle \end{array}\right] \end{array}\right]$$

The FRAMES value is the empty list, the INDEX value is notated as *there*[PER 3, NUM *num*]], and the LID is ⟨*there*[*expletive*]-*fr*⟩. Expletive *there* thus represents an exception to the usual identity of FRAMES values and LID values for lexemes. Such exceptions obtain only and always for listemes in which the FRAMES list is empty.

The Presentational *There* Construction adds to the Split Subject Constructi on the constraints that the mother's XARG is expletive *there* and the focal NP has a discourse-new referent.

(117) **The Presentational-*there* Construction**
(↑*split-subj-cxt*)

$$\textit{prst-there-cxt} \Rightarrow \begin{bmatrix} \text{MTR} & \begin{bmatrix} \text{ARG-ST} & \langle X{:}\textit{pron}\begin{bmatrix}\text{LID}\langle \textit{there[expl]-fr}\rangle\end{bmatrix}, \\ & \text{NP}_i, \ldots\rangle \\ \text{SYN} & \begin{bmatrix}\text{CAT} & \begin{bmatrix}\text{XARG} & X\end{bmatrix}\end{bmatrix} \\ \text{SEM} & Y \\ \text{INF-ST} & \begin{bmatrix}\text{NEW} & i\end{bmatrix}\end{bmatrix} \\ \text{DTRS} & \left\langle\begin{bmatrix}\text{SEM} & Y\end{bmatrix}\right\rangle \end{bmatrix}$$

2.7 Deictic Inversion

The Deictic Inversion[44] Construction, as discussed in detail by Lakoff (1987:468ff), specifies either *here* or *there* as XARG, and *be*[at] as the verb. Lakoff (1987:468) states that in deictic inversion clauses *here* or *there* is not the subject, which if correct would mean that they cannot be the XARG in our analysis. Lakoff offers two items of evidence for this view. The first is the alleged resistance of this pattern to Raising.

[44]This pattern is often referred to in the literature as presentational or "presentative" *there*, e.g. Keenan (2003:187fn). We follow here the terminology of Lakoff (1987:468).

This claim seems correct for many attempts to construct examples but still comes up against numerous attested counterexamples.

(118) a. Here seemed to come the proof, for on both feet the toes were joined by a thin membrane.

b. She told me on TV a number of hostages had escaped from the front doors. There seemed to be my look-a-like walking out of the hotel on live TV.

c. On two or three occasions — and here seems to come the "negligence" of the guest, if any — the plaintiff opened the box in the room, and counted the money in the presence of several persons.

d. And here seemed to be a much too up-close-and-personal view of LeBron James...

e. Scarcely had Don Quixote descried them when the fancy possessed him that this must be some new adventure; and to help him to imitate as far as he could those passages he had read of in his books, here seemed to come one made on purpose, which he resolved to attempt.

f. So here appear to be my options if I start a completely new library: ...

g. That's just what it seems like to me; first came the pain in my leg from the irons, and here seems to come following after it, pleasure.

h. In any event, there seems to go my theory that this quote could explain the 'Protestant Ethic' with its emphasis on material wealth...

i. there seems to go my thursday nite at the movies

j. so there seems to go my plan of reducing power-load from the tablet using it as a desktop PC with external monitor

k. There seems to go the connection of Isaac as his father. No documented proof.

l. So, here seems to be a strong cost driver pushing for an optimal connection of technology and business.

m. I didn't read it all, but here seem to be some latest edits:http://...

n. Here seemed to be a union from which jealousy had been leached.

o. The Medici, after all, had led the humanistic revival of Florence and here seemed to be a man who was preaching a new spiritualism

p. It's still early to say, but here seem to be the obvious pros and cons. Pro:...

q. I wrote for an appointment, and came to see the great master himself. My heart beat wildly. Here seemed to be my opportunity.

r. Here seemed to be a union from which jealousy had been leached.

s. I did some searching and here appears to be the large fig (Ficus carica) in California: http://www...

Despite the fact that DI examples clearly exhibit raising, the usual split-subject agreement with the postverbal nominal also occurs.

(119) a. Here comes the bus.

b. Watch Out, America: Here Come the Dallas Cowboys.

c. There goes John's old tutor.

d. There go two boys who just turned twenty...

e. Here is a situation where the Federal Reserve Board ruling ...

f. Here are several situations where there is an incorrect application ...

Lakoff's second argument that *here/there* is not the subject is that DI clauses resists tags. This predicts ungrammaticality for example (120).

(120) *There's Harry with his red hat on, isn't there? (Lakoff 1987:468, unnumbered ex.)

In an unsuccessful attempt to check the accuracy of this judgment, we found a plethora of web examples of a corresponding form (e.g., "There's * isn't there?") that however appear to exemplify the distinct existential construction. Our web search for deictic examples of this form was thus effectively swamped. Such examples are apparently too rare to show up in searches of corpora that permit more refined search syntax, in particular COCA, if they exist at all. Whether such examples are truly non-existent or just very rare, we are inclined to attribute their paucity to the illocutionary function of the construction rather than to a syntactic constraint. Similar considerations apply to the resistance of DI to negation and embedding (also noted by Lakoff 1987:469). The issue for our analysis, in any case, is not whether the initial *here* or *there* is 'the subject', but rather whether it has any subject properties – which the examples in (118) show to be the case.

As the initial element in a DI clause is limited to the locative prepositions *here* and *there*, so the verb possibilities are limited to *be*, *come*, and *go*. In an SBCG grammar, the semantic FRAMES form part of the overall multiple inheritance type hierarchy (Sag 2012; 88f, based on Davis & Koenig 2000). We assume the parts of the frame portion of the type hierarchy shown in (121). Accordingly, in the DI construction, the XARG is restricted to lexemes with [LID ⟨*axial-fr*⟩] and the verb itself is constrained by [LID ⟨*loc/move-fr*⟩].

(121) a. *loc/move-fr*: *come-fr*, *go-fr*, *be[at]-fr*

b. *axial-fr*: *proximal-loc-fr* [FORM ⟨here⟩], *distal-loc-fr* [FORM ⟨there⟩]

The listeme for the locative preposition *there* is shown in (122). We follow the terminology of Langacker (1986:7) in referring to the point of reference in the *distal-location-frame* as the LANDMARK and the located entity as the TRAJECTOR.

(122) **Locative *there* listeme**

$$
\left[\begin{array}{ll}
\textit{lexeme} & \\
\text{FORM} & \langle \textit{there} \rangle \\
\text{ARG-ST} & \langle\ \rangle \\
\text{SYN} & \left[\text{CAT}\ \left[\begin{array}{ll} \textit{prep} & \\ \text{LID} & L \\ \text{XARG} & \textit{none} \end{array}\right]\right] \\
\text{SEM} & \left[\begin{array}{l} \text{FRAMES}\ L{:}\left\langle \left[\begin{array}{ll} \textit{distal-loc-fr} & \\ \text{LANDMARK} & j \\ \text{TRAJECTOR} & i \end{array}\right] \right\rangle \\ \text{INDEX}\quad i \end{array}\right] \\
\text{CONTEXT} & \left[\text{C-INDS}\ \left[\text{UTT-LOC}\ j\right]\right]
\end{array}\right]
$$

In (122) the FORM value is, unsurprisingly, ⟨*there*⟩. The ARG-ST list is the empty list. The SYN value shows this lexeme to be an intransitive preposition whose XARG value is *none*. In the semantics the FRAMES list has a single member, a *distal-location-frame*, whose LANDMARK value is identified in the CONTEXT | C-INDS value as the utterance location, *j*, and whose TRAJECTOR value is the local index *i*.[45]

Contrary to some negative judgments in the literature, e.g. (123), DI is compatible with past tense, as shown in (124).

(123) *Here I came with a silly hat on. (Lakoff 1987:483 unnumbered ex.)

(124) a. Here came the waitress. She had on a mini-skirt, high heels, see-through blouse with padded brassiere.

b. So I looked, and here came a white horse!

c. Here came the entrails, to be scraped and washed clean for sausage casings; ...

[45] C-INDS stands for CONTEXTUAL-INDICES; other C-INDS features include SPEAKER and ADDRESSEE (Sag 2012:96, Pollard and Sag 1994). The listeme for *here* is similar, with [FORM ⟨*here*⟩] and *proximal-location-frame* in place of *distal-location-frame*.

d. Here came the Rabbi, his back bent, his face shaved, his pack on his back.
e. Here came the Princess, and as she passed hats were lifted.
f. Pretty soon here came the King on his horse...
g. We knew from parallax considerations that it had to be well outside the solar system, and so here was the mystery revealed.
h. Well there went George all the way down. Luckily a few friends pulled me out of the hole.
i. She watched the kids get on the bus one at a time. There went Alice and Jim.
j. Here came the Russians. Six museum directors from Russia visited Amish Acres in Nappanee, Indiana on December 18, 2014.
k. Everybody looked over, I can't say for sure but I think they were all thinking the same thing, there went your grandfather, there went George Porter, ...
l. My brother completely missed me so the coach started sending the other kids one at a time. I dodged them all. Then there went my brother with miss number two.
m. And there went Mrs. Gideon too, running awkwardly, puffing for breath.
n. There went Dr. and Mrs. Sorabjee, leaving little Amy alone at their table.
o. We had never heard of giant worms, but here was the fossil evidence.
p. But here was a visible symbol of the degradation of sin.
q. But, here was a curious thing.
r. And so here was the Rosetta stone for ICL perception of the Hagenbach case...

Like the OI and P-*there* constructions, the Deictic Inversion Construction defines a subtype of *split-subject-cxt*. The appearance of locative *there* or *here* in subject position is assured by the specification that the XARG's LID is ⟨*axial-fr*⟩. The identity of the verb is restricted to *be*, *come*, or *go* by the specification that its LID is ⟨*loc/move-fr*⟩. As frequently noted, DI is incompatible with progressive aspect.

(125) a. *Here is coming Kim.
  b. *There was going my last hope.

Consistent with its incompatibility with progressive aspect, the DI Construction imposes a stative interpretation on the reported SITUATION (eventuality) of location or movement. The SITUATION is also 'ongoing' in the sense that Reichenbachian event time includes reference time.

(126) **Deictic Inversion Construction** (↑*split-subj-cxt*)

$$
\textit{dx-inv-cxt} \Rightarrow \begin{bmatrix} \text{MTR} & \begin{bmatrix} \text{ARG-ST} & \left\langle X{:}\text{PP}_j \begin{bmatrix} \text{SYN} & \begin{bmatrix} \text{CAT} & \begin{bmatrix} \text{LID} \langle \textit{axial-fr} \rangle \end{bmatrix} \end{bmatrix} \end{bmatrix}, \; \text{NP}_i, \ldots \right\rangle \\ \text{SYN} & \begin{bmatrix} \text{CAT} & \begin{bmatrix} \text{XARG} & X \end{bmatrix} \end{bmatrix} \\ \text{SEM} & \begin{bmatrix} \text{FRAMES} & Y{:}\left\langle \begin{bmatrix} \textit{loc/move-fr} & \\ \text{TRAJECTOR} & i \\ \text{LANDMARK} & j \\ \text{SITUATION} & s \end{bmatrix}, \begin{bmatrix} \textit{state-fr} & \\ \text{INST} & s \end{bmatrix}, \begin{bmatrix} \textit{ongoing-fr} & \\ \text{INST} & s \end{bmatrix} \right\rangle \end{bmatrix} \\ \text{CTXT} & \begin{bmatrix} \text{C-INDS} & \begin{bmatrix} \text{UTT-LOC} & j \end{bmatrix} \end{bmatrix} \end{bmatrix} \\ \text{DTRS} & \left\langle \begin{bmatrix} \text{SEM} & \begin{bmatrix} \text{FRAMES} & \langle Y \rangle \end{bmatrix} \end{bmatrix} \right\rangle \end{bmatrix}
$$

The MOTHER of construction (126) defines the lexeme type *deictic-inv-v-lxm* as a subtype of *split-subj-i-v-lxm*, and further constrains it as follows. The XARG X is a PP whose LID value is a subtype of ⟨*axial-fr*⟩, which, according to (121a) limits the possibilities to *here* and (locative) *there*. The second argument is the non-XARG nominal of *split-subj-i-v-lxm*, whose INDEX i occurs also in the FRAMES value as the TRAJECTOR argument of a *loc/move-fr*. The FRAMES list, tagged Y, recurs in the value of the verb's LID, assuring by (121b) that the verb must be *come*, *go*, or *be*. The LANDMARK argument of the *loc/move-fr* is the INDEX j, which occurs in the CONTEXT value as indexing the location of the utterance. The two remaining frames predicate stativity and 'ongoingness'[46] of the SITUATION (event) variable s of the *loc/move-fr*.

2.8 Existential *There*

There is an extensive literature on existential sentences, which we do not review in detail here.[47] Existential *there* sentences in English accept the verbs *be*, *exist*, *remain*, and perhaps others. Zucchi (1995) goes so far as to include *arrive*, but we follow widespread usage in considering E-*there* sentences to have only stative readings. In fact we agree with the majority of authors (e.g., Milsark 1977, Barwise and Cooper 1981, Keenan 1987, 2003, and Abbott 1992, 1993, 1997, among others) that the verb of an existential sentence denotes an existence predicate. We note, however, following Abbott (1993, citing Karttunen 1969; see also Szekely 2015: 116), that this 'existence' may apply to referents that are in fact fictional. The interpretation of 'existence' to include 'discourse existence' is a key move in Abbott's accommodation of the major insights achieved in the strictly semantic view of (English) existentials (e.g., Milsark 1977, Barwise

[46] A situation is *ongoing* iff reference time is properly contained in event time.

[47] For a review article, see McNally 2016: for a monographic treatment, see Szekely 2015.

and Cooper 1981, de Jong 1987, Enç 1991, Keenan 1987, 2003), with a mixed semantic-pragmatic view that enjoys greater empirical coverage.

Abbott characterizes her view simply as 'pragmatic' but it includes the existence predication just mentioned. Her approach owes much to analyses based on observations of actual speech made by Prince (1981, 1992) and Ward & Birner (1995) and Birner & Ward 1998, and she cites a tradition of pragmatically based treatments of existentials, including Hetzron (1975), Bolinger (1977), Rando and Napoli (1978), Woisetschlaeger (1983), and Lakoff (1987). Abbott (1997) parts company with Ward and Birner with regard to the latter's adoption of Prince's concept of hearer new as the unique key to the illocutionary ("pragmatic") force of existential sentences. Abbott cites examples, similar to (127) and (128), with postverbal NPs of the form [demonstrative CNP], in which the demonstrative manifestly refers to an entity that is not new to the addressee, but rather contains an explicit reminder of the addressee's awareness of the entity's existence, and also the so-called list existentials, e.g., (130) and (131), in which what the speaker seeks to place in the focus of attention of the addressee is not only the denotation of the postverbal NP itself, but also the fact that it answers a question under discussion (QUD, Roberts 1998).[48]

(127) BS: There is an explosion of food culture in the United States at the moment...

MS: ...And while, as you say, there is this explosion of food culture in the US...

(128) A: One way that love works in this text is through subtle clairvoyance and the faintest suggestion of magic

B: ...But as you say, there is this "subtle clairvoyance" between the two of them, and yet we see them more fully than they see each other.

[48]In (130) and (131) the QUD is explicit, but in other cases, which we will see a few examples of below, the QUD is implicit. From now on, we refer to what have been called 'list' contexts in the literature as QUD contexts.

We should note that there are also existentials like (129), in which what the speaker wishes to draw the addressee's attention to is less the existence of the referent of the postverbal NP per se than the fact that some entity satisfies the secondary predication of an optional 'coda', in (129) the phrase *in a tutu.*

(129) People like to wear crazy outfits as well; there was *a man in a tutu* ... (italics added)

In (129) the man is, to be sure, asserted to exist, but the existence of the man is not the only thing the speaker seeks to draw to the attention of the addressee; a further intended focus of the addressee's attention is the fact that the man was wearing a tutu. In our view, by putting *a man* in focus position, the speaker seeks to bring into the addressee's attention the entirety of the tutu-wearing scene. Both the existence of the man and the matter of his wearing a tutu are new information. Example (129) might be glossed 'People like to wear crazy outfits as well; there was a tutu-wearing man' (modulo constraints on compound formation). Duffield and Michaelis (2011) suggest that sentences of this type are motivated by the tendency of speakers to avoid putting a focused constituent in a typically topical position, as would occur in the simple, declarative equivalent: A man was wearing a tutu. This kind of existential affords the speaker the opportunity to abide by the principle of separation of reference and role: "Do not introduce a new referent and talk about it in the same clause" (Lambrecht 1996:185). Abbott (1993:41) writes, "the function of existential sentences is to draw the addressee's attention to the existence and/or location of the entity or entities denoted by the focus NP." We would add to this basic insight that in addition to the existence or location of the postverbal NP, the speaker may also wish to focus the attention of the addressee on the state denoted by a secondary predication such as 'in a tutu' in (129).

This mixed, semantic-pragmatic approach allows Abbott to accommodate as data the unfortunately christened 'list' cases, like (130) and (131), and the reminder cases, like (127) and (128), which Keenan, for example, excludes from his analysis on the grounds that they allegedly resist polar interrogation and negation.

(130) A: Is there anything to eat?
B: Well, there's the leftover chicken from last night. (Abbott 1993:42 ex.4)

(131) A: I guess we've called everybody.
B: No, there's still Mary and John. (Abbott 1993:42 ex.5)

Keenan writes:

> List contexts:
>
> A: How do I get to UCLA from here?
>
> B: Well there's always the bus, but it doesn't run very often.
>
> Is there always the bus? (and There isn't always the bus) are unnatural in such contexts, so questioning (and negating) do not preserve the naturalness of DPs like the bus in such sentences (Anna Szabolcsi, p.c.) ... [Keenan proceeds to rule out what we have termed the Deictic-*there* cases.] Finally, "reminder contexts" do not naturally question or negate. They are cases where A reminds B of an already acknowledged reason for not doing X, one that A seems to have momentarily forgotten, and A responds, "Well, yes, there's always that." (Keenan 2003: 187, footnote).

Attested utterances like the following would appear to counter-exemplify the claim that polar questions and existentials with definite postverbal NPs are always unnatural in such circumstances.

(132) There isn't the Cat Suit because this image was made before the releasing of the game.

As we have suggested above, the so-called list cases are more adequately characterized as those in which a definite NP occurs in an existential sentence that proffers an answer to a QUD. Pace Keenan, negation and polar interrogation do appear to be acceptable in such cases.

(133) Bagg says ... it's a loss for Eastern Canada that there aren't silage corn trials here, but he doesn't expect to see anything change for the better anytime soon.
"It wouldn't take much to do corn-silage trials if farmers wanted; [QUD = What resources would be necessary for corn-silage trials in Eastern Canada?] the infrastructure is there, but *there isn't the stakeholder willingness to pay for it*," he says. (italics added)

(134) My favorite place to get books, though is ... actually in the garbage bins behind a regular bookstore called Pegasus books. They are a used bookstore which throws out so many things you wouldn't even believe – great works of fiction, encyclopedias, and even scholarly

books. Of course you have to be willing to take what is there, [QUD: What is the range of books available in the garbage bins behind Pegasus Books?] and *there isn't the selection of online bookstores* ... (italics added)

(135) I see. That WebJar points to: [URL]
You can grab the jar from: [URL]
And see what is in there.
[QUD: What is in the WebJar?]
So yes, *there isn't the file you are looking for in that WebJar.* Maybe you should... (italics added)

(136) The law was that there had to be two or three witnesses in agreement in order to establish guilt. The point here was not whether adultery was punishable, but [QUD: What was the point?] *were there the lawful number of collaborating witnesses to the act.* (italics added)

Keenan does not further elaborate his claim, so it is hard to judge with certainty what should count as counterexamples. On their face, examples (133)–(136) appear to counterexemplify the claim that negative and polar-question existentials with definite postverbal NPs are unnatural in QUD contexts.

As with the QUD contexts, we see that the reminder cases like (127) and (128) take in more than just reminders of a "reason for not doing [something]" (Keenan 2003:187, footnote). Speakers sometimes remind interlocutors of their words for the purpose of questioning or denying the claim those words express. The responses in the examples in (137) and (138), while invented, seem acceptable substitutes, grammatically speaking, for the responses in (127) and (128).

(137) BS: There is an explosion of food culture in the United States at the moment...
MS: Is there really this explosion of food culture you seem so anxious to dissect? (invented response)

(138) A: One way that love works in this text is through sub-

tle clairvoyance and the faintest suggestion of magic: ...

B: In my reading, there is in the novel not this "subtle clairvoyance" you describe but rather an exchange of explicitly lubricious messages. (invented response)

Some examples follow:

(139) but the Hospital say, '... We are very well satisfied with the decision thus far, that you,... have the power to enforce this servitude against those residing on the opposite side of the street...' My Lords... suppose it should turn out that they had no right — that *there is not this servitude* as to the tenants of the other side ... (italics added)

(140) I think you realize from this letter that *there is not the difference* that you imagined existing in our attitude towards the Indians... (italics added)

(141) ... *there was never this fuss* about Bob Dylan doing a tribute to Frank Sinatra. (italics added)

(142) *There was never that "space"* that you so beautifully defined where the relationship could grow & be nurtured... (italics added)

Speakers sometimes also remind their interlocutors of their own (that is, the speaker's own) recent utterances and in such reminders employ demonstrative determiners in negative existential clauses.

(143) a. According to the Scriptures, if a person touches another while the latter is in contact [with a corpse], he too is defiled for seven days; but if he touches him when *there is not this contact*, then he is only defiled until the evening. (italics added; [brackets] in original)

b. (The farer on the Great Way), the bodhisattva, comprehends the (ultimate) sameness of all deeds; and he does not take the good deed as meritorious and the evil deed as devoid of merit. (For, in the ultimate truth *there is not this distinction* of good and bad.) (italics added)

Keenan's justification for omitting as data the reminder and QUD cases on the grounds of non-productivity is thus empirically challenged. Moreover, as a matter of methodology, one is entitled to ask why unacceptability of a form in one context (negation, polar question) justifies not dealing with its acceptability in another context (declarative clause). Moreover, there is a productive formulaic template which juxtaposes two or more existential clauses and which distinctly favors proper names and definite descriptions.

(144) a. Before there was the internet there was the daily newspaper.
b. Before there was Beyoncé there was Madonna.
c. Before there were the New Casualists, there were the Provisional Painters, and before there were the Provisional Painters, there were the 1980s.
d. Before there were the Heartbreakers, before there were psychedelic music videos and Alice In Wonderland-like imagery, before there was "Mary Jane." Well, maybe not before there was Mary Jane, but before he was living "Like a Refugee," there was Mudcrutch. Featuring a Tom Petty no one knew about yet.
e. Before there was the Baby-Sitters Club, there were four girls named Kristy Thomas, Mary Anne Spier, Claudia Kishi, and Stacey McGill.
f. Before there was the CIA there was the OSS.

Finally, McNally & Van Geenhoven (1998:7), in arguing that the postverbal NPs in existential sentences are weak in that they are interpreted as denoting properties, point to the sentences in (145) (presumably invented), which they characterize as containing "necessarily quantificational NPs which quantify over kinds or similar higher order objects."[49]

[49]McNally & Van Geenhoven cite Lumsden 1988 (now 2014) as a source of similar

(145) a. There was every sort of complaint imaginable.
b. There was each type of question on the exam.
c. There were most varieties of tomatoes available in that seed catalogue.
d. There were both kinds of films on the program.

Unsurprisingly, attested examples like these are readily found as well:

(146) a. There was every variety of hats, with every imaginable slouch; and there was every cut and style of coat and pantaloons...
b. There is each sort of attire, prepared to wear, totes, footwear, ...
c. Among our dresses there were most kinds of shabby and greasy wear, and much fustian and corduroy that was neither sound nor fragrant.
d. There were both kinds of apples in the sauce.

To sum up so far, our analysis of existential sentences largely follows the mixed semantic-pragmatic analysis of Abbott, positing a basic existential predication with a possible secondary predication (contained in either the existence verb, the coda, or both) and a pragmatic specification that the postverbal NP is in focus. It appears that the reasons a speaker may have for wishing the postverbal NP to occupy the attentional focus of the addressee are many and may, in particular, include drawing the addressee's attention to the situation described by the secondary predication of the coda.[50]

We now turn to the syntactic properties of E-*there*, as a prelude to an analysis that formulates these properties, along

examples.

[50]As Abbott points out, persistent observations of definite NPs in postverbal position in existentials, ever since Milsark (1997) – including some of the kinds of examples noted above – pose a serious empirical challenge to any treatment in which such NPs violate in one way or another the Case Theory of transformational generative grammar, as in the analyses of Safir (1987) or Belletti (1988). For discussion, see Abbott (1993: 52-53).

with the semantico-pragmatic properties discussed above, in a construction that further constrains the type *split-subj-cxt*.

As we saw in (5), repeated as (147), existential *there* sentences exhibit both postverbal agreement and Raising.[51] E-*there*, like P-*there*, requires expletive *there*.[52]

(147) Existential *There* [E-*there*]

a. Is there really an elephant in the garden?

b. There are likely to be problems with the finale.

c. There remain three issues to be addressed.

d. There exist two possible solutions.

As mentioned, in an SBCG grammar, the semantic FRAMES make up part of the multiple inheritance hierarchy of typed feature structures. We assume that in the frame hierarchy one immediate subtype of *state-frame* is *existence-frame* and that *existence-frame* has at least three immediate subtypes, as indicated in (148).

(148)

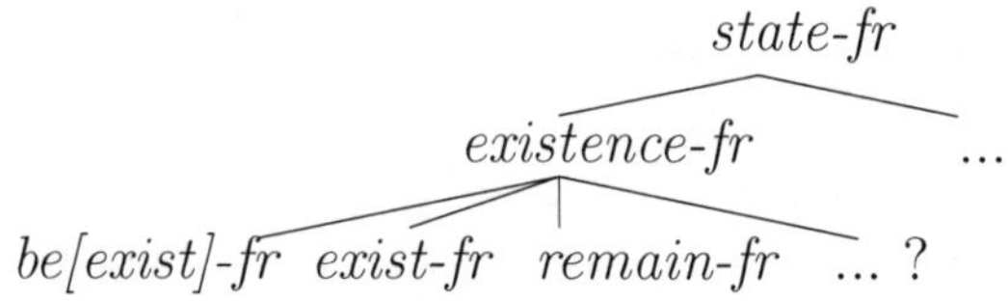

The FRAMES list of each existential verb contains a subtype of *existence-fr*. The Existential-*there* Construction specifies a subtype of *split-subj-cxt* whose mother's FRAMES list contains a (subtype of) *existence-fr*. The E-*there* construction also specifies that the mother's XARG is expletive *there*.

---

[51] We assume there is a separate lexical construction licensing sentences with singular verbal morphology and plural postverbal NPs, like (i):

(i) There's way too many ostriches.

Based on unsystematic observation it seems to us that there may be significant variation regarding (a) the restriction of the singular verbal morphology with plural postverbal NPs to *there's* versus *there is*, (b) whether either of these 'singular-for-plural' frames extend for any speaker to either *exist* or *remain*, and (c) how much variation there is within and across speakers with respect to all these matters and how such variation as does exist may be conditioned. We do not address any of these questions.

[52] See Szekely (2015:116 ff.) for several arguments that existential *there* is expletive *there*.

The mother's internal argument inherits the properties of pragmatic focus and determination of verbal agreement from *split-subj-cxt*. The mother's FRAMES value specifies an existence predication of the internal argument and leaves open the possibility, as in the case of *remain*, for the specification of further frames. We noted that existential *be* countenances discourse existence (130), (131), (139)–(144). It appears that existential *exist* does not have this property. Compare to (130) and (131), repeated as (149) and (150), the awkward examples (151) and (152), which substitute *exist* for *be* in B's reply. Real-world existence is the only available reading for these replies, which therefore can only be taken as indirect, possibly jocular or ironic, responses to A's question.

(149) A: Is there anything to eat?
B: Well, there's the chicken from last night. (Abbott 1993:42 ex.4)

(150) A: I guess we've called everybody.
B: No, there's still Mary and John. (Abbott 1993:42 ex.5)

(151) A: Is there anything to eat?
B: #Well, the leftover chicken from last night exists. (invented example)

(152) A: I guess we've called everybody.
B: #No, Mary and John still exist. (invented example)

(153) **Existential *there* Construction** (↑*split-subj-cxt*)

$$ex\text{-}there\text{-}cxt \Rightarrow \left[\text{MTR}\left[\begin{array}{ll} \text{ARG-ST} & \langle X{:}noun\left[\text{SYN}\left[\text{CAT}\left[\text{LID}\ \langle there[expl]\text{-}fr\rangle\right]\right]\right], \\ & \text{NP}_i, \ldots\rangle \\ \text{SYN} & \left[\text{CAT}\left[\text{XARG}\ X\right]\right] \\ \text{SEM} & \left[\text{FRAMES}\ \left\langle\begin{bmatrix} existence\text{-}fr \\ \text{ENTITY}\ i\end{bmatrix}\right\rangle\right]\end{array}\right]\right]$$

The Existential *there* Construction (153) adds to the information of *split-subj-cxt* only that the mother's XARG is expletive *there* and that the frame contributed by the daughter is consistent with *existence-fr*.

2.9 Reversed Specficational *be* (RS-*be*)

RS-*be* has the properties of canonical specificational *be*, plus two imposed by the Split Subject Construction: the non-XARG, postverbal, argument is (i) the agreement controller and (ii) specified as plural.[53] We follow Mikkelsen's (2002, 2005) analysis of specificational clauses except for implementing that analysis lexically in SBCG rather than in the Minimalism framework. Mikkelsen notes that the Minimalism implementation requires that the syntax rely on indications ("uninterpretable features") of topic and focus. The lexicalist, SBCG implementation we present below does not require that the syntax 'see' discourse properties of this kind.

According to Mikkelsen's analysis the key features of a specificational clause are that (1) the NP subject not be referential, (2) the NP subject express a (1-place) predicate, (3) the NP subject be TOPIC, (4) the postverbal NP denote the argument of the predicate, (5) the postverbal NP be in FOCUS. These properties hold for both "reversed" and "non-reversed" specificational clauses, the two versions differing only in the assignment of agreement control between the two arguments and the specification of plurality in the reversed version.[54]

The implementation of the Mikkelsen analysis in SBCG

[53]That is, we have found no examples with the structure of (i), in which the XARG/subject is plural and the verb agrees with a singular postverbal constituent. But it is admittedly risky to infer evidence of absence from absence of evidence in the case of such a highly marked construction.

(i)*?My worst problems is the IRS.

[54]With regard to the Mikkelsen analysis, the term "specificational" may be viewed as motivated by the relevant extensions. The extension of the clause-initial predicate is a set; the extension of the postverbal, referential NP is a member or a proper subset of that set. Thus the predication further 'specifies' the class denoted by the topical predicate.

proceeds as follows. We assume the lexicon furnishes a copula lexeme *be* that, when heading a standard *subject-predicate-construct* projects an ordinary predicational clause like that in (154a); compare to (154b) (= (6a) repeated).

(154) a. The injury risks are my biggest worry.
b. My biggest worry are the injury risks.

Following Mikkelsen's analysis, we analyze reversed specificational *be* as the result of applying the Split Subject Construction (70) to a copula *be* that licenses an ordinary predicational clause such as (154a) by identifying the predicational copula with the daughter of an SS construct. The MTR of the resulting construct class is consequently constrained to have all the properties required by Mikkelsen's analysis – that is, topical predicate projected by the Subject-Predicate Construction to clause-initial position with focused referential NP internal argument projected to postverbal position. In the reversed version, agreement is controlled by the internal argument. The copula *be* projecting a specificational clause is thus the MTR of a split-subject construct whose unique daughter is its predicational, truth-conditional equivalent. This approach relates a form of specificational clause directly to the truth-conditionally (but *not* discursively) equivalent predicational clause.

The parenthetical items in gray are not part of the construction depicted in (155). They are added to the diagram to illustrate the way the RS-*be* construction relates the copula of a reversed specificational clause such as (154a) to the truth-conditionally equivalent, predicational clause like (154b). Unofficially, a copula of the form of the daughter in which the 'risks' argument is specified as the XARG, hence subject-in-waiting, would license a predicational clause like (154a); a copula of the form of the daughter in which the 'worry' argument is specified as the XARG will license a specificatonal clause like (154b).

(155) **Reversed Specificational *be* Construction**
(↑*split-subj-cxt*)

$$
\textit{rev-spec-be-cxt} \Rightarrow \left[\begin{array}{ll}
\text{MTR} & Z!\left[\begin{array}{ll}
\multicolumn{2}{l}{\textit{rev-spec-cop-v-lxm}} \\
\text{FORM} & \langle \textit{be} \rangle \\
\text{ARG-ST} & \langle Y{:}\text{NP}_j\ \textit{(worry)}, \\
 & \quad X{:}\text{NP}_{i:[AGR\ w]}\ \textit{(risks)} \rangle \\
\text{SYN} & \left[\text{CAT}\left[\begin{array}{ll}\text{XARG} & Y \\ \text{AGR} & W\end{array}\right]\right] \\
\text{SEM} & Z \\
\text{CONTEXT} & \left[\text{INFO-ROLE}\left[\text{FOCUS}\ i\right]\right]
\end{array}\right] \\
\text{DTRS} & \left\langle Z{:}\left[\begin{array}{ll}
\multicolumn{2}{l}{\textit{pred-cop-v-lxm}} \\
\text{FORM} & \langle \textit{be} \rangle \\
\text{ARG-ST} & \langle X{:}\text{NP}_{i:[AGR\ w]}\ \textit{(risks)}, \\
 & \quad Y{:}\text{NP}_j\ \textit{(worry)} \rangle \\
\text{SYN} & \left[\text{CAT}\left[\begin{array}{ll}\text{XARG} & X \\ \text{AGR} & W{:}\left[\text{NUM}\ \textit{plural}\right]\end{array}\right]\right] \\
\text{SEM} & Z{:}\left[\text{FRAMES}\ \langle \textit{worry-fr(i)} \rangle\right]
\end{array}\right]\right\rangle
\end{array}\right]
$$

More generally, the MTR of the Specificational *Be* Construction is a *specificational-copula-be-verb-lexeme.* The XARG Y is a predicate, as shown in (155) in the shared FRAMES value Z, where this predicate is applied to the INDEX i of the external argument of the daughter (= the internal argument of the mother). As noted, the diagram in (155) is not a fully accurate representation of the RS-*be* construction because of the addition of the parts in gray. In an accurate representation ⟨*worry (i)*⟩ would be replaced by an expression like $l_0(i)$, where l_0 would represent the LABEL of the FRAMES value of NP_j. The RS-*be* Construction specifies that its MTR is a lexeme of type *reversed-specificational-copula-verb-lexeme*, which is capable of projecting a clause with the properties attributed to a specificational clause by Mikkelsen. The inherited Split Subject Construction does most of the work once the daughter is specified to be a copula lexeme that would project a predicational clause. The fact that the mother's XARG is predicated of the daughter's INDEX follows from the fact that the daughter predicates its internal argument on the INDEX of its external argument. The only added constraints are that the internal argument is controller of agreement and that the daughter's XARG's number is *plural*.

2.10 Conclusion

We have considered five clausal patterns in English in each of which certain of the properties that are standardly considered "subject" properties are distributed between two different constituents. To our knowledge, despite intensive analysis of several of these patterns, the group as a whole has not been subject to prior study. The SBCG approach has enabled us to see precisely what the five patterns have in common, namely the Split Subject Construction, and what is particular to each, revealing that a constructional, constraint-based approach like SBCG has the ability to extract the correct grammatical generalizations, not only in so-called "core" areas of a grammar, but in the hard cases, where concepts such as subject, which readily handle the more tractable facts, fail to fit comfortably the facts at hand. We see further that the five split-subject patterns, often identified as clausal, yield to a strictly lexical analysis (Kaplan & Bresnan 1982, Pollard & Sag 1994, Müller & Wechsler 2014, among many others).

Along the way we have noted that several of the intuitive acceptability judgments on which analyses of some of these patterns have depended fail to agree with observations of actual usage to a degree that is hard to reconcile with performance error or dialect diversity.

Appendix 1: Inflection

Our approach to morphology is realizational, following that of Sag (2012). (See Sag 2012: 107, fn. 54 and p. 113 for background). Affixes are not constituents, i.e., not signs. Affixation and other morphological processes are the result of morphological functions that have as input the FORM value of the daughter, called the stem of an inflectional or derivational construction and as output the FORM value of the mother. A derivational or inflectional construction specifies the relevant morphological function. The morphological function for pluralizing English nouns is given in (156).

(156) $F_{noun.pl}$

Stem	$F_{noun.pl}$(Stem)
ox	oxen
sheep	sheep
criterion	criteria
...	
Others	
x	x-s

The morphological function for third person singular present tense verbal agreement is given in (157).

(157) $F_{3sg.pres}$

Stem	$F_{3sg.pres}$(Stem)
have	has
be	is
do	does
will	will
...	
Others	
x	x-s

Inflectional constructions (in English) specify a lexeme daughter and a corresponding word mother, taking account of the relevant syntactic information in the daughter and applying the appropriate inflectional function to the daughter's FORM value to produce the mother's FORM value. In the case of verbal agreement inflection, the AGR value of the daughter is crucial. Recall that this value will be identical to that of the XARG in canonical verbs, but not in split-subject verbs.

(158) Third Singular Present Inflectional Construction
(↑*inflectional-cxt*)[55]

$$\textit{3-sg-pres-infl-cxt} \Rightarrow \begin{bmatrix} \text{MTR} & X!\begin{bmatrix} \textit{v-word} \\ \text{FORM } F_Y(L_0) \end{bmatrix} \\ \text{DTRS} & \left\langle X: \begin{bmatrix} \textit{v-lexeme} & \\ \text{FORM} & L_0 \\ \text{SYN} & \begin{bmatrix}\text{CAT} \begin{bmatrix}\text{AGR } Y\end{bmatrix}\end{bmatrix}\end{bmatrix}\right\rangle \end{bmatrix}$$

Appendix 2: Long-distance agreement (LDA) in split-subject structures

LDA occurs in split-subject structures such as existentials, as noted by Chomsky (2000)[56], illustrated in (159), and in OI, illustrated in (160), for formal register English.

(159) a. There seem to be numerous problems.
b. There seem to be a few trees between the green and your ball.
c. If there do not appear to be truffles beneath the oak, but there appear to be to X because X is under some

[55] We assume for convenience that there is an AGR(EEMENT) feature TENSE in English verbs which, among other things, specifies "present tense" morphology in conditional protases, narrative present, future reference with future adverbs (*She arrives tomorrow*), repeated or habitual events, *and* and *or* conditionals (*It moves and I shoot, She drops it or I shoot*), timeless truths, and perhaps more.

[56] This observation and related facts of Icelandic furnished the empirical basis of Chomsky's (2000) proposal of the Agree operation within the Minimalism framework. There has been extensive examination within that framework regarding LDA in general and the Agree operation in particular. See, for example, Polinsky & Potsdam (2001), Boeckx (2004), Bhatt (2005), Legate (2005), and Sigurðsson & Holmberg (2008), among others.

sort of illusion (or delusion) as to how things would appear if there were truffles, that is a matter of X's attitudes...

(160) a. From the base of the main sector below appear to arise two branches, the one at the extreme base being the stem of the wide fork...

b. But here may seem to arise two material objections...

Non-finite verbs do not inflect in English or Icelandic but in a language in which non-finite forms inflect, the non-finite verbal head of the lower VP or clause in an LDA structure may show the same agreement features as the matrix verb and the source argument. Example (161) of Hindi-Urdu is taken from Boeckx (2004) ex.5.

(161)

Vivek-ne	[kitaab	parh-nii]	chaah-ii
Vivek-ERG	book.F	read-INF.F	want-PFV.F

Vivek wants to read the book.

In (161) the infinitive parh-nii 'read-INF.F' agrees both with its nominal complement kitaab 'book.F' and the matrix verb chaah-ii 'want-PFV.F'. Example (162) is from Godoberi, a Nakh-Daghestanian language (Haspelmath 1999:131). In the [a] (sg) and [b] (pl) versions, respectively, the infinitive b–ax-i (sg)/r-axi (pl) agrees with its absolutive argument gyazeti (sg)/gyazeta-be (pl) and also with the matrix verb b-eʔu-č̌a (sg)/ r-eʔu-č̌a (pl).

(162)

a.

ʕali-č̌'u	gyazeti	b-ax-i	b-eʔu-č̌a
Ali-CONT	[paper(ABS)	N-take-INF]	N-forget-AOR

Ali forgot to buy a newspaper.

b.

ʕali-č̌'u	gyazeta-be	r-ax-i	r-eʔu-č̌a
Ali-CONT	[paper-PL(ABS)	PLN-take-INF]	PLN-forget-AOR

Ali forgot to buy newspapers.

Such facts suggest that the apparently long-distance relation between the matrix verb and the nominal in an infinitival or other non-finite complement may, in some cases, be composed of two local relations, one between a complement infinitive and its nominal complement and the other between the complement infinitive and the matrix verb.[57] For English it suffices to say that a subject-raising verb agrees with whatever its complement agrees with. In the usual case, when the matrix verb agrees with the unexpressed subject of the complement (*Fido (sg) seems (sg) to like bones (pl)*) this will have no effect different from the usual assumption that the matrix verb agrees with its subject. But in split subject cases like (159) and (160) the apparent long distance agreement is correctly predicted. Accordingly we posit the lexical class construction in (163), defining the type *subject-raising-verb-lexeme* as a subtype of *intransitive-verb-lexeme*. The parts of the AVM shown in gray indicate what is added to take care of LDA in English to what is otherwise a standard definition of a raising verb in a constraint-based approach.

(163) **Subject Raising Lexical Class Construction**
($\uparrow$*intrans-verb-lxm*)

$$\textit{subj-raising-v-lxm} \Rightarrow \begin{bmatrix} \text{ARG-ST} \left\langle X{:}\text{XP},\ \text{VP}\begin{bmatrix}\text{SYN}\begin{bmatrix}\text{CAT} & \begin{bmatrix}\text{XARG } X\end{bmatrix} \\ \text{AGR} & Y\end{bmatrix}\end{bmatrix}\right\rangle \\ \text{SYN} \quad \begin{bmatrix}\text{CAT} & \begin{bmatrix}\text{XARG } X\end{bmatrix} \\ \text{AGR} & Y\end{bmatrix}\end{bmatrix}$$

[57] We have not studied the facts of Hindi-Urdu or Godoberi and there may be relevant facts not taken into account in what follows. However, it appears from the description of Boeckx (2004: 25-27, examples 5-14) that the relevant facts of Hindi-Urdu LDA, for example, could be accounted for in SBCG by specifying a subtype of control verb whose infinitival complement (i) has exactly one internal (i.e., non-XARG) argument, (ii) that argument is not overtly case-marked, (iii) the GENDER value of the internal argument is identified with the corresponding value of the infinitive's AGR feature, and (iv) the AGR feature of the infinitive is identified with that of the matrix verb. (Given the larger generalization that Hindi-Urdu verbs only agree with case-marked subjects, this constraint would presumably be specified higher in the type hierarchy.)

3

Copy Raising as a Lexical Rule

Paul Kay

Introduction

There is compelling empirical motivation to define copy raising in English as a lexical rule that converts a perception verb with a stimulus subject (a so-called "flip perception verb") into a semantically bleached verb of mild evidentiary force, roughly equivalent semantically to *seem* in some uses. The derived verb does not subcategorize for a source of perception. It provides for a generic interpretation of the unexpressed experiencer of the awareness, and it identifies the index of its external argument with the index of the external argument of its clausal complement. Sign-Based Construction Grammar provides an apt formal framework for expressing this analysis.

Following Kim (2014), Landau (2011), and Potsdam & Runner (2001), among others, we observe that certain English perception verbs have two distinct senses: (i) a perception sense, in which the verb's external argument denotes an entity that plays a semantic role which might be called the 'perceptual stimulus' in a report of an experience in the perceptual mode denoted by the verb, and (ii) a different sense (or a homophonous verb) that does not assign a semantic role to its external argument and which figures in sentences like (1)–(4).[1]

(1) it's not difficult to work out why *Trump looked like he was going to win in January*: the stock market was booming, unemployment was low, crime low, there were no new wars... it's not a mystery.

(2) i have gone ahead and paid your parts because *the host of the giveaway looks like he disappeared ...*

(3) *the bill seemed like it would easily pass...*

(4) I'm so excited to get my copy of Sara's book ... *this one sounds like it's going to win an immediate place in my heart.*

In (1) Trump's visual appearance is patently not at issue. Similarly in (2) as regards the visual appearance of the giveaway host. In (3) any perceptual properties the bill might have had are almost certainly not related to its likelihood of passing. In (4), the information prompting the speaker's enthusiasm for a new cookbook is almost certainly not auditory. (All positive, numbered examples in this paper were attested on the web in the period 2021-2024, unless otherwise indicated.)

Sentences of this kind contain a subordinate clause complement, introduced by *like*, *as if*, or *as though*, the subject of which is a pronoun whose index is identified with the index of the matrix verb's external argument. The latter bundle of facts has given rise to the name Copy Raising (CR).[2] A key fact about CR sentences is that they have a paraphrase with an expletive subject and only one mention of the nominal

[1] The verbs with these two senses are not necessarily limited to those senses. For example, *seem* and *appear* may have additional senses associated with their raising and *it*-extraposition valences and *sound* has a hearsay sense (as suggested by Laura Michaelis) distinct from both its perception and copy raising senses (i).
(i) This 74-year-old pasta sauce recipe sounds incredibly delicious.

[2] The phenomenon was originally discussed for English by Andy Rogers (1971, 1973, 1974a, 1974b), who gave the transformation he proposed to model such phenomena the name "Richard", perhaps to convey with a somewhat whimsical flourish how different this phenomenon seemed from raising or any other familiar grammatical pattern of English.

expression in question. For example, a sentence such as (5a) has two distinct rough paraphrases (5b) (CR) and (5c) (perception report; perhaps Trump is watching Fox News and smiling).

(5) a. Trump looks like he will get the 2024 crowd he wants. [NY. Times, May 28, 2023, online]
b. 'It appears likely that Trump will get the 2024 crowd he wants' (CR)
c. 'Trump's visual appearance suggests that he will get the 2024 crowd he wants' (Perception report)

With regard to CR, the only structures that need special attention beyond the rest of the grammar are those in which (i) the subject pronoun of the *like*-phrase shares the index of the matrix subject and (ii) the meaning is that of the paraphrase just described. Sentences such as (6a) or even (6b) are widely understood to employ only the perception sense of the verb and be thus irrelevant to the analysis of CR, although there are certainly dissenters from this view (e.g., Melnik 2023, Asudeh and Toivonen 2012 and related papers, Lappin 1983, 1984, Heycock 1994, and Kim 2014).

(6) a. Pat looks like Marion is angry at him. (invented example)
b. Pat looks like Marion is angry. (invented example)

I do not discuss those dissents here. I find persuasive the arguments of Potsdam & Runner (2001), who conclude their examination of the relevant facts, "... true Copy Raising exists only where the pronominal copy is in subject position."

An essential observation relevant to the CR phenomenon is that an expression of the form *like/as if/as though* + S[fin] is an ordinary kind of subordinate clause, not limited to Copy Raising locutions. Such clauses can appear as complements to verbs like *act, behave* and *acquit (oneself)* as in examples (7)–(9).

(7) ... everyone high or low acquitted himself *(as if the

fortune of the field depended on his own individual prowess).

(8) Although it continued to float in midair, it acted *(like someone had cemented it to the ground).

(9) Americium, which is a pseudolanthanide, behaves *(as though it were roughly atomic No. 60).

As-if clauses can also serve as complements to perception verbs, as in examples 10 through 12.

(10) Doug Collins looked *(like someone had just slapped him). (Kevin Sullivan & Mary Jordan, *Trump on Trial: The Investigation, Impeachment, Acquittal, and Aftermath.* Washington Post/Scribner: 2020)

(11) The words sounded *(as if they were floating like flowers on water). (Virginia Woolf, *To the Lighthouse.* Oxford World's Classics: 1930)

(12) As for Ramsey... he had told me all along that his head was in danger, and he seemed *(as though the order was out for its removal).

Clauses of this form can also serve as adverbial modifiers of both transitive and intransitive verbal expressions.

(13) The man called her *as though he was calling a little cat.*

(14) This girl swims *like it was something she was meant to do.*

(15) She looked at him *like he had lost it completely.*

Kim (2014, among others) considers examples like (10)–(12) to be a kind of CR. The full range of examples like (7)–(15) suggests, on the other hand, that doing so complicates the full picture unnecessarily. There is no necessity to suppose that a sentence like (10), for example, has a grammatical form different from that of, say, (16).

(16) She looked like someone had died.

Let's call such clauses *as-if* clauses; as-if clauses possess the following properties: *like, as if*, and *as though* select a finite clause via the SELECT feature proposed by Allegranza (1989) and Van Eynde (2006), which groups determiners and modifiers together as *functors*. The finite S selectee is the head of the as-if clause and consequently its external argument (XARG) is visible externally. As-if clauses are accorded a dedicated MARKING value, *asif*, and apply an appropriate *frame* to the INDEX of the head finite clause. (The term *frame* is the SBCG name for an MRS elementary predication.) Huddleston & Pullum (2002:1151) argue for the lexical unity of *as if* and *as though*, which is also usual in the CR literature, and recognize the syntactic reality of as-if clauses. They assume that *like, as if,* and *as though* are prepositions and their relation to their clausal accompaniments that of complementation rather than modification. Unsurprisingly, given the relevant publication dates, they do not appear to have considered the possibility of a functor-type analysis.

3.1 Expletives

Before presenting an analysis of CR, it is desirable to look briefly at how expletives behave in CR contexts, since expletives and related forms have furnished key data for many analyses of CR. For example, Sag (2012) presents the examples in (17) and (18). His analysis of CR consists in proposing an illustrative lexeme type, as exemplified for CR *look* in (19).

(17) There looks like { there's going to be a storm / *it's going to rain / *Kim's going to win }

(Sag 2012:150, (110a))

The point intended is that the CR version of *look* requires identity between the matrix subject and that of the phrase following *like*.

(18) ?Kim looks like $\left\{\begin{array}{l}\text{there's going to be a storm}\\ \text{it's going to rain}\\ \text{Pat's going to win}\end{array}\right\}$

(Sag 2012:151, (110b))

Sag's implied interpretation regarding (18) is that all three cases must be perception reports (and not CR) because there is no identity of indices between the matrix and subordinate subjects, and the question mark indicates pragmatic oddity in the absence of a special context.[3] Sag's SBCG lexical analysis of CR is illustrated in (19).

(19) $\begin{bmatrix}\text{FORM} & \langle\ \textit{look}\ \rangle\\ \text{ARG-ST} & \left\langle \text{NP}_i,\ \overset{\text{PRT}}{\left[\textit{like}\right]},\ \overset{\text{S}}{\left[\text{XARG NP}_i\textit{pron}\right]} \right\rangle\end{bmatrix}$

(Sag 2012:151, (111))

This analysis is not persuasive.[4] The particle *like* serves only to make the XARG of the complement visible to the matrix XARG in the ARG-ST. It is otherwise unmotivated, performing no further function either in a CR environment or elsewhere in the grammar. On the other hand, we have seen that as-if clauses such as *like there's going to be a storm* in (17) and *like Pat's going to win* in (18) function as constituents in a range of non-CR examples, such as those exemplified in (7)–(15), with the same apparent semantic effects as in (17) and (18). Ideally, the as-if clause type should be recognized as such in an analysis of CR clauses.

As an initial step in investigating the role of expletives in

[3] Sag states that "the acceptability [of the examples in (18)] is slightly degraded." The alleged degradation, and the attendant question mark, need not be considered grammatically relevant, as these sentences appear to exemplify fully grammatical sentences that seem odd when presented in isolation only because the contexts in which they might be felicitously uttered do not spring readily to mind. Imagine in the first two cases of (18) that Kim is a farmer who has hurriedly thrown on his rain gear and is dashing out the door.

[4] We will see, however, that the analysis or CR presented below shares with that implied by (19) the properties of being strictly lexical and making strategic use of the XARG feature.

CR, we note that English so-called "weather-*it*" is not properly considered expletive. In a mostly forgotten paper of a half-century ago, Bolinger (1973) makes a compelling case that weather-*it* is not only not restricted to weather and time (*It's freezing; it's nearly 4:00 a.m.*) but rather denotes ambience generally. Some of Bolinger's initial examples imagine a phone conversation between two forest rangers in different stations.

(20) a. 'How's it down there?' – 'It's fairly calm.'
  b. 'How's it up there?' – 'It's practically ripping the trees out.'

Apparently, in (20) *it* includes the local wind conditions in its reference, but in a different location for each interlocutor. Bolinger continues:

(21) a. 'Isn't it nice out this afternoon?' – 'You must be crazy. It's so hot that it's giving me a headache.'
  b. 'It's cold enough to freeze the balls on a brass monkey.'

"Presumably in the last two sentences the *it* that refers to the weather is the same *it* that gives the headache and freezes the balls on the brass monkey." (Bolinger 1973:262). Ambient *it*, as Bolinger shows, is protean. The examples in 22 are also from Bolinger 1973.

(22) a. It's scary in the dark
  b. It's inspiring here at MIT.
  c. I'm climbing down. It's too exposed up here.
  d. It's her graduation next week.
  e. I like it in California.
  f. The noise makes it hard to study.
  g. It's all finished between us.

One might disagree with Bolinger that the examples in (23) exemplify the same *it* as those in (20)–(22), but in any case, these tokens of *it* are also clearly not expletive. He continues, "I would maintain that the same *it* turns up in the following:

(23) a. *Stop it!* (what you are obviously doing).
b. Don't do it! (what you are obviously about to do).
c. Come off it! (what you are obviously insisting on)" (Bolinger 1973:263)

We proceed on the hypothesis that the *it* subject of weather sentences is not expletive. This hypothesis is consistent with the tradition in HPSG that postulates three types of index for English: expletive *it*, expletive *there*, and referential. Ambient *it* is a subtype of *referential-index*.

That weather-*it* denotes ambiance entails that a weather predicate imposes a semantic role on its external argument. This in turn entails that a sentence like (24a) is three ways ambiguous. The lower *it* must be ambient because *rain* requires ambient *it* of its subject. The matrix *it* can be either ambient or expletive; if it is ambient the sentence can be CR, but it can also be a perception report with the two ambient *it* tokens referring differently, the matrix *it* to the current ambience and the lower *it* to an imagined future ambience, somewhat as we saw in (20) with contrasting wind conditions. If the matrix *it* is expletive, (24a) cannot be a CR sentence because in CR the matrix and complement subjects share an index and *rain* requires a referential (ambient-referring) subject. Instead, *seems* is the familiar raising verb in its alternate *it*-extraposition valence, and the sentence is interpreted like a sentence such as (24e). Example (24b) is bad because *rain* requires ambient *it*. Example (24c) is bad for the same reason; that reason also explains why CR is not possible, despite identity of the matrix subject's index and the complement's subject's index. Example (24d) is bad because it lacks the identity of indices required by CR and neither perception *seem* nor *it*-extraposition *seem* allows a *there* subject. Sentence (24e) is a perception report, with perception *seem* and ambient *it* subject. Example (24f) is boringly bad because there is no bound pronoun as required for CR, and both perception *seem* and *it*-extraposition *seem* reject *there* subjects. Finally, sentence (24g), which contrasts minimally with (24c), exemplifies CR, with matching expletives *there*; (*be a*) *storm* is not a weather predicate, which would require an ambience-referring subject.

(24) a. It seems like it's going to rain soon.
b. *It seems like there is going to rain soon.
c. *There seems like there is going to rain soon.
d. *There seems like it is going to rain soon.
e. It seems like rain is coming soon.
f. *There seems like rain is coming soon.
g. There seems like there is going to be a storm soon.

3.2 Analysis of Copy Raising

So far, nothing has been formally proposed regarding CR per se; as-if clauses are vanilla English grammar. The proposed analysis of CR is a lexical rule. SBCG expresses lexical rules as unary-branching, derivational constructions. The CR construction pumps a perception verb lexeme to a verb lexeme with a meaning that might be characterized as imparting a weak evidentiary force, perhaps similar to the meaning of *seem* in a sentence like (25), and whose output lexeme identifies the index of its NP XARG with the index of the pronominally specified XARG of the *as-if-cl* complement, as shown in (26).

(25) … the bill seems like a positive step for our state.

(26)

$$\left[\text{MTR}\left[\text{ARG-ST}\ \langle \text{NP}_i,\text{S}\left[\text{MRKG}\ \textit{as-if},\ \text{SYN}\left[\text{XARG}\ \text{NP}_i\textit{pron}\right]\right]\rangle\right]\right]$$

The expression in (26) describes informally the output of the Copy Raising lexical rule by specifying that the value of the MOTHER (MTR) attribute of the corresponding unary-branching derivational construction is constrained as follows: the value of the MOTHER's ARG(UMENT)-ST(RUCTURE) attribute consists of a list of length two, of which the first member is an NP with INDEX i and the second member is an as-if clause whose subject is a pronominal NP with INDEX i.

This analysis, despite departing from that of Sag (2012), shares with it both a strictly lexical approach and critical dependence upon the XARG feature: although the selectee finite clause in an as-if clause has empty VAL(ENCE), its XARG remains available to be coindexed with the matrix subject. The key points of this approach are (i) the empirical observation that all the verbs that participate in CR have a perception-verb double, (ii) that expressions such as *like he was going to win* in (1) occur freely in non-CR contexts, as illustrated in examples (7)–(15), (iii) the fact that the *it* subjects of weather sentences are best conceived as referential, (iv) the Allegranza-Van Eynde innovation of the Head-Functor Construction, based on the SELECT feature, which in the present context enables the subject of the as-if complement clause of an erstwhile perception verb to be visible to the subject in the latter's ARG-ST, and (v) that aspect of the architecture of SBCG (and of related forms of HPSG) that makes it possible for a *realized* external argument to nonetheless be visible in the ARG-ST of a governing predicator.

For illustration we consider the invented CR sentence (27). First, we take up the ordinary listeme *like*, which appears in examples (1)–(4), (10), (14), (15) and (27), recalling that examples (7)–(15) are not CR. (Since scope constraints play no direct role in the present analysis, I employ a kind of MRS Lite notation, in which constraints on relative scope, such as *qeq* constraints, are unexpressed, in effect ignoring the distinction between LTOP and GTOP.)

(27) Trump looks like he disappeared.

(28) **Listeme** *like*

$$\begin{bmatrix} \text{FORM} & \langle \textit{like} \rangle \\ \text{SYN} & \begin{bmatrix} \text{CAT} & \begin{bmatrix} \textit{adverb} & \\ \text{XARG} & \textit{none} \\ \text{SELECT} & \begin{bmatrix} \textit{verb} & \\ \text{SYN} & \begin{bmatrix} \text{CAT} & \begin{bmatrix} \text{VFORM} & \textit{fin} \\ \text{XARG} & \text{NP} \\ \text{INV} & - \end{bmatrix} \\ \text{VAL} & \langle\ \rangle \end{bmatrix} \\ \text{SEM} & \begin{bmatrix} \text{LTOP} & l \\ \text{INDEX} & e \end{bmatrix} \end{bmatrix} \end{bmatrix} \\ \text{VAL} & \langle\ \rangle \\ \text{MRKG} & \textit{asif} \end{bmatrix} \\ \text{SEM} & \begin{bmatrix} \text{FRAMES} & \langle \textit{as-if}(e',l) \rangle \\ \text{INDEX} & e' \end{bmatrix} \end{bmatrix}$$

The functor *like* is an adverb that SELECTs a finite clause ([VFORM *fin*, INV –]); the selected clause specifies a nominal external argument and an empty valence list. The semantics of *like* applies the *as-if-frame* to the LTOP of its selectee clause. Also, *like* is marked *asif*. As a functor, it will transmit [MARKING *asif*] to its MOTHER in a *head-functor-construct*.

The only addition we make to the grammar of English to account for the CR facts is the lexical rule in (29), which takes a perception verb lexeme as input and yields a CR verb lexeme as output. A CR verb (as specified by the mother in (29)) subcategorizes for an NP subject (Z) and an as-if clause complement. Semantically, it specifies a *seeming-frame* with three arguments: the Davidsonian event variable e, a human experiencer argument j, and the semantic information, labeled l of the *as-if* complement, which is the state of affairs that *seems* to j to be the case. Also – and essential to the CR phenomenon – the CR verb identifies the index of its external argument Z with the index of the pronominal external argument of the *as-if* complement.

(29) **Copy Raising Construction** ($\uparrow$*derivational-cxt*) [a lexical rule][5]

$$
\textit{cpy-rais-v-cxt} \Rightarrow
\begin{bmatrix}
\text{MTR} \;\; X! \begin{bmatrix}
\text{SYN} \begin{bmatrix}
\text{CAT} \begin{bmatrix} \text{XARG} \;\; Z{:}\text{NP}_i \end{bmatrix} \\
\text{VAL} \left\langle Z, \begin{bmatrix}
\text{SYN} \begin{bmatrix}
\text{CAT} & \begin{bmatrix} \text{VFORM} \; \textit{fin} \\ \text{XARG} \;\; \text{NP}_i\textit{pron} \end{bmatrix} \\
\text{VAL} & \langle\, \rangle \\
\text{MRKG} & \textit{asif}
\end{bmatrix} \\
\text{SEM} \begin{bmatrix} \text{LTOP} \; l \end{bmatrix}
\end{bmatrix} \right\rangle
\end{bmatrix} \\
\text{SEM} \begin{bmatrix}
\text{FRAMES} \; \langle \textit{seeming-fr}(e, \textit{human-fr}(j), l) \rangle \\
\text{INDEX} \;\; e
\end{bmatrix}
\end{bmatrix} \\
\text{DTRS} \left\langle X{:} \begin{bmatrix}
\textit{verb} \\
\text{SEM} \begin{bmatrix} \text{FRAMES} \; \langle \textit{perception-fr}(e) \rangle \end{bmatrix}
\end{bmatrix} \right\rangle
\end{bmatrix}
$$

By way of illustration, Figure 1 shows the derivation tree for invented sentence (27) *Trump looks like he disappeared.*

We take sentence (27) *Trump looks like he disappeared* to have the approximate gloss 'It seems as if Trump disappeared'. Starting at the bottom of the tree, consider the right (head) daughter sign. In the SEM(ANTICS) value, the FRAMES value specifies the *disappear-frame* applied to the event variable e, which is the INDEX of the sign, and the in-

[5]Comments on notation: For constraint descriptions (AVMs) [A], [B], the paired tags 'X! [A]' and 'X: [B]' indicate that [A] and [B] are identical in all respects in which they are not shown to differ. This abbreviatory notation is commonly used in SBCG for the statement of lexical rules, though not limited to that use. (See Sag 2012:125 fn. for further discussion.) AVMs in boxes represent model objects as against grammatical objects (feature structures, as against descriptions of feature structures, such as types and constructions).

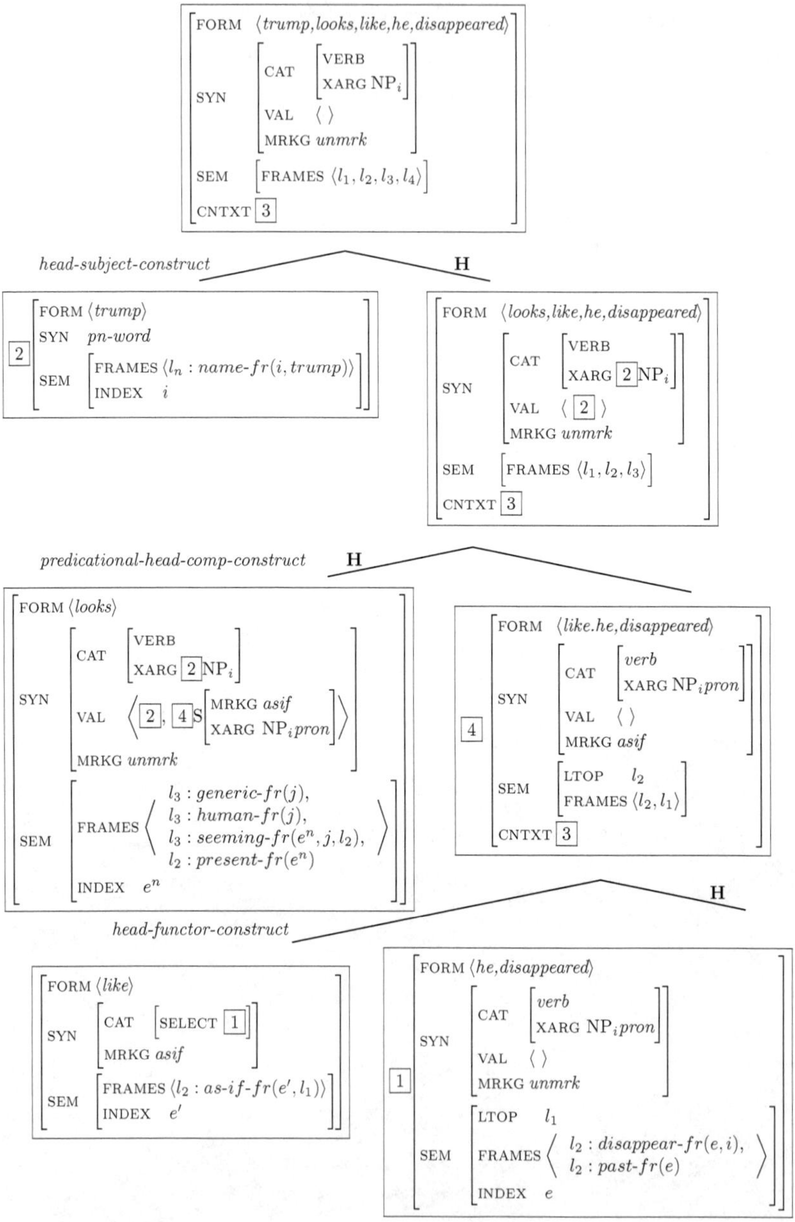

FIGURE 1 Derivation tree for *Trump looks like he disappeared*

dividual variable *i*. The FRAMES list also contains the *past-frame* applied to *e*. According to the tag [1] the right daughter is the value of the SELECT feature of the left, functor, daughter, *like*, in a *head-functor-construct*. The functor daughter's FRAMES feature applies the *as-if-frame* to the local INDEX *e'* and to the *disappear* and *past* predications jointly labelled l_1, the value of the LTOP of the head daughter. I suggest that the *as-if-frame* is interpreted as an epistemic operator of some kind, which I do not pursue further here. The *like* sign also introduces the MARKING value *asif*, which is passed up to the MOTHER sign, *like he disappeared*, in a *head-functor-construct*. The mother of that construct, *like he disappeared*, gathers up the frames of its two daughters and inherits the rest of its information from the head daughter.

To build the VP *looks like he disappeared* with the Predicational Head-Complement Construction, we note that we have employed the Copy Raising lexical rule (29) to build the CR form of *look* from perception *look*. Inflected *looks* introduces in its FRAMES list the *present-frame* predicated of the local index *e"*. In this example the semantic equivalent of so-called arbitrary PRO is introduced as the experiencer of the *seeming* predication by application of the *generic-fr* to the bound variable *j*, restricted by the *human-frame*. The *seeming-frame* specifies two arguments in addition to the event variable *e"*: *j* and the *asif-fr* predication l_2. The *seeming* predication thus specifies that the *as-if* predication l_2 is the state of affairs that seems to the generic human *j* to be the case. *Looks* also specifies in its VALENCE list the CR-characteristic coindexation of its NP XARG and the XARG of its *asif-clause* complement. The latter valent, bearing the tag [4], is discharged in the *predicational-head-complement* construct by the right sister of *looks*. We have already discussed this sign as the mother of the *like-he-disappeared* construct. As a head, the *looks* constituent bears the MARKING value *unmarked*, which it passes up to its mother, *looks like he disappeared*, in the *predicational-head-complement-construct.*

Finally, The Head-Subject Construction (aka Subject-Predicate Construction) realizes the remaining valent [2] as the subject *Trump.* The mother constituent of the *head-subject-construct, Trump looks like he disappeared,* gathers up the four frames of its daughters, inherits the marking value *unmarked* from the head VP, and expresses with an empty VALENCE set the fact that the NP *trump,* whose index *i* is identified with that of the pronoun *he,* has satisfied the last remaining valent.

3.3 Conclusion

The lexical rule analysis of CR presented here has benefitted particularly from three empirical observations and two formal aspects of SBCG and related versions of HPSG. The empirical observations are not necessarily new, but they have not to my knowledge been marshalled in this combination before. They are that (i) to each verb participating in CR there corresponds a homophonous perception verb, (ii) the pronoun *it* that serves as the subject of weather verbs is referential, and (iii) the word string initiated by *like, as if,* or *as though* in a CR sentence forms a constituent, a type of subordinate clause (christened here "as-if" clause) that occurs as both complement and modifier elsewhere in the grammar. The formal aspects of SBCG/HPSG that are strategically employed in the present analysis are as follows: (i) The SELECT feature makes it possible for the finite clause requirement of the CR-marking expression (*like, as if,* or *as though*) to be a selectee rather than a complement of that expression. This circumstance identifies the XARG of the finite selectee with the XARG of the as-if clause, and so renders its subject potentially (and actually) visible in the ARG-ST of the CR verb. (ii) Since the XARG feature, unlike the ARG-ST feature, percolates up the line of heads, the XARG of the as-if complement can be addressed in the ARG-ST of the CR verb and specified as a pronoun that shares its index with that of the matrix XARG. When the three empirical observations are considered, the SBCG/HPSG formalism enables an account of the CR facts with a lexical rule that inputs a perception verb and outputs a verb that identifies the index of its external argument with the index of the external argument of its as-if complement and whose semantics specifies a mildly evidentiary *seeming* meaning of which the experiencer argument may be covert and interpreted generically.

This paper has considered CR only for English. Future research will have to determine whether this approach is helpful in understanding CR in other languages.

Acknowledgements

An earlier version of this chapter was presented to the 2021 International Conference of Head-Driven Phrase Structure Grammar. I want to thank the participants of that conference, in particular Robert Borsley, Jean-Pierre Koenig, and Adam Przepiórkowski. I also thank Jong-Bok Kim and Eric Potsdam for helpful email correspondence. The story of CR presented here has arisen from many conversations on this subject with Laura Michaelis and I owe Rui Chaves an unpayable debt for his generous counsel. Flaws are mine alone.

References

Abbott, Barbara. 1992. Definiteness, existentials, and the 'list' interpretation. In *SALT II: Proceedings of the Second Conference on Semantics and Linguistic Theory*, pages 1–16. Columbus: The Ohio State University.

Abbott, Barbara. 1997. Definiteness and existentials. *Language* 73(1):103–108.

Abeillé, Anne. 1995. The flexibility of French idioms: A representation with Lexical Tree Adjoining Grammar. In M. Everaert, E.-J. v. d. Linden, A. Schenk, and R. Schreuder, eds., *Idioms. Structural and Psychological Perspectives*, pages 15–42. Lawrence Erlbaum Associates, Hillsdale.

Aissen, Judith. 1975. Presentational-there insertion: A cyclic root transformation. In *Papers from the Tenth Regional Meeting of the Chicago Linguistic Society*, pages 1–14. Chicago Linguistic Society.

Aissen, Judith and Jorge Hankamer. 1972. Shifty subjects: A conspiracy in syntax. *Linguistic Inquiry* 3:501–504.

Allegranza, Valerio. 1998a. Determiners as functors: NP structure in Italian. In S. Balari and L. Dini, eds., *Romance in HPSG*, CSLI Lecture Notes, pages 55–108. Stanford: CSLI Publications.

Allegranza, Valerio. 2007. *The Signs of Determination. Constraint-Based Modelling Across Languages*, vol. 16 of *SABEST: Saarbrücker Beiträge zur Sprach- und Translationswissenschaft*. Frankfurt am Main: Peter Lang.

Asudeh, Ash and Ida Toivonen. 2012. Copy raising and perception. *Natural Language and Linguistic Theory* 30(2):321–380.

Barwise, Jon and Robin Cooper. 1981. Generalized quantifiers and natural language. *Linguistics and Philosophy* 4:159–219.

Belletti, Adriana. 1988. The case of unaccusatives. *Linguistic Inquiry* 19:1–34.

Bhatt, Rajesh. 2005. Long distance agreement in hindi-urdu. *Natural Language and Linguistic Theory* 23:757–807.

Birner, Betty J. 1996. *The Discourse Function of Inversion in English*. New York: Garland.

Birner, Betty J. and Gregory Ward. 1998. *Information status and noncanonical word order in English*. Amsterdam: John Benjamins.

Boas, Hans C. and Ivan A. Sag, eds. 2012. *Sign-Based Construction Grammar*. Stanford, CA: CSLI Publications.

Boeckx, Cedric. 2004. Long-distance agreement in Hindi: Some theoretical implications. *Studia linguistica* 56(1):23–36.

Bolinger, Dwight. 1977. *Meaning and form*. New York/London: Longman.

Bond, Francis, Jia Qian Ho, and Dan Flickinger. 2015. Feeling our way to an analysis of english possessed idioms. In S. Müller, ed., *Proceedings of the 22nd International Conference on Head-Driven Phrase Structure Grammar, Nanyang Technological University (NTU), Singapore*, pages 61–74. Stanford, CA: CSLI Publications.

Borer, Hagit. 2005. *The Normal Course of Events: Structuring Sense, Volume II*. Oxford: Oxford University Press.

Bruening, Benjamin. 2010. Language-particular syntactic rules and constraints: English locative inversion and do-support. *Language* 86:43–84.

Burzio, Luigi. 1981. *Intransitive verbs and Italian auxiliaries*. Dissertation, Cambridge MA.

Chaves, Rui Pedro. 2012. On the grammar of extraction and coordination. *Natural Language and Linguistic Theory* 30(2):465–512.

Chaves, Rui Pedro. 2014. On the disunity of right-node raising phenomena: Extraposition, ellipsis, and deletion. *Language* 90:834–886.

Chaves, Rui Pedro, Paul Kay, and Laura Michaelis. submitted. Sometimes it goes without saying: English implicit arguments in Sign-Based Construction Grammar.

Chomsky, Noam. 2000. Minimalist Inquiries: The Framework. In R. Martin, D. Michaels, and J. Uriagereka, eds., *Step by Step: Essays on minimalist syntax in honor of Howard Lasnik*. Cambridge, MA: MIT Press.

Copestake, Ann, Dan Flickinger, Carl J. Pollard, and Ivan A. Sag. 2005. Minimal recursion semantics: an introduction. *Research on Language and Computation* 3(4):281–332.

Culicover, Peter. 1993. Evidence against ECP accounts of the that-*t* effect. *Linguistic Inquiry* 24:557–561.

Culicover, Peter W. and Robert Levine. 2001. Stylistic inversion in English: A reconsideration. *Natural Language and Linguistic Theory* 19:283–310.

Davis, Anthony R. and Jean-Pierre Koenig. 2000. Linking as constraints on word classes in a hierarchical lexicon. *Language* 76(1):56–91.

de Jong, Franciska. 1987. The compositional nature of (in)definiteness. In E. Reuland and A. ter Meulen, eds., *The Representation of (In)definiteness*, pages 286–317. Cambridge, MA: MIT Press.

Donohue, Cathryn and Ivan A. Sag. 1991. Domains in Warlpiri. Paper presented at HPSG-99 – University of Edinburgh. Non-final draft available at http://www.cs.toronto.edu/ gpenn/csc2517/donohue-sag99.pdf.

DuBois, John. 1987. The discourse basis of ergativity. *Language* 18:805–855.

DuBois, John, William Ashby, and Lorraine Kumpf. 2003. *Preferred argument structure*. John Benjamins.

Duffield, Jill. 2013. *Beyond the subject: The interaction of syntax and semantics in the production of English verb agreement*. Dissertation, University of Colorado Boulder.

Duffield, Jill and Laura Michaelis. 2011. Why subject relatives prevail: Constraints versus constructional licensing. *Language and Cognition* 3:171–208.

Engdahl, Elisabeth. 2006. Information packaging in questions. In O. Bonami and P. C. Hofherr, eds., *Empirical Issues in Syntax and Semantics 6*, pages 93–111.

Enç, Mürvet. 1991. The semantics of specificity. *Linguistic Inquiry* 22:1–25.

Falk, Yehuda N. 1983. Subjects and long-distance dependencies. *Linguistic Analysis* 12:245–270.

Fillmore, Charles J. 1982. Frame semantics. In *In Linguistics in the Morning Calm*, pages 111–137. Seoul: Hanshin Publishing Co.

Fillmore, Charles J. 1985. Frames and the semantics of understanding. *Quaderni di Semantica* 6:222–254.

Fillmore, Charles J. and Colin Baker. 2010. A frames approach to semantic analysis. In B. Heine and H. Narrog, eds., *The Oxford Handbook of Linguistic Analysis*, pages 313–340. Oxford: Oxford University Press.

Fillmore, Charles J., Paul Kay, and Mary C. O'Connor. 1988. Regularity and idiomaticity in grammatical constructions: The case of *let alone*. *Language* 64:501–538.

Gazdar, Gerald. 1981. Unbounded dependencies and coordinate structure. *Linguistic Inquiry* 12:155–84.

Goldsmith, John. 1985. A principled exception to the coordinate structure constraint. *CLS 21, Part 1* pages 133–143.

Haspelmath, Martin. 1999. Long distance agreement in godoberi (daghestanian) complement clauses. *Folia Linguistica* 33(1-2):131–152.

Hedberg, Nancy. 2000. The referential status of clefts. *Language* 76:891–920.

Hetzron, Robert. 1975. *SURFACING: From Dependency Relations to Linearity*. Liviana.

Heycock, Caroline. 1994. *Layers of Predication*. New York: Garland Publishing Co.

Heycock, Caroline and Anthony Kroch. 2002. Topic, focus, and syntactic representations. In *Proceedings of WCCFL*, pages 141–165. Cascadilla Press.

Huddleston, Rodney D. and Geoffrey K. Pullum. 2002. *The Cambridge Grammar of the English Language*. Cambridge: Cambridge University Press.

Jaeggli, Osvaldo and Kenneth J. Safir. 1989. The null subject parameter and parametric theory. In O. Jaeggli and K. Safir, eds., *The null subject parameter*, pages 1–44. Dordrecht: Kluwer.

Kaplan, Ronald M. and Joan Bresnan. 1982. Lexical-functional grammar: A formal system for grammatical representation. In J. Bresnan, ed., *The Mental Representation of Grammatical Relations*, pages 173–281. MIT Press. Reprinted in Mary Dalrymple, Ronald Kaplan, John Maxwell, and Annie Zaenen, eds., *Formal Issues in Lexical-Functional Grammar*. Stanford: CSLI Publications. Pages 29–130.

Karttunen, Lauri. 1969. Discourse referents. In *International Conference on Computational Linguistics COLING 1969: Preprint No. 70*. Sånga Säby, Sweden.

Kathol, Andreas. 1999. Agreement and the syntax-morphology interface in HPSG. In R. D. Levine and G. Green, eds., *Studies in Contemporary Phrase Structure Grammar*, pages 209–260. Cambridge and New York: Cambridge University Press.

Kathol, Andreas. 2000. *Linear Syntax*. New York, Oxford: Oxford University Press.

Kay, Paul and Charles Fillmore. 1999. Grammatical constructions and linguistic generalizations: The *what's x doing y?* construction. *Language* 75.1:1–33.

Kay, Paul and Laura A. Michaelis. 2019. A few words to do with multiword expressions. In C. Condoravdi and T. H. King, eds., *Tokens of Meaning: Papers in Honor of Lauri Karttunen*. Stanford: CSLI Publications.

Kay, Paul and Ivan A. Sag. 2012. Discontinuous dependencies and complex determiners. In H. C. Boas and I. A. Sag, eds., *Sign-Based Construction Grammar*, pages 211–238. CSLI Publications.

Kay, Paul, Ivan A. Sag, and Dan Flickinger. (this volume). A lexical theory of phrasal idioms.

Keenan, Edward. 1987. A semantic definition of 'indefinite NP'. In E. Reuland and A. ter Meulen, eds., *The representation of (in)definiteness*. Cambridge MA: MIT Press.

Keenan, Edward. 2003. The definiteness effect: Semantics or pragmatics? *Natural Language Semantics* 11:187–216.

Kim, Jong-Bok. 2003. English locative inversion: A constraint-based approach. *Korean Journal of Linguistics* 28:207–235.

Kim, Jong-Bok. 2014. English copy raising constructions: Argument realization and characterization condition. *Linguistics* 52(1):167–203.

Ladd, D. Robert. 1996. *Intonational Phonology*. Cambridge: Cambridge University Press.

Lakoff, George. 1986. Frame semantic control of the coordinate structure constraint. In *Papers from the Twenty-Second Annual Regional Meeting of the Chicago Linguistic Society, Part 2*, pages 152–167. Chicago: Chicago Linguistic Society.

Lakoff, G. 1987. *Women, Fire, and Dangerous Things*. Chicago: University of Chicago Press.

Lambrecht, Knud. 1994. *Information Structure and Sentence Form: Topic, Focus, and the Mental Representations of Discourse Referents*. Cambridge Studies in Linguistics. Cambridge: Cambridge University Press.

Lambrecht, Knud and Laura A. Michaelis. 1998. Sentence accent in information questions: Default and projection. *Natural Language and Linguistic Theory* 23:477–544.

Landau, Idan. 2011. Predication vs aboutness in copy raising. *Linguistics and Philosophy* 21(3):779–813.

Langacker, Ronald W. 1986. An introduction to cognitive grammar. *Cognitive Science* 10:1–40.

Lappin, Shalom. 1983. Theta-roles and np movement. In P. Sells and C. Jones, eds., *The Proceedings of NELS 13*, pages 121–128. Amherst MA: GLSA.

Lappin, Shalom. 1984. Predication and raising. In P. Sells and C. Jones, eds., *The Proceedings of NELS 14*, pages 236–252. Amherst MA: GLSA.

Lawler, John M. 1977. A Agrees with B in Achenese:: A Problem for Relational Grammar. In Brill, ed., *Syntax and Semantics 8: Grammatical relations*. Academic Press.

Ledgeway, Adam. 1998. Variation in the Romance infinitive: The cases of the Southern Calabrian inflected infinitive. *Transactions of the Philological Society* 96(1):1–6.

Legate, Julie A. 1995. Phases and cyclic agreement. Perspectives on phases. In *MIT Working Papers in Linguistics 49*, pages 147–156.

Levine, Robert. 1989. On focus inversion: syntactic valence and the role of a subcat list. *Linguistics* 27:1013–1056.

Lumsden, Michael. 1988. *Existential sentences: Their structure and meaning*. New York: Croom Helm.

Matsos, Gabriela. 2013. Quotative inversion in Peninsular Portuguese and Spanish, and in English. *Catalan Journal of Linguistics* 12:113–130.

McCawley, James D. 1981. The syntax and semantics of Enlish relative clauses. *Lingua* 53(2):99–149.

McNally, Louise. 2016. Existential sentences crosslinguistically: Variations in form and meaning. In M. Liberman and B. Partee, eds., *Annual Review of Linguistics 2*.

McNally, Louise and Veerle Van Geenhoven. 1998. Redefining the weak/strong distinction. url: http://www.upf.edu/pdi/louise-mcnally/pdf/publications/weaknps.pdf.

Melnik, Nurit. 2023. Copy raising reconsidered. *Journal of Language Modelling* 11:297–341.

Michaelis, Laura A. and Hartwell Francis. 2006. Lexical subjects and the conflation strategy. In N. Hedberg and R. Zacharski, eds., *The Grammar–Pragmatics Interface: Essays in honor of Jeanette K. Gundel*, pages 19–48. John Benjamins.

Mikkelsen, Line. 2002. Specification is not inverted predication. In *Proceedings of NELS*, pages 403–422. University of Massachusetts GLSA.

Mikkelsen, Line. 2004. Specificational subjects – a formal characterization and some consequences. *Acta Linguistics Hafniensia* 36:79–112.

Mikkelsen, Line. 2005. *Copular Clauses: Specification, Predication and Equation*. John Benjamins.

Milsark, Gary L. 1979. *Existential Sentences in English*. New York: Garland.

Müller, Stefan. 2002. *Complex Predicates: Verbal Complexes, Resultative Constructions, and Particle Verbs in German*. No. 13 in Studies in Constraint"=Based Lexicalism. Stanford, CA: CSLI Publications.

Müller, Stefan. 2006. Phrasal or lexical Constructions? *Language* 82(4):850–883.

Müller, Stefan and Stephen Wechsler. 2014a. Lexical approaches to argument structure. *Theoretical Linguistics* 40:1–76.

Müller, Stefan and Stephen Wechsler. 2014b. Two sides of the same slim Boojum: Further arguments for a lexical approach to argument structure. *Theoretical Linguistics* 40(1–2):187–224.

Napoli, Maria. 2013. Semantic constraints on the Latin impersonal passive. In E. Gelderen, J. Barðdal, and M. Cennamo, eds., *Argument Structure in Flux: The Naples-Capri Papers*. Amsterdam: John Benjamins.

Nikolaeva, Irina. 2013. The narrative infinitive construction in French and Latin. In H. Boas and F. Gonzálvez-García, eds., *Romance Perspectives on Construction Grammar*, pages 139–179. Amsterdam: John Benjamins.

Nunberg, Geoffrey, Ivan A. Sag, and Thomas Wasow. 1994. Idioms. *Language* 70(3):491–538.

O'Grady, William. 1998. The syntax of idioms. *Natural Language and Linguistic Theory* 16:279–312.

Osborne, Timothy. 2012. Edge features, catenae, and dependency-based minimalism. *Linguistic Analysis* 34:321—-366.

Perlmutter, David and Annie Zaenen. 1984. The indefinite extraposition construction in Dutch and German. In D. Perlmutter and C. Rosen, eds., *Studies in Relational Grammar 2*, pages 171–216. Chicago: University of Chicago Press.

Platzak, Christen. 1987. The Scandinavian languages and the null-subject parameter. *Natural Language and Linguistic Theory* 5:377–401.

Polinsky, Maria and Eric Potsdam. 2001. Long-distance agreement and topic in Tsez. *Natural Language and Linguistic Theory* 19(3):583–646.

Pollard, Carl J. and Ivan A. Sag. 1994. *Head-Driven Phrase Structure Grammar*. Chicago: University of Chicago Press.

Postal, Paul M. 2004. A paradox in english syntax. In *Skeptical Linguistic Essays*. Oxford: Oxford University Press.

Potsdam, Eric and Jeffrey T. Runner. 2001. Richard returns: copy raising and its implications. In *Proceedings of The Thirty-Seventh Regional Meeting of the Chicago Linguistics Society*, pages 453–468.

Prince, Ellen F. 1981. Topicalization, focus-movement, and Yiddish movement: a pragmatic differentiation. In D. Alford, ed., *Proceedings of the 7th Regional Meeting of the Berkeley Linguistics Society*, pages 249–264. Berkeley: BLS.

Prince, Ellen F. 1992. The ZPG Letter: Subjects, definiteness, and information-status. In W. C. Mann and S. A. Thompson, eds., *Discourse Description: Diverse linguistic analyses of a fund-raising text*, pages 295–325. John Benjamins.

Rando, Emily and Donna J. Napoli. 1978. Definites in there-sentences. *Language* 54:300–313.

Rappaport-Hovav, Makla and Beth Levin. 2008. The English dative alternation: The case for verb sensitivity. *Journal of Linguistics* 44(1).

Reape, Mike. 1994. Domain union and word order variation in German. In J. Nerbonne, K. Netter, and C. J. Pollard, eds., *German in Head-Driven Phrase Structure Grammar*, no. 46 in CSLI Lecture Notes, pages 151–197. Stanford University: CSLI Publications.

Richter, Frank and Manfred Sailer. 2009. Phraseological clauses in constructional hpsg. In *Proceedings of the 16th International Conference on Head-Driven Phrase Structure Grammar, University of Göttingen, Germany*, pages 297–317. Stanford: CSLI Publications.

Roberts, Craige. 2012. Information structure in discourse: Towards an integrated formal theory of pragmatics. *Semantics and Pragmatics* 5:1–69.

Rogers, Andy. 1972. Another look at flip perception verbs. In *Papers from the Tenth Regional Meeting of the Chicago Linguistic Society*, pages 303–315. Chicago Linguistic Society.

Rogers, Andy. 1974a. *Physical Perception Verbs in English: A Study in Lexical Relatedness*. Dissertation, UCLA.

Rogers, Andy. 1974b. A transderivational constraint on Richard? In *Papers from the Tenth Regional Meeting of the Chicago Linguistic Society*, pages 551–558. Chicago Linguistic Society.

Ross, John R. 1967. *Constraints on Variables in Syntax*. Ph.D. thesis, MIT. [Published in 1986 as *Infinite Syntax!* Norwood, N. J.: Ablex].

Safir, Kenneth J. 1985. Missing subjects in German. In J. Toman, ed., *Linguistic theory and the grammar of German*, pages 193–229. Dordrecht: Foris.

Safir, Kenneth J. 1987. What explains the definiteness effect. In E. Reuland and A. ter Meulen, eds., *The Representation of (In)definiteness*, pages 71–97. Cambridge MA: MIT Press.

Sag, Ivan A. 2010a. English filler-gap constructions. *Language* 86:486–545.

Sag, Ivan A. 2010b. Feature geometry and predictions of locality. In G. Corbett and A. Kibort, eds., *Features: Perspectives on a Key Notion in Linguistics*, pages 236–271. Oxford: Clarendon Press.

Sag, Ivan A. 2012. Sign-based construction grammar: An informal synopsis. In H. C. Boas and I. A. Sag, eds., *Sign-Based Construction Grammar*, pages 69–202. Stanford, CA: CSLI Publications.

Sag, Ivan A., Timothy Baldwin, Francis Bond, Ann Copestake, and Daniel P. Flickinger. 2002. Multiword expressions: A pain in the neck for NLP. In *Proceedings of the Third International Conference on Intelligent Text Processing and Computational Linguistics (CICLING 2002)*, pages 1–15. Mexico City, Mexico.

Sag, Ivan A., Thomas Wasow, and Emily M. Bender. 2003. *Syntactic Theory: A Formal Introduction*. Stanford: CSLI Publications, 2nd edn.

Sailer, Manfred. 2003. Combinatorial semantics and idiomatic expressions in Head-Driven Phrase Structure Grammar. Phil. Dissertation (2000). Arbeitspapiere des SFB 340. 161, Universität Tübingen.

Salzmann, Martin. 2013. Repair-driven verb movement in english locative inversion. In P. Brandt and E. Fuss, eds., *Repairs: The Added Value of Being Wrong*, pages 155–206. de Gruyter Mouton.

Schachter, Paul. 1992. Comments on Bresnan and Kanverva's 'Locative inversion in Chichewa: A case study of factorization in grammar'. In T. Stowell and E. Wehrli, eds., *Syntax and the Lexicon*, pages 103–110. New York/San Francisco/London: Academic Press.

Sigurðsson, Halldór Á. and Anders Holmberg. 2008. Icelandic dative intervention: Person and number are separate probes. In R. D'Alessandro and G. Hrafnbjargarson, eds., *Agreement restrictions*, pages 251–280. de Gruyter Mouton.

Soehn, Jan-Philipp. 2004. License to COLL. In S. Müller, ed., *Proceedings of the HPSG-2004 Conference, Center for Computational Linguistics, Katholieke Universiteit Leuven*, pages 261–273. Stanford: CSLI Publications.

Szekely, Rachel. 2015. *Truth Without Predication: The Role of Placing in the Existential There-Sentence*. New York and London: Palgrave Macmillan.

Tóth, I.C. 2000. *Inflected infinitives in Hungarian*. Dissertation, Tilburg University.

Ura, Hiroyuki. 1994. Varieties of raising and the feature-based bare phrase structure theory. In *MIT Occasional Papers in Linguistics 7*. Cambridge MA: MIT Working Papers in Linguistics.

Van Eynde, Frank. 2006. NP-internal agreement and the structure of the noun phrase. *Journal of Linguistics* 42(1):139–186.

Van Eynde, Frank. 2007. The big mess construction. In S. Müller, ed., *The Proceedings of the 14th International Conference on Head-Driven Phrase Structure Grammar, Stanford University*, pages 415–433. Stanford: CSLI Publications.

Van Eynde, Frank. 2015. Sign-based construction grammar: A guided tour. *Journal of Linguistics* 52:194–217.

Van Valin, Robert and Randy LaPolla. 1997. *Syntax, Structure, Meaning and Function*. Cambridge University Press.

Wasow, Thomas, Ivan A. Sag, and Geoffrey Nunberg. 1984. Idioms: An interim report. In S. Hattori and K. Inoue, eds., *Proceedings of the 13th International Congress of Linguistics (Tokyo)*, pages 102–115. The Hague: CIPL.

Webelhuth, Gert. 2011. Motivating non-canonicality in Construction Grammar: The case of locative inversion. *Cognitive Linguistics* 22:81–105.

Wechsler, Stephen. 2011. Mixed agreement, the person feature, and the index/concord distinction. *Natural Language and Linguistic Theory* 29:999–1031.

Wechsler, Stephen and Larisa Zlatić. 2001. A theory of agreement and its application to serbo-croatian. *Language* pages 391–423.

Wechsler, Stephen and Larisa Zlatić. 2015. *The Many Faces of Agreement*. Stanford: CSLI Publications.

Woisetschlaeger, Erich. 1983. On the question of definiteness in 'an old man's book'. *Linguistic Inquiry* 14:137–154.

Woolford, Ellen. 1987. An ECP account of constraints on across-the-board extraction. *Linguistic Inquiry* 18:166–171.

Zucchi, Alessandro. 1995. The ingredients of definiteness and the definiteness effect. *Natural Language Semantics* 3:33–78.

Name Index

Subject Index